The Enemies of Anarchy

Also by Robert Hunter

Storming of the Mind
Greenpeace (with photographs by Robert Keziere)

The Enemies of Anarchy

A GESTALT APPROACH TO CHANGE

ROBERT HUNTER

The Viking Press | New York

For Conan and Justine

309.104
H946e

Acknowledgments

Ballantine Books, Inc.: From *The Population Bomb* by Paul
Ehrlich, Copyright © 1968, 1971 by Paul R. Ehrlich. All rights
reserved. Reprinted by permission of Ballantine Books, Inc.

Dell Publishing Co., Inc.: From *Man Alone: Alienation in
Modern Society*, edited, with an Introduction, by Eric and
Mary Josephson. Copyright © 1962 by Dell Publishing Co., Inc.,
and used by permission of the publisher.

Doubleday & Co. Inc.: From *The Hidden Dimension* by
Edward T. Hall, Copyright © 1966 by Edward T. Hall.
Reprinted by permission of Doubleday & Co. Inc.

Harper & Row, Publishers, Inc.: From *The Meaning of the
20th Century* by Kenneth Boulding, Copyright © 1964 by
Kenneth Ewart Boulding. From *The Future of Man* by Pierre
Teilhard de Chardin, translated by Norman Denny, Copyright
© 1964 in the English translation by William Collins Sons
& Co. Ltd. and Harper & Row, Publishers, Inc. Originally
published in French and Copyright © 1959 by Editions du Seuil.
By permission of Harper & Row, Publishers, Inc.

Holt, Rinehart and Winston, Inc.: From *The Sane Society*
by Erich Fromm, Copyright © 1955 by Erich Fromm. Reprinted
by permission of Holt, Rinehart and Winston, Inc.

Page 254 constitutes an extension of this copyright page.

Preface

This book is an attempt to rough in the outlines of the greatest revolution in human history. Various dimensions of the revolution—economic, technological, religious, characterological, artistic, military, and political—have been examined in detail by writers whose works will be drawn upon here. But no one has, as yet, superimposed these various dimensions one on top of the other in order to see the picture in the largest perspective possible. What follows is an attempt to do just that. The effort, at this stage, can be compared to attempting to draw a map of New York City while standing in Times Square. I have no vantage point except a pyramid of books and my own experiences and observations. The results will, inevitably, be exploratory rather than definitive.

In the early and middle stages of all major revolutions in the past, the vast majority of the people involved were only vaguely aware of what was happening—and many were unaware that anything was happening beyond the sphere of their own immediate interests. Today, thanks to the greater prevalence of media of communication, this is less the case. Nevertheless, it remains true that while most of us are to some degree conscious of the changes that are taking place, our viewpoints are specialized or conditioned and, inevitably, selective. We live, as Lawrence Durrell once wrote, by selected fictions. Most change is therefore invisible to us.

My thesis is that we are collectively experiencing a process which I will refer to as "large-scale integration." This process can be compared to a drastic personality change. Viewed as the development of an aggressive-dominant personality, what we call "civilization" has slipped over the line from neurosis to pathology. Characteristics which at one time were essential to survival have now created a situation in which the continuation of such behavior is clearly suicidal. At this point, an abrupt and painful readjustment is required. The aggressive personality must be made to adjust to new realities —otherwise, it will destroy itself. Unfortunately, there is no omnipotent therapist around to effect the necessary adjustment. The adjustment, if it is to be made at all, must therefore be spontaneous. The aggressive, domineering personality must reshape itself into a cooperative and—by its former standards—meek individual.

The transition is similar to the problem faced by the Savage in Aldous Huxley's *Brave New World*. Huxley, however, failed completely to interpret the character of the brave new world into whose embrace we are being driven. Himself a product of a basically anarchic culture, he was unable to perceive human dignity except in terms of anarchic behavior. The Savage was an anarchist. The citizens of Brave New World were cooperative, well-integrated human beings. But they were unreal, because Huxley was unable to escape his conditioning sufficiently to see that a cooperative, integrated society did not necessarily exclude the possibility that human dignity might be preserved *in new forms*. That such a society could be existential, humanistic, autonomous, gestaltian, creative, and post-literate did not occur to the inner-directed, literate Huxley. His was a failure to appreciate the meaning of new dimensions of consciousness.

The Savage was dangerous. He personified the values of Western culture as they have evolved over the centuries, the very values which now threaten us with extinction. And *Brave New World* was a dangerous book, because it made so many of us afraid of the very possibilities which are now our only hope of preserving both our lives and our dignity. As I will attempt to show, however, it will be possible, in a brave new world, to be liberated—as individuals in no other culture in history have ever had the chance to be liberated

—rather than imprisoned. We are approaching a new kind of existence, a "post-civilized" world as Kenneth Boulding calls it, the main features of which will be large-scale integration at every level, from the purely political and economic to the psychological and even characterological. It will involve controls over our existence which are more pervasive than those that have existed in any earlier culture. Yet the nature of the controls and the way in which they will function will *free* us—and free us not only from economic slavery, but from ideological, cultural, and emotional slavery as well.

The process of large-scale integration is a preliminary step in this direction. Large-scale integration leads to "convergence." The process is already taking place, not only at the political level, but at every other level—more or less simultaneously and almost completely spontaneously. I will explain later the way in which the word "spontaneously" is to be qualified. For the moment, suffice it to say that I use the word to indicate that the process is not being organized, directed, or controlled by any particular group.

The argument presented here is that civilization is coming to an end. In making this assertion, I am using Arnold Toynbee's definition of civilization. Toynbee points out, in *A Study of History,* that some twenty-one civilizations have existed in the last 6000 years, and he treats them all as being "philosophically *contemporaneous"* or "philosophically *equivalent."* In other words, from ancient Sumeric civilization to modern Western civilization, the differences are marginal, while the matrix of civilization remains the same. However, modern Western civilization is now undergoing several unprecedented experiences. As I will attempt to show in the course of this book, the matrix is breaking up and a further continuation of the processes of civilization is no longer possible. The accumulated evidence strongly suggests that ours is the last civilization. Whether it will emerge as the first "post-civilization" is another question. Such historical precedents as there are would indicate that our chances are negligible—but the imponderables of unprecedented experiences cannot accurately be weighed.

The processes which I choose to call large-scale integration and convergence, although not recognized in so many words by Toynbee, are salient examples of these unprecedented experiences. But before such processes can be appreciated, I believe it is necessary to understand fully that civilization, as it has manifested itself throughout recorded history, is finally finished as the vehicle of human development. Many suspect this—and not a few say it as a matter of course—but I have yet to see the various crises with which we are confronted added up so that we may look at the sum total.

Part I of this book is a clearing operation, intended to show that we cannot hope to survive by making minor adjustments here and there. The problems, it will be seen, are too tightly woven into the basic patterns of civilization—and particularly of industrialization —to be solved by tinkering. A reversal of our *basic premises,* behavior, and methodology is necessary at this stage if we are to survive. Part II of the book is an attempt to document, in similar fashion, the extent to which large-scale integration has already taken place, and, further, to show how the problems outlined in Part I force a further evolution of the process of large-scale integration. At the same time, I will try to show just how far advanced the process of convergence already is.

Contents

PART II—LARGE-SCALE INTEGRATION *105*

PART III—CONVERGENCE *221*

Introduction

Synergy is the only word in
our language that means *behavior
of whole systems unpredicted by
the separately observed behaviors
of any of the system's separate
parts or any subassembly of the
system's parts.* There is nothing
in the chemistry of a toe nail
that predicts the existence of
a human being.

—R. Buckminster Fuller
  Operating Manual for Spaceship Earth

1

A Computer Metaphor

In 1948 the transistor was discovered. The discovery started a revolution in electronics. The valve of the old radio gave way to small slivers of semiconducting material. Almost overnight the electronics industry moved from the centimeter scale to the micron. Left behind was the old technique of joining electronic components— valves, resistors, or capacitors—with wires. The shift can be compared to the jump from a walled village of mud huts to a modern metropolis.

The technological tidal wave set in motion by the transistor had barely broken when, ten years later, the first integrated circuit appeared. A number of devices could now be formed in the same microscopic silicon wafer. This was microelectronics, which seemed at first to represent the ultimate dimension of miniaturization. This, however, was not to be the case. In 1965 three American firms proposed to take the step *beyond* microminiaturization. Motorola called its method the "Polycell" technique; Texas Instruments referred to its method as "Discrete Wiring"; and Fairchild Semiconductor chose to call its own system the "Micro-matrix" technique. Each employed an approach generally referred to as planar diffusion. What this amounted to was large-scale integration (LSI). It meant that whole arrays of circuits could be made from the same microscopic piece of semiconductor material. While a conventional integrated circuit could pack fifty to a hundred active and passive components on a chip three millimeters square, the new LSI techniques allowed three hundred to one thousand components to be packed into the same space. The whole of a 76-millimeter silicon slice could contain about 500 memories or 52,400,000 components. In an article in the August 1968 edition of *Science Journal,* A. T. Lawton and G. E. Abrook point out that by using LSI techniques, "it has proved possible to construct a 1024 bit memory with a total power consumption of 0.25 watt, or about one fifth as much as must be dissipated with the latest bipolar transistor memory." By comparison, the original computer constructed by Charles Babbage in 1844 used heavy cast-iron counting drums and required sixty horsepower from a large steam engine to perform even the simplest decade calculation. Using LSI techniques, the American firms involved expected to have transistor radio-sized computers on the market in the 1970s. Computers, for the first time, could become truly portable. Some would even fit into one's pocket. And the cost was expected to be not much more than two cents per memory bit.

Large-scale integration cannot be carried out without the assistance of the earlier generation of computers, automatic drafting machines, and so on. The process is, of course, complex. Its main characteristic, however, is that it involves intensely accurate *definition* of the specific functions of various circuits. The *interconnections* between these circuits must also be accurately defined. Each array comprises groups or cells of circuits which are coupled together to form complex functions. Individual elements are packed tightly together. "Defects," write Lawton and Abrook, "cannot yet be excluded in manufacture. . . . To overcome this problem . . . Texas Instruments evolved Discretionary Wiring or unique interconnection. . . . The array is built up from a large number of cells or circuits which are then interconnected. But with the discretionary technique, each cell is tested prior to interconnection and only the good ones are coupled into the final array."

Elements and interconnections are unique. They are kept that way. The main features of LSI techniques are an "extremely high component density" and complex interconnected networks. It is the very opposite of mechanical technologies which involve homogenization and repetition of functions. So sensitively structured are LSI techniques that a whole "package" has to be designed, right from the beginning, around a customer's specific requirements. The fact that must be kept in mind is that large-scale integration *demands unique components, unique interconnections, and, further, unique interconnections of networks composed of unique interconnected components.* The parts are *not* interchangeable. They cannot be envisioned as mere cogs, since each contributes a highly defined function to the whole.

I propose to let the concept of large-scale integration stand as a metaphor. for our time. Moreover, apart from its metaphorical value, there is in the specific technique of large-scale integration as applied to computer technology a *pattern* that has far wider, possibly universal, application. Just as an apple falling from a tree betrayed a pattern which, when interpreted, revealed the law of gravity, so too the development of large-scale integration as a computer technique reveals a principle of social development. This principle, like the law of gravity, functions without human guidance, even though it represents the total integral functioning of human society.

Dr. Renatus Hartogs has written that "a total upheaval of values [is] now sweeping the Western world." Marshall McLuhan says that "after three thousand years of explosion, by means of fragmentary and mechanical technologies, the Western world is imploding." Carl Jung wrote in the 1920s, at least as apocalyptically as McLuhan did in the 1960s, that "we are only at the threshold of a new spiritual epoch." John Kenneth Galbraith refers to the "matrix of change" which we are well into and which is "more than the sum of its parts." Historian Arnold Toynbee says that we are being carried toward an "inevitable ordeal" which threatens to tear "the Ark of civilization" to pieces. Naturalist and historian Richard Carrington says that we are at the final stage of the "psychozoic era." Kenneth Boulding has written that we are experiencing a "major revolution" in the human condition, involving the agonizing transition from civilization to post-civilization. If nothing else, it can be seen from the above that we live in a time of apocalyptic social commentary. This book will be no exception. As Boulding says, "the present moment indeed is unique in the whole four billion years of history on this planet." John H. Storer, author of *The Web of Life,* puts it simply and accurately: "Humanity is crossing the threshold into a new world."

The computer metaphor of large-scale integration is intended as a frame of reference which provides an overview of the great process of change that we are collectively experiencing. The process of large-scale integration which is taking place in all human affairs amounts to the greatest revolution in history. The word "revolution" is used here to indicate, not so much an overthrow of existing systems, as an abrupt, even cataclysmic speed-up in an evolutionary process which has been going on during the whole of human history. In effect, evolution becomes revolution—or, more exactly, a restoration of certain fundamental behavioral and characterological traits that have been submerged during the long anarchic period known as "civilization." The route has been Rube Goldberg-like rather than sequential. It is, moreover, a *total* revolution, which means that it is unprecedented. Conceivably, such a thing could not happen until total warfare becomes impossible (except through accident or miscalculation). As McLuhan notes in *Understanding Media:* "When we have achieved a worldwide fragmentation, it is not unnatural to think about a worldwide integration." The process of large-scale integration is, finally, global. Unlike the "integrated circuit" phase of history that is embodied in the tight organization of nation-states, the phase of large-scale integration—which is just now getting under way—represents a great convergence of forces not only in the political sphere, but in the psychological, economic, urban, religious, behavioral, and technological spheres as well.

The crisis has not yet come into focus. The stage is too cluttered. Our view of what is happening to date has been fragmentary, disconnected, and kaleidoscopic. We see ourselves reflected in a mirror that is broken into a thousand pieces. It has not yet dawned on us that, in effect, the process of large-scale integration is taking place at every level. It *is* dawning on us, however, that in order to survive, we must replace our existing competitive and exclusive system —which can be compared, at least on the international level, to the pretransistor radio valves—with systems that are based on cooperation, coordination, and integration. To many, this will appear obvious. But what is less obvious is that a growing consciousness of the need for change in basic group-behavior patterns is the triggering mechanism for most revolutionary activity in the world today. The consciousness need not be this broadly defined, and almost never is. Yet whether it is a revolution in computerization, a ghetto rebellion, student occupation of an administration building, the emergence of what Galbraith calls "technostructures," the nuclear deterrent, the formation of a political New Left, increased use of drugs, the collapse of old authoritarian morality and the rise of a humanistic morality, the rapid spread of group psychotherapeutic techniques, the growing popularity of dropout communities, greatly heightened interest in Oriental philosophies, astrology, and psychic phenomena, a revolt by the clergy, a revolution within schools, or even an increase in divorce rates—whichever of these it is, the underlying imperative remains demonstrably the same. It is the process of large-scale integration at work.

It is important to understand that *total* revolution, unlike political or even spiritual revolution, cannot be led by any one man or even a group of men. It is beyond the scope of any single organizational approach—at least, it is as yet. The jelly-like computers made up of macromolecules that will be with us by the 1980s may solve some of the problems of organization and control that are beyond our abilities at the moment. But as things stand now, the process of large-scale integration (which is unprogrammed, except in the loose sense that spontaneous combustion is "programmed" by a complex interplay of forces) is going on at too many levels and is moving in too many directions to be contained by any one formula. It moves as much against the Pentagon as it does against the Kremlin, the Vatican, and even Buckingham Palace. It presses forcefully against almost all the familiar landmarks of our world. Only a maiden aunt could believe that the revolution will be anything other than bloody, disruptive, agonizing, and bitterly fought. Predictably, the individuals who are in the vanguard today will be resisting further extensions of the process of change tomorrow. There are no historical precedents to refer to, since the over-all situation is unique. The activating mechanisms of social change have, through a process of metamorphosis, taken on new shapes and dimensions.

Civilization, as we know it, is indeed being destroyed. A more appropriate word would be "replaced"—in the sense that the integrated circuit is about to be replaced by the process of large-scale integration. Anyone who would "save" civilization, however, must face the fact that a revolution which is neither led nor organized, which (like the war in Vietnam) has no Maginot Lines but has fronts that lie in every direction, which rears its head on the side of industry as much as it does against it, which emerges in the central nervous system of government as well as thrusting up in the form of radical anti-establishment groups, which works as much for Black Power as it does against it, which takes the form of a tool in the hands of politicians and advertisers as much as it takes the form of a weapon in the hands of renegades and rebels, is a very difficult —in fact, impossible—revolution to resist.

2

Self-Regulated Revolution

Large-scale integration is offered as a frame of reference. It is intended to describe a process which needs to be identified. It is mainly a label—a "package description" or "handle." In the way in which LSI is applied in computer technology, some guiding genius lies behind it. The process is laboriously engineered and controlled. The efforts of draftsmen, electronic technicians, and an earlier generation of computers are coordinated within an organizational framework, and the process is guided step by step from conception to realization. At the point at which we begin to deal with the mechanics of social large-scale integration, however, the metaphor fails. There is no comparable guiding mechanism in society. In the social sense, the process of large-scale integration is neither guided, orchestrated, nor programmed. In place of a team of technicians and managers, the process is initiated and orchestrated in society by the mechanism of self-regulation.

This will seem, at first, too simple. Sweeping generalizations about social behavior tend to break down rather quickly when applied to specific situations, where random factors, coincidence, and personality combine to give each situation a certain uniqueness. Some social processes, however, can be perceived only in the aggregate sense and have little apparent bearing on individual cases. As French philosopher Jacques Ellul phrases it: "There is a collective sociological reality, which is independent of the individual. . . . Individual decisions are always made within the framework of this sociological reality, itself pre-existent and more or less determinative." This kind of awareness dominates the economic planning of mature corporations. Likewise, it is well understood by physicists. In industry, the need to regulate total or aggregate demand is conceded. It means, in effect, that as long as a corporation is large enough to deal with its customers by the hundreds of thousands or millions, it need only concern itself with over-all patterns of consumer response. And aggregate consumer patterns can be worked out in considerable detail, even though the behavior of any individual will remain more or less unpredictable.

Generalizations, despite their bad press, can be valid—even though in specific instances they fail to stand up. In the case of quantum phenomena, the German physicists Heisenberg and Born argued long ago that it is pointless for a physicist to worry about the properties of a single electron, since in the laboratory he is working with beams or showers of them, each containing billions of individual particles or waves (whichever they may be). The physicist, like the economist, is concerned only with mass behavior, statistics, and the laws of probability and chance. It makes no difference that within one household or one batch of electrons the behavior of individual electrons does not always conform to a given pattern. Aggregate behavior is not affected. Likewise, a general social mechanism of change may be seen to function in the aggregate sense without its being applicable in every specific instance of change. And it is in this general or aggregate sense that I refer to the concept of self-regulation.

The concept was made popular in the field of progressive education by the radical British educator, A. S. Neill, founder of Summerhill. Self-regulation, in terms of child rearing and education, refers to a natural and harmonious balance, within the child, between the rate at which he learns best and the rate at which learning should be offered to him. Neill argues that forced education defeats itself by producing scholars who are poorly educated because they have not absorbed knowledge at the rate that is best suited to them. The process of self-regulation therefore involves not forcing a child to learn, but helping to develop his personality as a whole and allowing him to absorb knowledge at his own rate. This method presupposes an internal equilibrium between emotional and intellectual development. It views the child as a whole—or, in Alfred Korzybski's phrase, as an "organism-as-a-whole." A self-regulated child is supposed to know when he needs knowledge just as he is supposed to know when he needs food or sleep.

This idea is also known as "homeostasis," or "equilibrium." McLuhan refers to it in *Understanding Media* as "a strategy of the staying power of any body. All organizations, but especially biological ones, struggle to maintain constant in their inner condition amidst the variations of outer shock and change. The man-made social environment, as an extension of man's physical body, is no exception." Put another way, society tries not to "learn" anything—or rather, rejects learning, even if the rejection is imperfect—until it is either ready to absorb new knowledge or is forced to do so.

The Industrial Revolution stands as an historical example. The Greeks and the Romans stood on the verge of an industrial revolution. Hero of Alexandria understood the force of steam and how to use it. Likewise, a steam engine was invented by Worcester in the seventeenth century. A Frenchman, Papin, invented another at about the same time. Yet none of these was put to use. It was not until Savery's version was put to work in mines and Newcomen corrected its weaknesses that the steam engine finally came into its own. The machine built by Watt was designed for use in mines, was later adapted to corn-grinding, and finally—about 1790—was put to use in textile industry. The point here is that inventions cannot function in a vacuum. In this respect, they resemble political ideas and movements. The work of da Vinci is a further, if obvious, example. His ideas could not be used because culturally and industrially his society was not ready for them. The process of self-regulation or homeostasis was working against them.

Similarly, great social change springs not out of a void. A whole matrix of pressures must be at work before any significant change occurs. Institutional, political, cultural, economic, technological, industrial, and psychological factors are all involved, and these—or some significant combination of them—must come together at some point if social inertia and the inherent resistance of institutions to alteration are to be overcome. A major social change is precipitated only as a result of a fusion or convergence of many crucial factors. In *Law in History* Edward Cheyney notes that "everything is the outcome of something preceding," and that "the immediate, sudden appearance of something, its creation by an individual or a group at some moment of time, is unknown in history." Carl G. Gustavson adds, in *A Preface to History,* that "no single cause ever adequately explains an historical episode. A 'cause' is a convenient figure of speech for any one of a number of factors which helps to explain why an historical event happened. . . ." Historical events are precipitated by a "medley of causes." In short, no one man or group of men ever triggers a major revolution—though the relative role of various individuals, books, ideas, and so on will vary considerably, depending on the extent to which they mirror various factors in the medley of causes.

This has been the case throughout history, and it is more than ever the case today—particularly in the more advanced nations. Thorstein Veblen has pointed out in *The Engineers and the Price System* that "the present industrial system and the manner of close-knit community life enforced by this industrial system have no example in history." The sheer complexity of the system reduces, to a very great extent, the likelihood of its being "taken over" by revolutionaries. The actions of individuals and groups of individuals have always been factors in any equation of change. The fewer the factors that one is working with, the greater the possibility that one or two factors will have a decisive effect. As the factors multiply, the influence of each factor diminishes. In a highly industrialized society, where economic and technological factors assume greater dimensions of importance, the factor of individual or even group behavior loses more and more of its potency. Submerged in the medley of causes, having become a part of a larger aggregate, individuals or groups are severely limited in their ability to initiate, control, or terminate social processes.

Veblen continues: "Wherever the mechanical industry has taken decisive effect, as in America and the two or three industrialized regions of Europe, the community lives from hand to mouth in such a way that its livelihood depends on the effectual working of its industrial system from day to day." This *dependence* on the system for survival means that any revolution would not only have to be able to replace immediately all the highly skilled and specialized technocrats who are required to run the machine of society, but it would also have to have very nearly unanimous support from the populace. The chances that support will materialize are negligible, if for no other reason than that the normal process of rationalization makes people support that which they are dependent upon. This problem of a society that is too complex to be taken over is what Herbert Marcuse describes as "the System." Its development is what he refers to as "the passing of historical forces which, at the preceding stages of society, seemed to represent the possibility of new forms of existence." In other words, the contemporary industrial society has absorbed and abolished the historic means of revolution.

As things stand now, Erich Fromm duly notes in *The Revolution of Hope,* it is "not possible [to have] a violent revolution in the style of the French or Russian revolutions, which means the overthrow of the government by force and the seizure of power by the revolutionary leaders. . . ." Victorious revolutions can take place with relative ease in simple societies. In a society where the "megamachine" is emerging, revolutions cannot take place without a total breakdown—and this is something that the vast majority of the populace would not support. It was Mao Tse-tung who observed that guerrillas can be successful only if they work within a population which is favorable to them.

At this point society becomes less responsive to leadership, particularly revolutionary leadership. Even "accepted" leadership can no longer function in the traditional way. The factor of the individual has been reduced to the point where it is no longer decisive.

I agree with Marcuse that the historical means of revolution have been absorbed by society. This does not mean, however, that the possibility of change has been abolished. Rather, the self-regulating features of social change become, in this context, more pervasive and decisive than they were in simpler societies—societies, that is, in which the human factor was large in comparison with, say, the technological and economic factors. In previous historical periods, the process of self-regulation served a chiefly negative function. In attempting to maintain equilibrium, the homeostatic mechanisms in any social body operated mainly to resist disruptive changes, most of which were initiated by individuals or groups. The human factor, in short, played the most positive role and homeostasis was the aggregate response, functioning as a sort of social thermostat, the main task of which was to turn off the furnace when the temperature got too hot. Now, however, the process has been more or less reversed. As it becomes more and more difficult to "lead," the pressure for change comes less from the human component in the social equation and more from the industrial, economic, technological, and psychosocial components. The "societal thermostat," adjusted in an aggregate sense to maintain the most comfortable temperature, is reacting as though the temperature had dropped too low and the furnace were being turned on, not off.

The self-regulating features of society—the interplay between conservative forces and radical forces, between institutional inertia and innovation, between cultural conditioning and intolerable social conditions—have, until our era, worked to slow down the pace of change. Now, in response to new and powerful pressures, the process of self-regulation is stepping up the rate of change, rather than slowing it down, and thus forcing changes on us whether we like it or not. The brake has become an accelerator. This is not to say that it has ceased to function as a brake at all. Far from it. But our over-all social position, at least in the industrially advanced nations, may be viewed not unrealistically as a situation resembling that of an automobile in which the brake and the gas pedal are both rammed to the floorboards. The brake lining, however, is being burned to a frazzle.

The interplay of forces—whether political, economic, biological, gravitational, or whatever—is always at least a two-way street. There is no reason to suppose that the self-regulating features of society—any society, not just the highly industrialized ones, in which the process is aggravated—are somehow dissimilar and that they operate on a unique, one-way basis. Put simply, given a medley of causes, given widely based pressures for which—particularly in the case of population—there are historical precedents to indicate social responsiveness, the self-regulating aspects of society can operate as much *for* change, revolution, innovation, and adaptation as they do *against* all of these things.

Another way of approaching the idea of self-regulated revolution is from the standpoint of the biologist, who speaks in terms of "environmental resistance." Biological laws, he informs us, impose strict behavioral rules on all animals. In *Man in the Web of Life*

John H. Storer describes environmental resistance as "a rough working balance . . . achieved between the population and carrying capacity of the environment."

The relationships between animals and their environment is thermostatically controlled by large-scale management. Nature, in fact, may be described as being more totalitarian than any dictatorship that has ever been created by man. Natural laws are not open to interpretation, there is no recourse to a higher court, and no species can violate biological law without paying the death penalty. The management of nature is carried out, however, without any central authority as we know it. Rather, the forces of instinct, need, ability, tenacity, and vulnerability converge to strike a rough but effective balance. Human beings, at least as judged by themselves, are thought to be independent of biological management. Yet they are as dependent on the four basic natural resources—water, soil, vegetation, and other animal life—as any lower form of life. "These basic resources," notes Storer, "are not separate entities, independent of each other. Each is dependent on the others for its own successful functioning. Man himself is dependent for his existence on the proper functioning of them all, as parts of an organized whole."

It is clear that through technology, medicine, and social organization, man is capable of immunizing himself against the immediate effects of his actions. But the process of immunization, it can now be seen, is far from complete. And what is known as "environmental collapse" is really a drastic reaction on the part of brutalized nature, an extreme form of environmental resistance. It is a homeostatic process in which human beings are pawns—though they once thought that they were the players. The revolutions in which we take part or which we attempt to resist are forced upon us—as this book will attempt to show—in almost exactly the same way that a "revolution" takes place in a lemming community when the lemming population outstrips the carrying capacity of the environment and sends thousands of the animals on a forced march into the sea. The march of the lemmings is a response to a self-regulating process, as much as is the rebellion of youth today. It is a homeostatic response to an intolerable environmental situation.

There is yet another approach to the idea of a self-regulated revolution, and it is one that must be clearly understood. In *The Technological Society* Jacques Ellul refers to the process of "self-augmentation." He is speaking in terms of techniques which he believes are becoming all-pervasive, to the point where a "technological" civilization—the first truly global society—is taking form, based entirely on "an ensemble of techniques" which, taken together, overwhelm and determine the behavior and goals of every culture it comes into contact with. "Technique," he writes, "has arrived at such a point in its evolution that it is being transformed and is progressing almost without decisive intervention by man. . . . Technique indeed progresses by means of minute improvements which are the result of common human efforts and are indefinitely additive until they form a mass of new conditions that permit a decisive forward step." Technique advances in every nation on earth because of "collective, anonymous research advances," driven by identical impulses. The process of self-augmentation, he argues, can be formulated in two laws: (I) in any given civilization technical progress is irreversible; and (2) technical progress tends to accelerate, not according to an arithmetic progression, but according to a geometric progression.

Technique sharply reduces the role of human invention and makes human decisions subordinate to the imperatives of technique itself. "Almost without deliberate will, by a simple combination of new data, incessant discoveries take place everywhere; and whole fields are opened up to technique because of the meeting of several currents." The implication of self-augmentation is that the role of the individual is less and less important. *"A whole new kind of spontaneous action is taking place here, and we know neither its laws nor its ends."*

In the present book this "whole new kind of spontaneous action" will be referred to as self-regulated large-scale integration.

3

Beyond
Specialization

This book is written from a generalist point of view. The picture will tend to be coarse-grained rather than finely detailed, but the lens has been adjusted for a panoramic view. I have attempted to take as many contemporary developments as possible and stack them together in a single deck—like so many transparent cards—so that similarities, parallels, and interrelationships can be readily perceived.

So far, the approach of most writers has been to isolate the germs of change and to examine them as separate entities. While it is true that in this way subtleties can be pried loose which might otherwise be missed, no clear over-all picture emerges. Moreover, the principle of microscopic examination leads to distortion the moment that the specialist, saturated with the details of one aspect of change, attempts to apply his specialized viewpoint elsewhere. Everything else is interpreted in terms of the metaphors, terminology, dynamics, and mechanisms of the researcher's major field of investigation. The problem has been clearly phrased by C. D. Darlington, a professor of botany at Oxford University. In *Genetics and Man* he writes: "Everywhere in the study of life for the last hundred years, attempts, successful attempts, have been made to simplify the situations which it is the business of scientific inquiry to reduce to order, to put in terms of cause and effect. The attempts are usually made by specialists, by experts supreme in each field, who are bound to ignore the methods, the assumptions, and the knowledge acquired in other fields. . . . We find the documentary historian expelling the small men from his thoughts, the archeologist expelling the big men. We find the social anthropologist, the economist, and the psychiatrist reducing men to a level and mankind to a predictable pulp."

The approach of the generalist—as opposed to that of the specialist—is to avoid becoming so conditioned by one field of study that when he attempts to look elsewhere he is, consciously or unconsciously, interpreting everything in terms of his acquired prejudices and reflexes. "Ethnocentrism" is the word used to describe the foreshortened global perspective characteristic of nationalists. Ethnocentrism has its parallel in the world of ideas and study, in which context we might call it "speciocentrism." For example, a highly trained economist, like a highly trained Englishman, can seldom avoid believing that economic influences (the equivalent of British influences to the Englishman) are a more dominant force than, say, psychological forces.

It is not my wish to compartmentalize developments or to put parentheses around anything. The truth is, as Alan Watts has written, "that in looking at the world bit by bit, we convince ourselves that it consists of separate things, and so give ourselves the problem of how these things are connected and how they cause and affect each other. The problem would never have arisen if we had been aware that it was just our way of looking at the world which has chopped it up into separate bits, things, events, causes and effects." We do not see this, as Watts suggests, but certainly the *consciousness of interrelationships* is one of the chief characteristics of the era which we are now entering. Interdependence is coming to be accepted as the basic fact of life. It is no coincidence that at the same time that the importance of ecology is finally being recognized, public relations is just beginning to hit its stride. "Consensus" becomes the operative political term; the word "group" precedes more words than ever; computers become as necessary as telephones; mutual-defense pacts proliferate like tacit price-fixing agreements between large corporations; priests, rabbis, and preachers alike grudgingly learn to pronounce the word "ecumenism"; and educators begin to talk about developing the personality as a whole. A true consciousness of interrelationships is subversive, at least insofar as existing institutions are concerned, because it eats at the very basis for their existence. Human existence has been compartmentalized, fragmented, and atomized to the point where societies—especially the most industrially advanced societies—have come to resemble almost infinitely complex labyrinths. The twentieth century, assuming that we survive the process of metamorphosis, will eventually come to be recognized as the period in which the long historic process of fragmentation began to reverse itself. For an assortment of economic, social, psychological, technological, organizational, and behavioral reasons, further fragmentation became intolerable. An "implosion," as McLuhan calls it, began to take place. My thesis, which can be phrased simply (at the risk of distorting the complex reality), is that we are collectively going through an experience similar to childbirth—an experience which, like childbirth, *can* be painless. A few simple adjustments could be made to spare us all the agonies of the major conflict which is just beginning. But this is the same as saying that a marriage which is in the process of being torn to ribbons can be saved by the simple act, on the part of one partner or the other, of changing his or her personality. It is a simple solution, but one that is all but impossible to achieve.

Organized Anarchy

Every tumor is a law unto itself. In every case of cancer it would seem as though the docile and subservient protoplasm of the cell had taken over the reins of government from the normally dominant nucleus. In consequence, one disobedient cell has escaped from the coordinated discipline of the tissue and of the organism as a whole.

—C. D. Darlington
  Genetics and Man

4

Change:
The Only
Constant

All human societies, insofar as they can be seen to have been separate from one another, have been transitional—some have simply been more transitional than others. The only thing certain about a *status quo* is that it will not endure. The forces that produce a "new" culture are the very forces that guarantee its collapse. They cannot be turned off. Every civilization, society, or culture eventually attempts to deny its essential energies, and in the process is destroyed—hence, the myth of the Phoenix, the most recurrent of all social myths.

Carl G. Gustavson makes the point in *A Preface to History* that any realistic study of history must take into consideration, at the very least, six major factors—economic, religious, technological, institutional, ideological, and military. These "furnish the power for the loom of history." In fact, language also plays a crucial role and so do population pressure, characterological conflict, and resources. We are dealing, when we speak of "history," with a four-dimensional tapestry. To single out any one point in the broad sweep of history—for example, the Renaissance or the Reformation—is automatically to distort the over-all view. As Gustavson explains:

The process of causation is at work in each change that occurs in social forms; the never-ending sequence of changes under the impact of social forces. Occasionally, as in the Reformation, the normal equilibrium of forces is destroyed and many pressures, hitherto diffused, are galvanized into unusual overt action. Their influence is speedily reflected in a rapid series of formal changes in government. Those comparatively sudden, cataclysmic revolutions that have occurred must not be allowed to overshadow or distort the obvious fact that most changes occur almost imperceptibly, so much so that they are scarcely visible from year to year, sometimes not for decades. . . . Where revolutions do seem to transform the political face of a country, the appearances are deceptive; less visible developments nearly always led up to the climactic events.

In our time, we see that changes move less imperceptibly. The pace of technological change is the most obvious example. In the 1920s the lag between discovery and general use was considered to average thirty years. Today it is less than nine. We are just beginning to appreciate the pervasive effect of new technologies and how other major forces are affected by them. It has been pointed out, in the context of population increase, that if you start with two drops of water in a bucket and double them every year, it may take you ninety-nine years to get the bucket half full. However, it will take only one more year to fill it right up. In an article published in *The Bulletin of the Atomic Scientists,* Kenneth Boulding noted that:

> . . . the first five hundred thousand years or so of man's existence on earth were relatively uneventful. Compared to his present condition, he puttered along in an astonishingly stationary state. . . . Whatever changes there were, they were almost unbelievably slow. About ten thousand years ago, we begin to perceive an acceleration in the rate of change. This becomes very noticeable five thousand years ago with the development of the first civilization. . . . Civilization represents a further acceleration of the rate of change. . . . Beginning about 1650, however, we begin to see the organization of science into a community of knowledge, and this leads again to an enormous acceleration of the rate of change.

The tempo, as we can see, has been picking up fairly steadily. According to the Ford Foundation, more than half of the research and development work carried out by mankind was accomplished between 1950 and 1970. In short, as much data was accumulated in twenty years as was accumulated in the whole of previous human history. One researcher predicts that knowledge is accumulating so rapidly that it will double itself again in the next ten or twelve years. Similar snowballing effects may be seen in the field of education, where in the United States alone there has been a twentyfold increase in the number of college and university teachers since 1900 and a similar explosive increase in the number of students— an increase that is paralleled, to varying degrees, in every other industrially advanced country. The stockpiling of weaponry has paralleled the stockpiling of academic degrees. In all cases, it is clear that the rate of change has accelerated enormously—to the point where a new fighter jet is obsolete by the time that it rolls off the assembly line.

The only constant, throughout history, is change. The rate has altered, but in the long run it has tended to accelerate—moving faster in some periods than in others, but steadily gaining momentum. Today, when we examine each of what Gustavson refers to as the "six major social forces," we find that it is moving in high gear. And the same can certainly be said of the four additional major forces that I have added to the list. Later, we shall see that new, unimagined, and unprecedented social forces are taking shape.

In the example of the bucket filling up, we see the simplest explanation for this unprecedented rate of change. In this context Buckminster Fuller's following observation does not come as a surprise: "All the trend curves which we may examine show rates of acceleration which underline the unprecedented nature of changes to come." Boulding adds, probably accurately, that "if the human race is to survive . . . it will have to change more in its ways of thinking in the next twenty-five years than it has done in the last twenty-five thousand." In the space of less than thirty years we have proceeded technologically almost a century into the future. There is a metaphor to be found in Einstein's theory that as an object approaches the speed of light, time dilates. Change in our society is, in a metaphorical sense, approaching the speed of light. To pursue the analogy further, we might note that our existing institutions are built more like Spanish galleons than like interstellar spaceships, and the vibrations and strains imposed by the present velocity of change are shaking them apart at the seams. However, while it is easy to see signs of dissolution and breakdown on every hand, we can, with effort, perceive in the accumulating wreckage the patterns of the future. And these patterns are more pervasive and consistent than a quick glance at the Bosch-like landscape would seem to indicate.

The question we are faced with now comes down to a choice between two ancient myths. On the one hand, we have the Greek myth of the Phoenix arising from its own ashes. On the other, we have the Hindu myth in which, as time passes, life gets worse and worse—until finally the god Shiva, the destructive aspect of the world, begins a terrible dance that destroys everything in fire. We cannot avoid the fire. The only question is whether or not we will emerge from it.

5

The
Population
Push

The Great Famine has begun, and it is a major factor in the crisis which is upon us. *The New York Times* noted a few years ago: "The belief that a world food crisis is still two decades off is proving a miscalculation. . . . The decisions, it is now evident, have not been made in time. The generals on the economic front have made the classic mistake of their military counterparts—fighting the last war too long. The shift from a four-decade war against surpluses to a new war—against world hunger—is under way, but it started too late. . . . The food crisis predicted for the 1980s is beginning to confront the world right now." As Dr. Paul Ehrlich put it in *The Population Bomb:* "The battle to feed all of humanity is over. In the 1970s, the world will undergo famines—*hundreds of millions* of people are going to starve to death in spite of any crash programs embarked upon now. At this late date, nothing can prevent a substantial increase in the world death rate. . . . Nothing could be more misleading to our children than our present affluent society. They will inherit a totally different world, a world in which the standards, politics, and economics of the 1960s are dead. . . . We are today involved in the elements leading to famine; tomorrow we may be destroyed by its consequences."

The rate of population increase has been accelerating for a longer period—and more in the form of a geometric progression —than has technology. Only in the past hundred years, and particularly in the past thirty, has the pace of technological acceleration begun to come from behind and surge forward. At the dawn of the 1970s, we found that it had drawn neck-and-neck with the furiously racing world population. At this stage, the two—population and technology—are tightly interwoven. Without technology the great population explosion could not have occurred. And the population problem forces technology to proceed far more rapidly than it would have done had population remained static.

Likewise, major economic changes take place in response to demand. As the market expands—or, more accurately, explodes—so too does the supply. Small rubber-manufacturing factories grow into corporate oligopolies. This, in turn, forces government to revise its political stance in relationship to industry, and this is reflected in an increased interdependence between government and corporations. The need for *further* technologies to cope with the new problems of size and organization creates whole new industries —IBM and Xerox, for example. As size increases and organization deepens, more technological breakthroughs (such as space flight) become possible. In the process, information is accumulated which can be applied in hundreds of different fields, not a few of them related to medicine—at which point, new means of cutting down the death rate are found and population pressure is further intensified.

Some global population figures are necessary at this point. Although population has been written about at great length since 1824—at which time the Reverend Thomas R. Malthus published his famous essay, "A Summary View of the Principle of Population," as a supplement to the *Encyclopædia Britannica*—the principle of population increase is still not as widely appreciated as it ought to be. As concise an explanation as any was given by Dr. Ehrlich in *The Population Bomb:*

> It has been estimated that the human population of 6000 B.C. was about five million people, taking perhaps one million years to get there from two and a half million. The population did not reach 500 million until almost 8000 years later—about A.D. 1650. This means that it doubled roughly once every thousand years or so. It reached a billion people around 1850, doubling in some 200 years. It took only

80 years or so for the next doubling, as the population reached two billion around 1930. We have not yet completed the next doubling to four billion, but we now have well over three billion people. The doubling time, at present, seems to be about 37 years. [In a footnote, Dr. Ehrlich adds: "Since this was written, 1968 figures have appeared, showing that the doubling time is now 35 years."] Quite a reduction in doubling times: 1,000,000 years, 1000 years, 200 years, 80 years, 37 years. Perhaps the meaning of a doubling time of around 37 years is best brought home by a theoretical exercise. Let's suppose what might happen on the absurd assumption that the population continued to double every 37 years into the indefinite future.

If growth continued at that rate for about 900 years, there would be some 6,000,000,000,000,000 people on the face of the earth. Sixty million billion people. This is about 100 persons for each square yard of the earth's surface, land and sea. A British physicist, J. H. Fremlin, guessed that such a multitude might be housed in a continuous 2000-story building covering our entire planet. The upper 1000 stories would contain only the apparatus for running this gigantic warren. Ducts, pipes, wires, elevator shafts, etc., would occupy about half of the space in the bottom 1000 stories. This would leave three or four yards of floor space for each person.

The way in which technology is related to the population situation needs to be examined. With the aid of DDT, for instance, it has been possible in various countries to cut the death rate from 25 per 1000 to 9 or 10 per 1000 in a matter of a few years. One of the main factors here is the way in which DDT contributes to the control of malaria. This cuts the death rate and, at the same time, allows a higher birth rate. The use of DDT covers only a quarter of a century, but already it is possible to see a dramatic shift in population patterns, with the age distribution in most societies being tilted abruptly toward the younger ages.

Today roughly 40 per cent of the population of the underdeveloped world is made up of people under fifteen years old. "As that mass of young people moves into its reproductive years during the next decade," says Dr. Ehrlich, "we're going to see the greatest baby boom of all time. Those children are the reasons for all the ominous predictions for the year 2000. They are the gunpowder of the population explosion." In short, the population crisis has not yet hit us—and, already it has been estimated that a total of 3.5 million people die annually from malnutrition. This figure, provided by the Population Crisis Committee, may even prove to be a conservative estimate, despite the recent talk of "zero population" figures in the United States and the Census Bureau's reduced population projection for the year 2000. Senator George McGovern has referred to hunger as "the chief killer of man."

Famine, of course, is not the only result of overpopulation. Other results are lack of shelter, low income, high incidence of disease, lack of medical facilities, and a high death rate among infants. To view the undeveloped nations strictly in terms of degrees of starvation is to overlook several wide bands on the spectrum of existence. Misery does not limit itself to the stomach.

In an article in *Scientific American* David Simpson asked the question: "Where is poverty most serious? How many people in the world are critically deprived of food and the other necessities of life?"

In terms of lack of food, Asia proves to be the most impoverished area in the world. A full two thirds of the world's undernourished are to be found in four countries: India, Pakistan, Indonesia, and China. The word "undernourished" is used here to include the 300 to 500 million who suffer calorie deficiency and the one third to one half of the world's population who suffer protein deficiency. Latin American countries turn out to be better off than their African and Asian counterparts. Yet Simpson's review showed that in terms of the infant mortality rate Latin American countries were in the worst shape. In Chile, Ecuador, Peru, and Guatemala, for instance, roughly 100 out of every 1000 infants die within the first year. This compares with an infant death rate of only 25 out of 1000 in North America and Western Europe.

The population of such cities as Nairobi, Calcutta, Caracas, Bogotá, and São Paulo is growing faster than the rate at which even rudimentary housing facilities can be provided. An account of housing conditions in Calcutta illustrates the magnitude of the problem there. A recent development plan of the Calcutta Metropolitan Planning Organization stated that adequate housing was "not within the bounds of feasible achievement over a 25-year period." The dimensions of the problem are so enormous that the plan did not anticipate the provision of houses but rather the construction of open-sided sheds to serve as shelters. One estimate suggests that 77 per cent of the families in Calcutta at present have less than 40 square feet of living space per person—an area, that is, only little more than six feet square.

Closely related to the lack of shelter is the lack of sanitation and the incidence of certain diseases—hookworm, trachoma, malaria, typhoid, dysentery, gastroenteritis, kwashiorkor, goiter, beriberi, and rickets. These are also indicative of a lack of nourishment and medication. Recording their incidence, however, was impossible, because "the countries require notification of only a limited number of illnesses and the reporting of these is incomplete. It is of interest, however, that the global incidence of malaria, a disease that is prevalent in tropical Africa, East Asia, and South America, has been estimated to be about 140 million cases per year, from which result just under a million deaths per year."

Simpson found that only 46 nations out of 124 had a per capita income of over $300 per year. A total of 2.1 billion people—almost two thirds of the world's population—live in those countries where the annual income per person is under $300. Of these, some 1.9 billion live in countries where the income is less than $100 per year. Only 18 countries in the world have a per capita annual income of over $1000—Canada, Czechoslovakia, Denmark, Finland, France, East Germany, West Germany, Hungary, Israel, Kuwait, the Netherlands, New Zealand, Norway, Sweden, Switzerland, the USSR, the United Kingdom, and the United States. Their total population amounts to 726.9 million.

Thus, if one were to step back from the earth, as astronauts have done, and attempt to describe it in terms of its over-all wealth or poverty, one would have to describe it as an impoverished planet. The impression of material wealth and well-being which exists in the handful of industrially advanced nations is, to say the least, misleading. It may be compared to the impressions received by those who live inside a feudal castle, oblivious to the sufferings of the peasants outside. The princes and princesses of the affluent society are living in a fairyland. Outside the customs and immigration gates, the world is a squalid, sprawling slum. The earth may be accurately described as a global ghetto, with only a few ornate mansions thrusting up here and there among the shacks and tenements and with the streets crammed with starving, crippled people.

The root cause of all this suffering is, of course, the population explosion, population trap, or population bomb—or, as it is also known, the Malthusian nightmare. All these terms, it will be noted, are negative descriptions of a process which, it can be shown, has some positive results. Invariably, these results are long-term, and the only short-term result is misery. This point has been made by Dr. Colin Grant Clark of Oxford University.

Dr. Clark was director of the Institute for Research in Agricultural Economics at Oxford and also served on the staff of England's Economic Advisory Council. Before presenting his case, however, I must point out that his attitude toward the problem of population growth can be described as an excellent example of the process of viewing situations in isolation. On the basis of existing Dutch and Japanese standards of agricultural productivity, he cheerfully predicts that the earth has the capacity to feed a population of as much as 92 billion persons. Beyond that, he refers vaguely to spaceships—"large artificial satellites on which people can live"—and the colonization of inhospitable planets.

Unfortunately, Dr. Clark makes no allowance for soil depreciation, the depletion of resources, and the failure to make technological adjustments at a pace rapid enough to match the rate of social decomposition which is brought on by population pressure coupled with these other factors. The word "pollution" is not a part of his vocabulary. He seems not to be worried at all about radiation, pesticide poisoning, the extinction of certain sea foods by residues, ecological disruption, or tipping of the carbon-oxygen balance due to atmospheric pollution. Moreover, he makes no allowance for the aggressions and tensions that are generated by conditions of overcrowding. Dr. Clark has apparently read none of the literature that deals with studies of overcrowding and the evidence that it contributes to aggressive behavior, a breakdown of social order, and increased instances of pathological behavior. He seems to think that 92 billion human beings could somehow live cheek-to-jowl in perfect harmony, without driving each other mad.

"Experts" such as Dr. Clark can perform the same acrobatic feats of rationalization in other fields—such as the area of pollution —and arrive, as he does, at the conclusion that the problems are greatly exaggerated. But, like Dr. Clark, they are working within an imaginary realm, one where a specific problem—population, pollution, depletion of resources, whatever—is somehow isolated, removed from any relationship with other problems, neatly boxed off in a corner where it can be easily dealt with. This specialized approach to problems leads to distortion. It takes the problem out of context and transforms it into an abstract issue for which there are obvious answers. This makes for a tidy thesis, but has little to do with the larger, more complex, and less manageable realities of the situation.

However, Dr. Clark does make the point that population pressures can be counted on to force changes that might otherwise never be made. Population pressure, he writes, has been the driving force of not a few major historical shifts. It is "probably the only force powerful enough to overcome the intense conservatism of peasant populations, whether they be Indian, Japanese, British, or Greek." Population pressure, for instance, initiated the Neolithic Revolution, that remarkable shift in cultural patterns in which our early ancestors were forced to move from a hunting-gathering economy to an agricultural mode of existence. Civilization, in short, came into being as a more or less direct result of population pressure. And the process was pushed still further—with the development of commerce and the production of specialized crops for export—when the population of seventh-century Greece began to outrun its agricultural resources.

"The great achievements of medieval civilization, particularly in France, came at a time of rapid population growth," writes Dr. Clark. The next key instance of a people's outrunning its agricultural resources was that of the Dutch at the beginning of the seventeenth century. "This pressure of population on resources provoked one of the most astonishing outbursts of national vigor which the world has ever seen"—resulting in the founding of New York, Cape Town, and Jakarta, as well as the discovery of Australia. By the second half of the eighteenth century, it was Britain's turn to feel the pinch of population pressure. In addition to the colonizing of North America, this led to "a radical transformation of [British] society—economic, political, and cultural—outstripping the achievements of the Dutch." Japan is also cited as an example. And the decline of French influence in the nineteenth century is blamed by leading French economists on the check in population growth. "In all these changes," Dr. Clark notes, "population increase has been the principal driving force."

There is no reason to suppose—at this particular juncture, when population pressure is being felt on a global scale for the first time —that it will suddenly cease to be a principal driving force in human affairs. On the other hand, it should be obvious that the changes that will be forged by population pressure this time cannot be the same as those that were forged in the past.

For the most part, the result in the past was an improvement in techniques of food production (something we are already well on the way to doing) and the stimulation of exploration and colonization. Clearly, this second reaction is no longer a viable option. The world is getting too close to being full, and the colonization of other planets is a long way off. Furthermore, even if it were logistically and financially possible to shoot people into space, it would take only eight thousand years, by most estimates, before the whole astronomical universe—two billion light-years in diameter—was packed solid with humanity, assuming that our present rate of reproduction was maintained.

Allowing that space exploration and colonization will never be a "solution" to population growth, it can also be pointed out that merely providing enough food is no solution either. It was the "unrealistic" Godwin who, in opposing the great Malthus, suggested that some day we would be able to grow all the world's food in a flowerpot. Technologically, the "flowerpot" is close to being within our grasp. Yet, clearly, the provision of food alone is not the answer to overpopulation. There are psychosocial problems, just beginning to be understood, which result from overcrowding. Moreover, the chances that the "flowerpot" will be built before the great famines of the 1970s have run their terrible course are not very good. The social upheavals that will be set in motion by these famines will have to be endured.

The third typical reaction to population pressure mentioned by Dr. Clark is "radical change in society," in terms of economics, politics, and culture. This is one place where the casual thread of historic continuity cannot be snipped. That population pressure is *already* forcing radical adjustments is clear. Perhaps the best illustration of the way in which population pressure succeeds in overwhelming institutional inertia is to be found in the response of Roman Catholics in North America to the Church's stand against birth control. A study published by Raymond H. Potvin, Charles F. Westoff, and Norman B. Ryder in the *Journal of Marriage and*

Family shows that by 1965, despite the Church's unrelenting position, a majority of Catholic women—in the United States, at any rate—were using artificial birth control devices. The study indicates that in 1955, 43 per cent of Catholic women never used any method of contraception. By 1965 this could be said of only 22 per cent. In the same ten-year period, the percentage of Catholic women using artificial birth control methods increased from 30 to 53 per cent. This was found to be happening among all types of Catholics, from blue-collar families to university graduates. It was happening despite Pope Paul VI's affirmation that "the thought and norm of the Church are not changed; they are those forces in the traditional teachings of the Church." The study included cross sections of various ethnic groups, many recently arrived from countries like Italy, Ireland, and France—so that the results likely represent at least the direction of an international trend, rather than a purely American trend.

I am not suggesting that population pressure—or, more specifically, the urge to limit one's family—accounts in itself for this breakdown in the authority of the Church. Other factors, which are clearly reflected in the breakdown of authoritarian structures in almost every other major Western institution, are also at work here. But the pressure of population, as it manifests itself in economic, social, and psychological terms, is without doubt a large contributing factor in the collapse of the old authoritarian Church structures. If it can work with so powerful and corrosive an effect on one of the most tradition-bound institutions on earth (i.e., the Catholic Church), it can reasonably be expected to work even more effectively on more responsive institutions such as governments. The refusal of *more than half* the Catholics in America to listen to the magisterium, the ultimate worldly teaching authority, can be described as amounting, at the very least, to a radical change in society.

Population can be seen, in this context, not only as a trap, a crisis, and an explosion, but also as a powerful lever of change. Rapidly accelerating population pressure will inevitably force rapidly accelerated change. There are further dimensions to the kinds of changes forced by population pressure, but these must be seen in the context of changes that are being forced by other rapidly accelerating pressures.

6

Not with
a Roar, but
a Hacking
Cough

Pollution enjoys—if such a word can be used—the same incestuous relationship with technology as does overpopulation. Furthermore, pollution can be blamed as much on overpopulation as it can on technology. The cumulative effect of all three factors, however, is usually not experienced until the damage is done. What we refer to separately as pollution, technology, and overpopulation can all be seen to derive from the same basic impulse to *grow*—to "fill up every ecological niche," as biologists put it. The more people there are, the greater the need for new technologies to keep these people alive. And the more technologies there are, the more pollution there is. In short, the root of all pollutant evil is not money, but people.

Marshall McLuhan notes in *Understanding Media* that "the drive toward unlimited growth [is] inherent in any kind of crowd, heap, or horde." Nature, it has been said, abhors a vacuum. What has been called the "will to live" can also be described as the "will to grow." Dr. Erhlich refers to our "evolutionary values," meaning that during all the centuries of our past "the individuals who had the most children passed on their genetic endowment in greater quantities than those who reproduced less. Their genes dominate our heredity today. All our biological urges are for more reproduction."

Biologists have often been stunned by the raw power of the drive toward growth that is manifested throughout the whole of the animate world. The science of ecology concerns itself wholly with the study of the ways in which this drive is at times released and at other times contained, thus maintaining the infinitely complex, interwoven balance of nature. There is another aspect of growth, however, which is not so marvelous and which has a strong bearing on the sequence which we describe as overpopulation-technology-pollution. This aspect was examined by John Davy, science correspondent for the London *Observer,* in an article dealing with the urgent global dangers created by human waste and ignorance. Davy concluded that:

> Certain remedies are obvious—more research, more education, more conservation. But in one sense this is a trivial answer, for the problem has much deeper roots. It is closely linked with the central dogma of civilization, which asserts the overriding necessity and desirability of "growth."
>
> Obviously, growth is a good thing insofar as it helps to feed, clothe, and house people, and reduce hunger and misery. But we are now being forced to realize that we are buying growth by squandering planetary capital at a frightening pace—fuel capital, mineral capital, water capital, soil capital, even animal capital (many whale and fish populations, for example, seem likely never to recover from our triumphs of fishing technology). In this connection, it is perhaps worth remembering other kinds of growth. In a medical context, the word has very sinister associations indeed. A tumor is a highly efficient, expansionist biological enterprise, recklessly exploiting the resources of its living host. With unswerving entrepreneurial drive, it soon establishes subsidiaries throughout its environment, which grow as industriously as the parent company. The result is familiar—suicide for the tumors through death of the host. During the past couple of centuries, we have been very busy creating a civilization which is now dangerously malignant. We have got to find a cure. We shall be compelled, I think, to look not only to more research and investment, but also within ourselves.

The earth, like any other host, has its limits. The growth of humanity, if it remains unchecked, cannot help but lead to suicide through death of the host. No understanding of the problem of pollution—the fallout of the population explosion which has been triggered by the warhead of technology—can be achieved until the limits of the host are established. These limits are not very flexible. The earth's weight is fixed at 6,000,000,000,000,000,000,000,000 (or 6×10^{21}) tons. It has a surface area of about 197 million square miles, three quarters of which is covered with water. One half of the land area is, as yet, uninhabitable, which leaves about 25 million square miles as the cradle, playpen, sandbox, or killing-ground of humanity. The earth has been the home of some 2500 species, of which about one third have survived—the rest dying out, leaving no descendants, only fossils. It has, at the moment, a population of 3.7 billion, which is increasing at the rate of 167,000 persons each day. In other words, each week we add to that population the equivalent of a metropolis of roughly one million inhabitants. Each person—at least, those who are North Americans—can be expected to consume some 26 million gallons of water in a 70-year lifetime, as well as 21,000 gallons of gasoline, 10,150 pounds of meat, 28,000 pounds of milk and cream, 9000 pounds of wheat, and whole warehouses full of other goodies—from food and drink to tobacco and furniture. In the process of gorging himself on this mountain of goods, he can be expected to produce some 21,000 pounds of carbon monoxide, at least 1000 pounds of nitrogen oxide, 4200 pounds of hydrocarbons, and so on. Two hundred million Americans, living out their natural lives, collectively consume eight billion five million tons of food. They also manage to produce twelve billion tons of solid garbage and at least—this is a conservative estimate—two and a half billion tons of raw sewage.

It has been said of the great ape, with contempt, that he is the only creature that will lie down in his own feces. It may be said of man, not so much with contempt as with horror, that he is the only creature whose wastes are not reprocessed in the ecological cycle. His is the only waste which is, in fact, "wasted." Not only is it wasted, but it also accumulates and becomes in itself a massive disruptor. Waste, for the first time in history, begins to become a social force. Further, it is a force which, like population and technology, is accelerating—and at roughly the same speed.

R. D. Lawrence reports in *The Poison Makers* that the typical American leaves behind him some 10,000 nondisposable bottles in his lifetime. Moreover, some 6000 tons of lead are pumped out of gun barrels in North America every year and left deposited in waterfowl habitats all over the continent. A single city such as metropolitan Toronto is expected, by 1986, to be producing a grand total of 3,111,400 tons of garbage per year. Already, in addition to garbage, Toronto must each year get rid of four million gallons of inflammable liquids, six million gallons of acid wastes, seven and a half million gallons of alkaline wastes, and 600,000 gallons of inert solutions—thus making up a total of more than eighteen million gallons. With these figures, we have just scratched the surface of the wastes that are accumulating throughout the industrialized nations. In one industry alone—namely, photography—Canadian companies, which are small in comparison with their American parent companies, dump some $25,000 worth of silver down the drain each year—and this at a time when mining experts predict that the world's supply of silver will be exhausted in five years.

There is, moreover, the problem of scrap. New York City alone produced in 1972 some 72,000 scrapped automobiles—almost double the figure of only six years before. On top of this heap, one must add the weight of scrapped refrigerators, stoves, pots, pans, washing machines, and so on. William May, chairman of the American Can Company, estimates that Americans every year dispose of 48 billion cans, 65 billion plastic and metal bottle caps and crowns, and 25 billion bottles and jars. According to the World Health Organization, "no environmental health problem has greater significance than the disposal of man's liquid and solid wastes."

Pollution—at this stage thrusting up everywhere in the form of smog, slimy beaches, radioactive harbors, stinking rivers, acidic rain, chemical poisons in our foods, a fantastic increase in cancer, and so on—can only be seen as the tip of a sludge-colored iceberg. It is much more pervasive than we wish to think, to the point where there is almost no pure air left on earth. In early 1968 Dr. Edgard E. Picciotto of the University of Brussels was forced to journey to McMurdo Station, the most remote research station in Antarctica, in order to obtain snow that had not been contaminated by pesticides and air pollution. The snow was to be used for a study of the fall of microscopic dust particles from space. It could not be obtained anywhere else on earth, because, as Picciotto said, "man has contaminated the whole earth—it's impossible to find water without carbon monoxide from automobiles and industrial waste."

It has been pointed out that the seas themselves are well on their way to becoming cesspools, to the extent that residues of pesticides have been found in the bodies of deep-sea fish which never come any closer than one hundred miles to shore. On the Antarctic Continent, residues of DDT have been found in the fat deposits of penguins and seals—residues that had drifted on ocean currents from the civilized world and had been absorbed through food and drink into the bodies of these birds and animals.

Robert and Leona Rienow, authors of *Moment in the Sun: A Report on the Deteriorating Quality of the American Environment,* wrote in *The Nation* in August 1968:

> Conservation is no longer a "cause"; it is a crisis. Its features are drawn in taut lines by forces unprecedented in human history, like the human face contorted by foreboding and strain. Conservation today bears scant resemblance to the historic pattern of the familiar wallflower at the on-going dance of material progress. Under the impact of a rocketing population, an insatiable spiral of economic expansion, as well as a gargantuan and pitiless technology, the very character of the concern of conservation has shifted. Once preoccupied with the quality of resources, its attention now is focused on the quality of environment. Once a question of supply, conservation is now an issue of survival—of species, of habitat, of mankind. . . . Calamities and crises which now tread on one another's heels are symptoms, environmental warnings. We are burdening the land with more people, production, and machines than it can possibly sustain.

During the course of the "on-going dance of material progress," we have, according to one estimate, annihilated some 450 species of animal. In the next fifty years more species of North American birds will become extinct than have in the past five thousand years. About that time, however, man himself will likely become extinct. A few years ago Dr. Richard Felger, then Senior Curator of Botany at the Los Angeles County Museum of Natural History, said: "Life will probably persist on earth for millions of years. But as things are now, it is not likely that man will be among the surviving species. If he continues poisoning the environment at the present rate, he won't have much more than half a century or a century left." Dr. Felger feels we are now facing the most serious evolutionary crisis in our history. And he is not, of course, alone in this view. A Greek chorus of biologists, botanists, ecologists, chemists, and demographers has been heard of late, all echoing Dr. Lamont C. Cole's plaintive question: "Can man domesticate himself ?" The evidence suggests, he said, that "the answer . . . is in the negative."

The domestication of man, as this book will attempt to show, has just begun. Our problem at the moment is to understand the dynamics of this process and the reasons for it. Pollution, like population and technology, is only one of the reasons. But before we can understand these phenomena as major social forces, we must gain some appreciation of their dimensions. Robert and Leona Rienow describe the present situation graphically. "This generation," they write, "is experiencing the convulsions of a dying nature." And biologist Hugh H. Iltis of the University of Wisconsin adds: "Never before in history has there been concern over the ability of nature to defend herself. But it is abundantly clear that one of the most important jobs of the conservation movement today is to expose the fallacies of the indestructibility of nature."

This fallacy can be exposed most readily by an examination of our atmosphere. Each of us breathes in some 18,000 lungfuls of air each day, amounting to between 25 and 50 pounds. By comparison, we take in only two to four pounds of food daily and a roughly equal amount of water. For the past 400 million years the level of oxygen in the atmosphere has remained constant at just a little over 20 per cent. Green plants absorb carbon dioxide and give off oxygen during the day, thus maintaining the balance. This fundamental process, known as "photosynthesis," is based squarely on the balanced relationship between carbon and oxygen. "Should this relationship be altered," says Dr. Cole of Cornell University, "life as we know it would be impossible. Man's actions today are bringing this imbalance upon us." When we reach the point where our rate of combustion exceeds nature's rate of photosynthesis, "we shall start running out of oxygen." It could happen, Dr. Cole adds, in a couple of decades. Or it could happen suddenly next year. And at the moment, we are adding carbon to the atmosphere much more rapidly than it is being absorbed by the oceans, and the oceans are the main reservoirs of carbon.

A 1967 study of 65 major manufacturing areas in the United States revealed that all 65 exceeded "acceptable limits of air pollution." Former Surgeon-General Dr. William H. Stewart reported that a four-engine jet liner expels 88 pounds of pollutants during each takeoff. There are more than 2000 commercial airlines adding to this sort of pollution in the United States every day. Authorities in Los Angeles estimate that for every 1000 gallons of gasoline used by cars, some 1000 pounds of carbon monoxide are discharged. At the same time, 200 to 400 pounds of hydrocarbons are also discharged, along with 50 to 150 pounds of nitrogen oxide and other compounds. In a city with a population of only one million, some 200,000 gallons of gasoline are used every day, releasing 20 to 40 tons of hydrocarbons, 5 to 15 tons of nitrogen dioxide, one ton of sulphur dioxide, and 100 tons of carbon monoxide. In all, almost 100 million tons of these compounds are released into the atmosphere in the United States each year.

In terms of cost, it has been pointed out that air pollution in North America causes some two billion dollars a year in crop and property damage. In terms of health, the cost is infinitely greater. Hydrocarbons cause cancer. Sulphur dioxide not only damages plants, but eats away such materials as stone, metal, cement, leather, paint, and textiles. It also causes respiratory diseases, including bronchitis and lung cancer. After being inhaled into the lungs, nitrogen oxide is readily absorbed by the blood and combines with the hemoglobin to form an additional complex which is similar in its effects to carbon monoxide. Carbon monoxide, of course, is poisonous. It is, however, an insidious poison. In high or acute levels in the air, it is deadly. Recent evidence suggests that in low but constant levels it may be a large factor in motor vehicle accidents and heart disease.

The use of lead in gasoline has increased tremendously, to the point where roughly two pounds of lead per capita are blown into the air in the United States every year. That puts the total at well over 400 million pounds. And, as in the case of carbon monoxide, lead is commonly known to be a poison. Until restrictions were imposed on the use of lead in paints, there were numerous cases of brain damage to youngsters who had nibbled lead-based paint from peeling toys and walls. Recent studies have shown that the feeding of lead to mice and rats in quantities comparable to the present human intake results in a shortening of the life span through a loss of vigor. Red blood cells are the principal victims of low lead intake, and the brain, kidneys, and other organs are affected by larger doses.

The average healthy individual in North America now has from 100 to 300 parts per billion of lead in his blood—a two- to fivefold increase over the levels which could be expected without artificial contamination. This is in addition to the carbon monoxide, hydrocarbons, and, as we shall see shortly, the accumulating residues of nitrates, DDT, and so on, which can also be found in comparatively large quantities in our bodies.

It must be remembered, at this point, that it is only the technological proficiency of modern medicine that prevents us from feeling the full effects of living in what has been described as "a frightening gas chamber." The protective umbrella of medicine shields us to an extent that keeps many of us alive. Despite the umbrella, however, the cancer rate among men in North America has increased by 23 per cent in the past twenty years. Medical experts point out that the increase is due mainly to lung cancer. In the same period the death from emphysema has increased to the point where Dr. Benjamin Burrows of the University of Chicago has said that it now "undoubtedly exceeds that from lung cancer." And emphysema ranks second to heart diseases as a cause of disability among adults. Emphysema, like lung cancer, and also like bronchitis— which is the fastest-growing ailment in North America—has been shown to be far more common in areas where the pollution level is high.

It has been estimated that roughly five million Americans are alive today—despite the poisons in the air, some fifty different kinds of which are pumped into it daily—thanks largely to drugs which were unknown even twenty-five years ago. At the same time, however, drugs also increase the dimensions of health problems. In *The Pill Conspiracy* George Johnson notes that "one in ten general hospital beds is occupied by someone suffering from the efforts to treat him, often involving misuse of modern drugs. . . . More than half of all recorded suicides in 1962 were caused at least partly by barbiturates unknown in 1940. . . . Some one-and-one-half million Americans now depend on the 'minor' tranquilizers and other habit-forming sedatives. One out of six of us reaches for the pill bottle at the first sign of stress." Dr. Herbert Ratner of Chicago's Loyola University has remarked that "we are becoming a pill-swallowing civilization. None of these pills is innocuous, and the damage they do frequently outweighs the good they intend." There are an estimated one million cases of drug poisoning in the United States each year, with roughly two thousand of them fatal. "Furthermore," as Johnson reports, "the United States Public Health Service lists 1.3 million *reported* cases a year of 'therapeutic misadventure'—a polite term for adverse reaction to drugs wrongly or improperly prescribed and given."

Misuse of modern drugs amounts to a form of internal pollution that is matched in scope and impact only by the pollution that affects our air, water, food, and soil. At the same time that we are poisoning our environment, we are frequently poisoning ourselves by ingesting potent pills whose long-range effects have not yet been tested. To cite the thalidomide tragedy is to point to only the most obvious example. Dr. Hollis Ingraham of the New York State health commission states: "Our interest today is not only with the pace of chemical synthesis, but with the character of it. With sulfa drugs and antibiotics we were concerned with toxicologic effects that were symptomatic and usually reversible. But [now] we're dealing more frequently with profound and irreversible effects. To questions of acute toxicity we must now add a concern with chronic and cumulative effects."

As will be shown later in this book, the conditions of life in large urban centers, into which more and more people are packed every day, leads to synergistic and cumulative effects that take the form of nervous and physiological illness, forcing the medical profession to come up with more and more drugs to combat the effects of atmospheric pollution, overcrowding, pesticide poisoning, and so on. While the new drugs do help to counteract the effects of the other forms of pollution, they act in two ways to worsen the situation: first, they lower our resistance, thus making us increasingly dependent on drugs; and, second, they frequently—either by themselves or in combination with other drugs—make us even sicker.

The extent to which society is affected by drugs is rarely understood. In 1939, as Johnson notes in *The Pill Conspiracy,* pharmaceutical sales in the United States for prescription and nonprescription drugs totaled $300 million at manufacturers' prices. The retail value was $800 million, which, as Johnson remarks, "may suggest to you where your friendly neighborhood druggist's interest lies." By 1970, however, pharmaceutical sales had swollen to $12 billion at retail. In roughly thirty years drug sales had increased 1600 per cent. A survey conducted by *Fortune* in 1964 indicated that the five hundred largest American drug companies showed profits of 10.6 per cent, the highest profit ratio of any industry. That the picture had remained basically the same was shown by *Forbes*'s "25th Annual Report on American Industry" published on January 1, 1973. "Consumer Goods: Health Care"—*Forbes*'s euphemism for drug companies—ranked first of all American industry groups in profitability. *Forbes*'s calculates profitability on the basis of return on both equity and capital. On both bases, the "Health Care" companies ranked number one, both for 1972 and during the five year period 1968–1972. Current trends indicate at least another 50 per cent increase in drug sales by 1978. Today there are 45,000 drugstores in the United States. And whereas twenty-five years ago the actual sale of drugs accounted for only about 20 per cent of the druggist's profit, by 1972 it accounted for almost half. Moreover, it has been noted that the number of drugstores owned by doctors has doubled since 1960, a strong indication that the number of prescriptions being handed out is not likely to drop suddenly.

Johnson writes: "Among the more common side effects drugs can induce are allergies, serious changes in the body's blood-making functions, liver and kidney changes, teratogenic effects (adverse influence on the development of unborn children, as exemplified by thalidomide), changes in behavior, drug dependence, and drug addiction. All of the above effects are toxic, meaning that they are forms of drug poisoning. Most of them can be fatal." Keeping this in mind, we begin to perceive the awesome dimensions of the problem: "Experts have estimated that from 90 to 95 per cent of the 1250 *tons* of antibiotics being used annually are prescribed unnecessarily—which is a familiar form of abuse." In one city alone—St. Louis (where atmospheric pollution has already contributed significantly to the incidence of emphysema, lung cancer, and bronchitis)—some 16,000 persons are reported to be using amphetamines and stimulants "in a potentially harmful manner."

Drug pollution—like the increase in disease (both mental and physical), to which it is partly a response—cannot be separated from the more general problem of atmospheric and chemical pollution. And long before there can be any reasonable chance of reversing this downward trend, the larger question of environmental pollution must be dealt with.

It can easily be shown that, so far, any attempts to control the cloud of poisonous gases that now envelops the earth have, on the whole, been miserable failures. In Los Angeles in 1960, automobiles by themselves spewed 1870 tons of cancer-causing hydrocarbons into the air each day. "Controls" were brought in. The result: by 1970 the level had *risen* more than 500 per cent. Moreover, the pace of building—factories, homes, automobiles, in short, everything that contributes to pollution—is expected to increase by five times before the century is out. Americans seem charmed by the vision of 244 million cars on the roads by the year 2000.

A further drain on the world's carbon-oxygen balance comes from the fact that each year some three million acres of land in the United States are torn up and replaced with asphalt and concrete, thus decreasing the number of oxygen-manufacturing plants by that amount. As pesticides and herbicides drain from the land into rivers and are washed out into the ocean, the phytoplankton of the sea (which produce 70 per cent of the world's oxygen supply) are being interfered with massively. Dr. Cole has estimated that if a ship the size of the *Torrey Canyon,* loaded with concentrated herbicides instead of crude oil, had sunk off the coast of North America, it would have erased these phytoplankton—with the result that almost overnight everyone in the Northern Hemisphere would be gasping for breath. And the day when we *will* be gasping for breath may not be far off. Austin N. Heller, former Pollution Control Commissioner for New York, has estimated that unless air pollution can be brought under control within twenty years, North American city dwellers will have to walk around wearing gas masks. Where their food will come from, of course, remains to be seen.

The first tangible signs of a global shift in atmospheric conditions as a direct result of pollution came to light in February 1968. At that time, R. A. Bryson, director of the Center for Climatic Research at the University of Wisconsin, reported that the average world temperature had dropped about seven tenths of a degree. This was caused by an increase of only 2 per cent in the amount of pollutants in the earth's atmosphere. "That doesn't sound like much," said Bryson in an interview with the Los Angeles *Times.* "But it is enough to change the pattern of heat exchange between the equatorial area and the polar areas of the earth, setting in train causes and effects that are bringing about shorter, cooler summers and longer, colder winters. For example, an increase of 30 per cent in the turbidity of the atmosphere would lengthen the winter in the northern tier of Midwestern states about six weeks. Lengthening the northern winter that much would mean there wouldn't be much summer left." Prior to industrialization, Bryson pointed out, the chief source of atmospheric "dust" (meaning any particle, organic or inorganic, that gets into the air and stays there for any length of time) was volcanoes.

Many scientists believe that the ice ages were originally caused by volcanic eruptions which filled the atmosphere with fine, floating dust. This cover of dust shaded the earth from the sun's radiation and thus lowered its temperature. In January 1969 the first official acknowledgment that such a process is now taking place in our own atmosphere came from Washington. Government meteorologist J. Murray Mitchell, Jr., reported that both American and Russian meteorologists believe that the poisonous clouds hovering over industrial centers are now spreading themselves out into a nebulous veil that virtually encircles the planet. Mitchell admitted that the veil "may indeed be responsible for a slight cooling trend noted in the earth's climate in the last quarter century." Harsher winters in North America and Europe in recent years are "linked" to the cooling-off, and the cooling-off is in turn linked to the planetary veil, which is the sum of industrial pollution. "Man is loading the atmosphere with an increasing tonnage and ever-widening variety of other chemical wastes, including smokes, dusts, . . . toxic fumes, and occasionally radioactive materials."

Along with poisoning our atmosphere to the extent that we are likely to trigger another ice age, we have also managed to poison our soil and water. In 1970 almost 100 million pounds of pesticides and herbicides were dumped on the soil in North America alone. In *Silent Spring* Rachel Carson shows that these pesticides and herbicides do not merely "evaporate" after being used. They remain in the soil until they seep down into the water tables. In large quantities they are also carried by erosion, run-off, and underground rivers directly into other rivers, streams, and lakes.

Soil is composed of millions of tiny organisms—from bacteria to worms, grubs, and insects. Studies have shown that the use of poisons—usually to get rid of only one kind of insect or weed— succeeds in poisoning dozens, sometimes hundreds, of other species, including man. The poisoning need not be direct, since nature works on the principle of "the house that Jack built." The birds that feed on grubs and worms are poisoned; the fox that feeds on the bird that fed on the grubs and worms is poisoned; and so on. The chain of life is easily disrupted by the introduction of poison at any point along the line. Likewise, when rivers are contaminated, the fish are sooner or later poisoned too. And if the fish are caught and eaten, the poison is passed on to us.

Tests have shown that vegetables and fruits are similarly affected by chemical poisons. Carrots, for instance, have been found to absorb more insecticides than any other crop. Over a period of ten years even seemingly moderate applications of insecticides to the soil can build up incredible quantities. Potato soils in the United States and Canada have been found to contain concentrations of up to fifteen pounds of DDT per acre. Corn soils have had as much as nineteen pounds. In apple orchards, DDT residues have been found to be present in concentrations up to 113 pounds per acre. And DDT, after all, is only a mild chemical poison in comparison with some of the ones that are now being used. Some, such as Aldrin, have been shown to be 100 to 300 times as toxic as DDT.

That these chemicals find their way into our bodies is beyond doubt. The average North American today—you, me, your wife, your children—has eleven parts per million of DDT concentrated in the fatty tissues of his body. Israelis, heavy users of artificial fertilizers, have been found to have as many as 19.2 parts per million. In fact, the use of artificial nitrogen fertilizer—more than six million tons per year in North America—has produced a problem of concentrations even in baby foods. The Montreal Department of Health not long ago found 642 parts per million in squash. The "acceptable health limit" of nitrates in drinking water, for instance, is considered in some areas to be no more than forty-five parts per million, and in others, no more than ten parts per million. An almost complete ban on the use of DDT in the United States was ordered by the Environmental Protection Agency in 1972. But these residues will remain for a long time to come. What is more, pressures are already being exerted to repeal the ban on DDT at least in certain sectors.

An article in the March 1969 issue of *Scientific American* began: "Man's injection of excess nitrogen into the biosphere is not only seriously polluting rivers and lakes but also has greatly increased the frequency of a rare form of poisoning in both humans and domestic animals." The concentration of nitrates in drinking water already exceeds the health limit in a quarter of the shallow wells in Illinois and in many other wells in California. In one Minnesota town, the concentration of nitrates "has forced complete replacement of the water system. . . . The danger to health from nitrate-polluted water arises not from the nitrate, which is relatively innocuous, but from the fact that certain intestinal bacteria convert nitrate (NO_3) into nitrite (NO_2). Nitrite combines with hemoglobin and destroys its oxygen-transporting properties."

Water, of course, is not the only source of nitrates. According to Barry Commoner of Washington University, "poisoning from an overabudance of nitrate in foodstuffs has been reported in Europe; children under the age of three months are particularly vulnerable. One French pediatrician has set the maximum permissible concentration of nitrate in foodstuffs at 300 parts per million." In addition to the levels of nitrate concentration found in baby foods, other studies found—again in baby foods—443 parts of nitrate per million in wax beans, 977 in beets, and 1373 in spinach.

During a meeting of the American Association for the Advancement of Science, Commoner also noted that nitrogen production in the United States, due to fumes from power plants and automobile exhausts, has increased 300 per cent in the last twenty-five years. In the same period, the use of nitrogen fertilizers has increased 1400 per cent. "The last two processes," reported *Scientific American,* "add some ten million tons of nitrogen compounds to the environment each year, more nitrogen than is cycled annually within the U.S. by all the processes of nature combined." The magazine concludes by taking note of "the painful dilemma presented by fertilizers: high agricultural yields and thus the whole of the farm economy depend on fertilizers, yet it is physically impossible to prevent the escape of nitrates from field to water table. To impose limitations on the use of fertilizers would be to reduce food supplies at a time of mounting worldwide needs, *as well as to engender fierce opposition from farmers and the chemical industry* [my italics]." Is this not the "painful dilemma" presented by every other form of pollution—whether caused by pesticides, herbicides, automobile exhausts, industrial fumes, sewage disposal, or whatever?

The causes of pollution are lock-stitched into the basic material of our economy, and nothing short of a basic change can ever successfully unravel the problem.

The problem, as has been pointed out earlier, is now global. Rainfall over Sweden becomes increasingly acidic. In the Philippines, a single spraying of a pond to get rid of mosquitoes results in the death of 60,000 milkfish. And it must be remembered that two thirds of the world's sea life breeds in the shallow estuaries that are polluted directly by rivers, spraying, and development.

In September 1968 sixty-six nations sent representatives to the UNESCO conference on conservation in Paris and even agreed in principle to a blueprint for planetary management—a development which, as we shall see later, ties in closely with developments in a wide range of different fields. The blueprint, called the International Biological Programme, has so far scarcely gotten off the ground, even as nothing more than a project-launching agency. But at the conference Fraser Darling, vice-president of the United States Conservation Foundation, expressed an opinion that is worth recording. There is a strong possibility, he said, that as a species we might eventually sterilize ourselves out of existence with an overload of chemical pollutants such as residual pesticides. This is a possibility that is not as remote as it might seem.

A few months after the Paris conference, the 135th Annual Meeting of the American Association for the Advancement of Science was held in Dallas, Texas. In symposium after symposium, scientists repeatedly warned of impending danger as we continue to pollute the air, the land, and the sea. Dr. Irving S. Bengelsdorf, former senior scientist with the Borax Research Corporation, then working as a science writer for the Los Angeles *Times,* pointed out that "when a swamp in Ceylon is sprayed with DDT to eliminate insect pests, we somehow affect the amount of DDT stored within the livers of snowy owls in the Arctic, penguins in the Antarctic, and people everywhere. There are more than 20 tons of DDT 'on the hoof' in this country, 'walking around' stored within the fatty tissues of 200 million Americans." At the same meeting Dr. John L. Buckley of the United States Office of Science and Technology pointed out that about one half of the pesticides that are sprayed end up in areas for which they were not intended, thus affecting plants and animals which are not considered targets. He estimated that there are now some 300 to 500 million pounds of DDT "floating around" in the earth's atmosphere.

In *Man in the Web of Life* John Storer reports that Dr. M. M. Hargraves of the Mayo Clinic, "referring to some 200 case histories of cancer and blood diseases, expressed the conviction that they show a direct cause-and-effect relationship to the chlorinated hydrocarbons which include DDT and many others. There have also been instances where people exposed to organo-phosphorous insecticides have developed schizophrenic and other reactions, including impairment of memory." Storer mentions a 1963 pesticide research program in which the Department of the Interior reported that oysters exposed to DDT in their environment accumulated within their bodies concentrations that were 70,000 times as strong as those normally accumulated within a month. "As Dr. LaHam points out, we just don't know what is happening within the human body as a result of exposure to pesticides and their relatives. On the other hand, it has been conclusively proven that DDT, DDD, and other similar poisons that accumulate in the fat have led to the sterility of certain species, and we have found this out because the species in question are relatively short-lived and therefore breed more rapidly than the larger animals, affording more generations for study." It must be remembered, R. D. Lawrence adds, that "in Canada and the U.S. 7 parts per million of poison in edible substances is tolerated by our authorities. That is, cabbages can come to our table containing 7 p.p.m. of herbicides. Apples may also contain that proportion, so may lettuce and beets and practically everything else that we eat. By this means, the so-called safe level of poison may be multipled to levels that may be extremely unsafe, because, as I have already said, many of these poisons become absorbed and stored in our fatty tissues."

The hydrogen bomb—the threat of nuclear war in general—is one of our "lesser worries." So long as it does not happen, and so long as excessive testing of nuclear weapons does not take place, we are not killed off. In order for us to be annihilated by nuclear fallout, a war must first take place. This is not the case with industrial fallout, otherwise known as pollution. It is a "war" which has been going on for more than a century. Its cumulative effects are just beginning to be felt. There is no proof that the damage done so far is even reversible. Conceivably, chain reactions may already have been set in motion which cannot be halted. Whatever the case, life on earth as we now experience it will not be possible any longer than fifty years—assuming that the rate of the pollution remains the same. This is not, however, to be the case. At this point, we are sucked back into the vortex of the population increase. As the population curve rises, so too does the curve of pollution. Daniel O. Price says in *The 99th Hour: The Population Crisis in the United States:* "At the present rate of population increase, we will have to approximately double all our school facilities in the next sixty years if we are to maintain the present level of educational facilities."

The same, of course, can be said about factories, aircraft, automobiles, refineries, incinerators, houses, smelters, processing plants, and garbage-disposal complexes—all sources of pollution. As the sources double, so too does the amount of pollution. More sophisticated control devices may reduce the rate of increase, but given the doubling of sources of pollution, it is highly unlikely that the present rate—the rate that will lead to our doom in fifty years—can be reduced. A 50 per cent increase in the efficiency of pollution control methods—which would be an incredible leap forward, considering the failure of almost all methods so far—would succeed in doing nothing more than leveling off the rate of pollution increase. And this would do nothing to avoid the disaster.

Nor is it enough to hope that population increase will suddenly cease. Boulding points out in *The Meaning of the Twentieth Century:*

> A generation ago it seemed reasonable to suppose that this problem [i.e., the problem of population increase] would solve itself with the increase in income. It was observed that the richer countries had lower birth rates than the poorer countries and that the richer classes within each country had a lower birth rate than the poorer classes. The recipe for the control of population then seemed merely to make everybody rich. . . . In the 1930s in many parts of the developed societies the net reproduction rate was actually less than one. [This refers to the ratio of one generation to the preceding generation. When the ratio is one, it means that as one generation dies off, it leaves an equal number to replace it.] In the 1940s, however, there was a change. . . . In almost all societies today, the net reproduction ratio is much greater than one. At its present rate of increase, for instance, the United States will reach a billion people in a little over a hundred years.

What we have been examining so far—overpopulation, pollution, and, briefly, the way in which they are related to technology and to each other—is not yet an over-all process. We have been discussing only two major parts of a much larger problem—a problem that is referred to as "environmental collapse." Environmental collapse, we shall see, is rapidly becoming a social force greater than any other in the whole of human history. It is much more than the sum of its parts. So long as pollution and overpopulation are the only factors considered, the topography of environmental collapse—its scope and meaning—cannot be understood. Thus, we turn now to a further dimension of environmental collapse, one which is as closely related to pollution, overpopulation, and technology as these three are related to each other.

7

The Gored
Earth

The average automobile is made up of 2600 pounds of iron and
steel, 76 pounds of aluminum, 36 pounds of copper and copper alloys, 32 pounds of lead, 23 pounds of zinc, and 2 pounds of magne-
sium. In 1972, 10.7 million cars were sold in the United States,
about 85 per cent of which were built here. This means that in the
course of that one year the automobile industry gobbled up some 23
billion pounds of iron and steel and 700 million pounds of aluminum. This says nothing about the drain on resources made by the
construction industry, the military, the aircraft industry, or any of
the other major users of ores. By the end of the century, according
to the Department of the Interior, the American population will be
nearly twice its present size and "automobile production may have
tripled."

Fairfield Osborn has noted that Americans have used up more of
the world's resources in the past forty years than all of the human
beings on earth were able to use in the past 4000 years. While
Americans account for only one fifteenth of the world's population,
they manage to consume *one half* of the world's total annual product. By the year 2000, if current trends were somehow to continue,
the United States would be consuming 83 per cent of the world's

total output of goods. We see here, in addition to a rapidly accelerated pace of technological change, an accelerated population increase, and an accelerated rate of pollution, an accelerated assault
on natural resources.

The relationship pointed out earlier between technology and population, between technology, population, and pollution, and between
all three interacting together, can now be seen to have extended itself to include depletion of available resources. As population increases, the pressure on resources mounts. And as technology
advances, the methods of getting at the resources are improved. Not
only are more resources used up at a faster rate in response to a
greater demand, but in the process of extracting the resources, the
technological base is expanded—thus making it possible to extract
more resources at an even faster rate and, further, to use the resources in more ways, thereby creating whole new industries with
appetites for yet more resources. In the process, we incidentally
make it possible for more people to live longer and more infants to
survive, thus technologically stimulating the increase in population
and making the demand for resources even greater. At the same
time, in the process of getting at the available resources and processing them, we increase the level of pollution. This tends to diminish the quality of the resources which remain, so that we are
subtracting from them indirectly at the same time that we are rapidly multiplying the demands for them. And as the pollution level
rises like a cloud of dust in the wake of technology, the rate at
which resources are disrupted, diminished, and in some cases wiped
out almost entirely increases in direct proportion.

Vance Packard reports in *The Waste Makers* that when the President's Material Policy Commission surveyed consumption patterns
in the United States, it found that every man, woman, and child was
using up an average of eighteen tons of material each year. In a
study of existing resources, Packard found that "the amount of . . .
rich iron ore left in known deposits in the United States would not
meet American needs for even a decade." Already, American steelmakers have been driven into Canada, South America, and elsewhere in the search for high-grade ores.

Foreign sources are supplying a third of the iron-ore needs of the
United States (the percentage of iron ore imported quadrupled within

a decade) and the percentage will continue to mount. . . . Of the seven metals most needed in making steel alloys, only two are in adequate supply from domestic sources. . . . The once-rich United States reserves of zinc and lead have become so low that they are rapidly approaching the point of being uneconomic to work. . . . Many mining companies are being forced to process six times as much ore to get a ton of copper as they did at the beginning of the century. Partly as a result, copper costs have risen about 600 per cent in three decades. Meanwhile, the U.S. has changed from being the world's leading exporter of copper to being the world's leading importer of copper. . . . United States consumption of oil, the chief source of the nation's energy, has tripled since the end of World War II. With only one seventh of the world's proven reserves of oil, the United States has been consuming considerably more than half of all the world's production. . . . At today's rate of consumption, not tomorrow's, the United States has proven reserves of oil sufficient to meet the nation's needs for thirteen years.

Packard takes note of the further "violently accelerated demands upon resources [being made] by the other nations of the world." The demand for petroleum, for example, is rising faster in the rest of the free world than it is in the United States. Italy's landscape is starting to show many great, gleaming gasoline stations. In Britain the number of cars on the road has doubled within a decade. And there is a fantastic world population growth. . . .

An excerpt from this section of *The Waste Makers* is worth quoting in whole, since it focuses on the central dilemma of unorganized or unintegrated—as opposed to organized and integrated —global society:

Further, many nations have desperately ambitious plans to industrialize; and their people have learned from American movies, tourists, and advertisements to desire such things as telephones, refrigerators, television, and motorcars.

Joseph Spengler, Duke University economist, specializing in world population trends, points out that shortages of materials available in the United States "will be greatly intensified by the progress of population and aggregate consumption in other parts of the world, since these other areas will be drawing increasingly upon relatively limited sources of supply, major access to which has heretofore been enjoyed by Americans."

As industrialization spreads in Asia, Africa, and other areas where per capita consumption of materials has been extremely low by

American standards, demand for raw materials and energy will expand swiftly and produce scarcities that will force rises in price. *If the rest of the world—even with its present population—were to achieve the level of material wealth enjoyed by the people of the United States, there would be a sixfold increase in need for materials. Actually, there is no longer enough copper, tin, and lead left in the world to permit such a duplication on the basis of today's technology.*

Obviously, as resources diminish and the rate of industrialization increases in other countries, the amount of competition will also increase. Already, India, looking ahead to a technological future, has clamped down on thorium export. Canada, becoming increasingly aware of her own water needs of the future, and uncomfortably aware of the growing thirst of the United States, is already resisting pressures to "sell" water across the border. The time may not be far off when Venezuela will begin to hoard her iron ore and oil, or at least sell it to other customers. Likewise, Canada will soon probably begin to resent the mining of her rich deposits by American steelmakers. "It would seem inevitable," writes Packard, "that if the world's population and the resources are not soon brought into a more tolerable balance, some of the competition by nations for badly needed resources is likely to generate ugly frictions that could explode into warfare."

While we are dealing here mainly with American problems—the most aggravated in the world as yet—it should not be hard to see that the United States, due to its technological superiority, is merely the first nation to stumble so heavily into a trap which inevitably awaits any industrially advanced country. Other nations, particularly Russia, are pressing hard on American heels. All large nations, India and China being the most obvious examples, aspire to create an industrial base equal to that of the United States. That they have no hope, on the basis of existing technologies, of achieving it, should be clear.

The Chinese, like the Indians, have only begun to strip their resources American-style. At Wuchang in Central China, the Wuhan Iron and Steel Company was a complex with a total personnel of 200,000, as of 1965. Yet only seven years before, in 1958, no iron was being produced in the area at all. According to Robert Guillain, author of *When China Wakes,* Chinese production of steel reached twelve million tons in 1961. A year earlier, coal production had reached between 350 and 400 million tons. Petroleum production rose to six million tons in 1962. In all cases, bad slumps followed as a result of Moscow's withdrawal of her technicians at the beginning of the Sino-Soviet split. But production steadily began to pick up afterward and is now presumably at much higher levels. Heavy rolling mills, steel works, blast furnaces, factories of every kind spring up across the length and breadth of China.

A few more figures are in order before we turn to yet another aspect of environmental collapse. These other figures—related, like everything else, to population and the problems of technological advance—concern the soil. In December 1967 Dr. Lamont Cole told the American Association for the Advancement of Science that "we have lost many thousands of acres to erosion and gullying, and many thousands more to strip mining." Strip mining, in fact, had by the end of 1972 defaced some 3.6 million acres of American land, and, with the aid of machines equipped with 200-ton jaws, the rate of disfigurement is now 165,000 acres per year. That rate is expected to double soon. "It has been estimated," continued Dr. Cole, "that the agricultural value of Iowa farmland, which is about as good land as we have, is declining by one per cent per year. In our irrigated lands of the West there is the constant danger of salinization from rising water tables, while elsewhere, from Long Island to California, we have lowered water tables so greatly that in coastal regions salt water is seeping into the aquifiers. Meanwhile, an estimated two thousand irrigation dams in the United States are now useless impoundments of silt, sand, and gravel."

It has also been shown that the United States has lost roughly nine inches of the rich topsoil it had when the Pilgrims landed—which is about one third of the topsoil at that time. Back in 1948, quoting from a report by the Soil Conservation Service, Fairfield Osborn noted that the soil losses by erosion from all lands in the United States total 5,400,000,000 tons annually. "From farmlands alone, the annual loss is about three billion tons, enough to fill a freight train which would girdle the globe eighteen times. . . . In a normal production year, erosion by wind and water removes twenty-one times as much plant food from the soil as is removed in the crops sold off this land. . . . The total annual loss to the United States as a result of uncontrolled erosion and water runoff is estimated at $3,844,000,000."

We cannot discuss soil erosion without at least touching on the closely related problem of shrinking forests, a problem that contributes enormously to further erosion as well as adding to the danger of an eventual collapse of the oxygen-carbon balance in the atmosphere. In *The Plundered Planet* Osborn mentions that other than forests, there are about a billion acres of land in the United States that fall into the three categories of farm pasture land, farm croplands, and open-range grazing lands. Of this billion acres, he says, "considerably more than one quarter have now been ruined or severely impoverished." Turning to the problem of the forests, Osborn notes an even more drastic rate of impoverishment. In its natural state, about 40 per cent of the American land mass was covered with forest. "Today the primeval or virgin forest has been so reduced that it covers less than 7 per cent of our entire land area."

Even taking into consideration forested areas consisting of second- or third-growth forests, many in poor condition, and scattered farm woodlots—as opposed to healthy "virgin" forest—the total of forested areas adds up to only 20 per cent. "The situation in our remaining forests is becoming serious," wrote Osborn. He notes that in 1909 the estimated total stand of saw timber in the country was 2826 billion board feet. By 1945 that total had been reduced by 44 per cent to only 1601 billion board feet—at the very time that population was rising in a curve that was almost as steep as the one that measured the fall of timber stands. "The annual drain on the nation's forests approximates 54 billion board feet, while the annual growth is only approximately 35 billion board feet. In other words, the loss exceeds growth by more than 50 per cent. It does not take much mathematics to prove that our country cannot go on this way much longer. We are repeating the errors . . . that have undermined so many other countries in earlier periods of history."

A final point needs to be made here. "Our present technology is fundamentally suicidal," writes Kenneth Boulding. "It is based on the extraction of concentrated deposits of fossil fuels and ores, which in the nature of things are exhaustible. . . . If the rest of the world advances to American standards of consumption, these resources will disappear overnight. On this view, economic development is the process of bringing closer the evil day when everything will be gone—all the oil, the coal, the ores—and we will have to go back to primitive agriculture and scratching in the woods." Having said this, Boulding then acknowledges that a detectible "anti-entropic movement in technology" likely foreshadows "a technology in which we shall draw all the materials we need from the virtually inexhaustible reservoirs of the sea and the air and draw our energy from controlled fusion—either artificially produced on earth or from the sun."

The earth *is* being gored and plundered and exhausted at a fantastic and ever-increasing rate. That this will lead inevitably to further misery, deprivation, and a progressive deterioration in the quality of our environment (and therefore in our experience of life) cannot rationally be denied. However, it must also be pointed out that alternate sources of energy and power have already been found in unlimited abundance and that it is just a matter of time before they are put to work on a large scale. Unfortunately, there is a snag here, and the snag is in those words, "a matter of time." There is a deadline—one that is probably most tangible in the form of the danger of an irreversible disruption of the oxygen-carbon balance in the atmosphere, described in the previous section. It may be seen eventually that the greatest damage done by destruction of natural resources was to cut deeply into the world's total number of plants, upon which the vital process of photosynthesis depends. The gouging of 165,000 acres of land each year in the United States for surface mining, the gobbling up of land by urban sprawl—at a rate that is expected to increase shortly by five times—and the removal of forests at a rate that has seen the American timber stand shrink to less than one half of what it was in Teddy Roosevelt's day, all serve to cut down the total amount of photosynthesis taking place.

At the same time, the pollution caused by the production of petroleum, the mining of coal, the smelting of steel and iron, and so on, contributes to the rate of combustion and causes more and more pollution. In short, the effects of the *process* of depleting resources may have a cumulative impact which will hit us long before we make the slow, disrupting, and agonizing transition to other sources of power. Having made that clear, hopefully—and having already dealt with hunger, possible strangulation in waste, and poisoning—we turn now to the problem of thirst.

8

Revenge of
the Automatic
Washers

If I seem so far to have been placing undue emphasis (and perhaps blame) on the United States, it is simply because I believe, as does researcher and author Zbigniew Brzezinski, that the United States today is "the first society to experience the future." Richard Kostelanetz points out in *Beyond Left & Right* that "the power of new technologies is so fundamental and autonomous that a particularly crude machine seems to have more or less the same effect upon both individuals and the environment in every culture that adopts it." And further: "As America is technologically the most advanced of cultures, what happens here, for good or ill, is liable to happen in staggered succession everywhere around the world."

If this is, in fact, the case, then the Chinese, Indians, Russians, Europeans, and Latin Americans would do well to adopt the cautious, hoarding attitude of Canadians toward their water supplies. Canada, of course, is a logical alternate source of water for thirsty America. And the pressure is already mounting for the purchase of Canadian waters. Technology, overpopulation, the exploiting of resources (particularly mineral resources) all combine to drain available water supplies at a furious rate. While at the same time, pollution and pesticide poisoning combine to diminish or make useless the remaining supplies.

Americans use more than 350 billion gallons of water every year. As of 1972, the country contained more than 40 million bathrooms, about 75 million washing machines, and 20 million dishwashers, not to mention the millions of car washers, lawn sprinklers, and so on. Twenty to thirty gallons of water are used up in each load handled by a washing machine or in the course of a single shower. It takes about 1000 gallons of water to produce a single pound of irrigated sugar or corn, 10,000 gallons of water for a single pound of cotton fiber, 1500 gallons of water for a single pound of wheat, 25 gallons of water to turn out a pound of paper, 65,000 gallons to make a ton of steel, and 660,000 gallons to produce a ton of synthetic rubber. To produce a gallon of alcohol requires 100 gallons of water. A modern oil refinery uses as much water as a city of two million people. Moreover, a 1968 report turned over to Congress by then President Lyndon B. Johnson said that by the year 2020 the United States is expected to be drawing off nearly five times as much water as it is today.

The incredible demands being made on American water resources are mounting steadily—and meanwhile the supplies are steadily diminishing. Water tables all over North America are falling. People living in western New York State already pay a dollar for one five-gallon jug of drinking water, while several communities in Texas have been abandoned for lack of water. In the Midwest underground water tables have sunk so low that further draining is prohibited. Dallas, Texas, is already being forced to pump water from the salt-tainted Red River. New York at one point a few years ago considered trying to purify the polluted Hudson in order to slake its thirst, an attempt shelved only because of a long period of heavy rainfall. But with the next drought? . . . Wells in Chicago which a century ago flowed under their own pressure today go down more than 2000 feet to reach the water table.

A short, optimistic answer to this problem lies in the word "desalination"—i.e., the process of changing the salt water of the oceans into drinkable water. The reality of the situation, however, does not leave room for such simple, one-technology answers. The worldwide desalting capacity is expected to be twenty billion gallons a year by 1984—a considerable quantity. The trouble is that by 1984 the United States alone will need 600 billion gallons a year. The maximum global desalting capacity, in short, will meet only one thirtieth of the needs of this one country.

Apart from problems in the future, the present situation is already at the point of being nearly intolerable. It was reported in April 1964 that some 320,000 acres of Arizona farmland had been withdrawn from production because of the water shortage. R. D. Lawrence tells us that already more than 100 million acres of water have been drained for agricultural purposes, "that untold other millions of acres of water have been filled in to control mosquitoes, that countless more have been drained for roadways and buildings." And apart from the fact that more and more water is being used at a time when less and less water is available, we must, at this point, further complicate matters by reintroducing the factor of pollution.

Ships sailing on Lake Erie have been urged by the United States Public Health Service not to use lake water taken from within five miles of the American coast either for drinking or cooking. The water is so fouled with chemicals and wastes that not even boiling or chlorination can make it safe to drink. Not surprisingly, the catch of blue pike in Lake Erie dropped from 6.9 million pounds in 1956 to less than 200 pounds in 1963—another reminder of the way in which resources, including food resources, are diminishing at the same time that demand is multiplying. Dr. Barry Commoner, director of the Center of the Biology of Natural Systems in St. Louis, has pointed out that artificial nitrogen fertilizers—seeping through the soil, being carried by runoff, and so on—have been accumulating in vast amounts of organic waste in the lake, making it a kind of "huge underwater cesspool." A recent Federal Water Pollution Control Commission survey of Lake Erie showed that municipal sewage added some ninety million pounds of nitrogen to the lake each year. Fertilizer runoff from surrounding farms added another seventy-five million pounds of nitrogen.

Dr. René Dubos has noted that Lake Erie—the most obvious example—is not the only lake undergoing a "biological cataclysm." "The growing burden of urban wastes," says Dubos, "will by 1980 be sufficient to consume the total oxygen content of the entire river system of the United States during the summer rate of flow." It was recently noted that in the United States more than 1500 communities with a population of thirteen million people were discharging untreated sewage and detergents into their streams. Another 1500 communities were discharging "inadequately treated" sewage from some seventeen million people. And more than 2700 small towns with a total population of six million people had no sewage treatment facilities at all.

Further dimensions of the water problem are perceived when we refer to the point made earlier about the eventual shift from fossil fuels to controlled fusion. While such a transition would help to avert a collapse of the social machine from lack of energy due to exhaustion of mineral resources, we cannot depend on atomic power unless we have a tremendous amount of water to spare. As Packard notes in *The Waste Makers,* "most of the developments which are supposed to produce a golden era require fantastic amounts of fresh water. . . . Nuclear power plants are drawing oil from shale, and plants for preparing low-grade iron (taconite) for the steel mills are voracious gulpers of water." The nuclear power plant at Haddam on the Connecticut River, for instance, uses 370,000 gallons of coolant water *each minute.* By the end of 1972 there were twenty such nuclear power plants with a total capacity of almost 12 million kilowatts in operation in the United States. Fifty-one other plants with a total capacity of 43,992,100 kilowatts are under construction; 66 plants, totaling 65,884,000 kilowatts, are in the planning stage, with reactors already ordered.

Keeping in mind the present and anticipated levels of pollution mentioned earlier, we now have to consider the impact of what is called "thermal pollution." For not only are nuclear power plants "voracious gulpers of water," they are also incredible sources of thermal pollution. In an article in the March 1969 issue of *Scientific American,* John R. Clark points out that "the use of natural water to cool the condensers [of nuclear power plants] would entail the heating of an amount of water equivalent to a third of the yearly freshwater runoff in the U.S. During low-flow periods in summer, the requirement would be 100 per cent of the runoff." And the problem is not simply a matter of cool waters becoming uncomfortably warm. The problem is one of "an ecological crisis."

Temperature is considered by ecologists to be the primary control of life on earth, "and fish, which as cold-blooded animals are unable to regulate their body temperature, are particularly sensitive to changes in the thermal environment." The Federal Water Pollution Control Administration has noted that waters with temperatures above 93 degrees F. "are essentially uninhabitable for all fishes in the U.S., except certain southern species. Many U.S. rivers already reach a temperature of 90 degrees F. or more in the summer through natural heating alone."

The cooling of steam condensers in generating plants accounts for about three quarters of the total of 60,000 billion gallons of water used in the United States for industrial cooling, Clark notes. A ninefold expansion of electric-power production is expected, due mainly to the construction of large generating plants fueled by nuclear energy. "Within 30 years, the electric-power industry . . . will require the disposal of about 20 million billion B.T.U.'s of waste heat per day." Moreover, the waste heat from a single power plant producing 1000 megawatts is expected to raise the temperature of a river carrying a flow of 3000 cubic feet per second by ten degrees. "It is obvious," writes Clark, "that many U.S. waters would become uninhabitable."

In short, the nuclear horn of plenty does not function without snags. And one of the snags may well be to wipe out American fish populations, thus further disrupting a large slice of the ecological balance, causing jellyfish to explode in abundant growth "making some estuarine waters unusable for bathing or other water sports," increasing the likelihood of more and more "red tides" of dinoflagellates along the coasts, causing algae to proliferate in warm estuaries to the point where they "clog the filtering apparatus of shellfish and cause their death."

9

Wavelengths of Death

We live in a sea of electromagnetic waves. We are exposed from birth—earlier, from the moment of conception—to natural radiation from the sun in the form of cosmic rays, radio waves, and light. We are similarly affected by the moon and stars. Moreover, we are exposed to "background radiation" which emanates from the soil itself, rocks, water, and even the air we breathe. There is even a certain amount of natural internal radioactivity in our own bodies. But an increasingly large proportion of the radiation to which we are exposed is man-made. It includes radar waves, radio waves, X-rays (including some from television sets), and other "hard radiation" used in therapy, industry, and scientific research. In addition, there is radioactive fallout from military and civil processes and the problem of disposal of radioactive wastes from atomic energy plants. With the development of high-voltage direct current transmission systems, there is also the new problem of ion leakage. In *New Scientist*, C. Maxwell Cade, chief research engineer and manager with Smith Industries Limited, wrote: "We know now that even the most innocent-seeming [electromagnetic] waves may have unexpected and sometimes tragic biological effects. But we were slow to learn."

The introduction to Cade's article read: "It is time we examined the possible hazards of the 'radiation environment'—much of it man-made—in which we live, rather than wait until dangers of particular radiations become known. Such a study is necessary because of new knowledge about the biological effects of radiation and *the interactions between effects* [my italics]." Cade said that "within the last seven years there have been many reports concerning previously unnoticed effects of radio waves on animals." He cites the Canadian National Research Council's use of microwave fields to clear airport tarmacs of birds. "Dramatic nervous system disorders" were produced in the birds. Further experiments have shown the irradiation of the heads of Rhesus monkeys with weak 91-centimeter waves killed the animals in two minutes. Irradiation of rats for prolonged periods with very weak radiation made them "lethargic, irritable, and more susceptible to seizures induced by noise or electric shock." Even at the risk of making a parallel which may not necessarily be valid—but which, on the other hand, may be—one might note that the symptoms shown by the rats sound extremely familiar. In fact, they sound very much like symptoms experienced by most of us who live in urban centers, and who are therefore constantly exposed to radio waves and such.

Cade also notes the discovery that "different radiations acting simultaneously or in sequence can produce effects which are different from those caused by either radiation alone." This sounds very much like the problem of synergistic effects noted earlier in the section dealing with chemical pollution, wherein two or more compounds can act together to produce a reaction which neither would produce on its own. Another point worth noting here is the fact that "the interaction of man with his radiation environment is not just a question of the presence of harmful waves: the absence of certain wavelengths can also be injurious. . . . Heavy doses of any very short wavelengths are fatal, and ill-health, if not death, will result from an insufficiency of visible light and also from lack of the near-infrared and near-ultraviolet rays." French toxicologist J. Sterne has discovered that the resistance of mice to poisons is proportional to the hours of daylight to which they are exposed. Various investigators, Cade points out, have found that light entering the eyes of animals is directly concerned with stimulation of the pituitary and hypothalamus. At a time when atmospheric pollution is lowering the amount of direct light to which we are exposed, and the amount of poisons to which we are exposed is constantly increasing, this problem needs to be seriously considered.

Again, we must note the relationship between problems of radiation and problems of chemical pollution and atmospheric changes, and must remember that these are woven inextricably into the overlapping webs of population increase, technological advance, and depletion of resources. Technology advances in response to the needs of an increased population and itself stimulates further population increase. Technology is the means of producing more sources of radiation. And as natural-fuel sources dwindle under the impact of a technology that is stimulated to greater efforts by population, the amount of radiation increases proportionately—more radios, more television sets, more nuclear reactors, more transmission systems, more X-ray machines, radar traps, sonic booms, ionizing rays, low-frequency vibrations, and so forth.

Many of these dangers are just beginning to be recognized. In the case of noise, for instance, it has been shown that protracted exposure to high noise levels can produce not only deafness but nervous disorders. And experiments have shown that mutated children may be born, in Cade's words, "as a result of the mother being exposed to sonic bangs during pregnancy." The area known as "infrasound" is likewise just beginning to be studied—so far, only negatively. In France the Center for Scientific Research has developed an "infrasonic death-ray" which, working at very low frequencies, causes the organs of the body to resonate and thus rub against each other. Even at low power levels it makes victims seriously ill. Cade concludes:

> It is becoming clear that man today, as a result both of his exploration of new environments in space and of his technological command of a rapidly widening spectrum of radiation, is exposing himself increasingly to dangers which are rarely understood and often unsuspected. . . . It is time that we seriously asked whether we are not in danger of drowning in the new sea of man-made waves.
>
> When radiation hazards are mentioned, it is the effects of ionizing radiations which are normally understood. This shows how we are in danger of losing sight of the woods (problems of interaction between man and environment) because of the trees (specific risks). Various organizations are studying different kinds of risk—sonic bangs, ioniz-

ing rays, low-frequency vibration, and so on—but the over-all problem of the total radiation environment is largely overlooked. . . .

We are remarkably careless in some ways. . . . Certainly we do not want to become radiation hypochondriacs. But if we are to avoid a repetition of the tragedies which followed the early unprotected use of X-rays, we must be much more careful in our employment of radio waves as well as of ionizing radiations. A thorough study of the radiation environment, including interaction effects between radiations, will involve administrative as well as technical difficulties, but a more complete knowledge of the sea of waves in which we live may well be a matter of life and death.

To illustrate the statement about how "remarkably careless" we are, one has only to turn to the report made by Dr. Ernest J. Sternglass in late 1968. Since the beginning of nuclear testing in 1951, an increase of 25 *per cent* was reported in the rate of baby deaths in the United States alone. Between 1951 and 1966, the deaths of infants under one year of age increased by 375,000. The rate of infant mortality, growing by 34,000 deaths a year, has fallen off slowly since the ratification of the 1963 test-ban treaty. Dr. Sternglass said that his studies indicated that *fallout has already caused long-range damage to human reproductive systems.*

As in the case of high or acute levels of carbon monoxide in the air, radiation is deadly. But—like carbon monoxide—in low or chronic levels, it may contribute to long-range or largely invisible effects. A case in point was the flap about television radiation. In 1966 a Florida researcher discovered that television radiation shortened the life span of rats, reduced their litters, and, if they were placed close enough to the source of radiation, burned their skins. Any similar danger to human beings was, of course, dismissed. Until July 1967, that is—at which time General Electric admitted that there *was* a danger to human beings. The problem, as it was described in the newspapers, centered around a number of color sets whose shunt regulator tubes were capable of emitting X-rays above the recognized international safety limits. The level of radiation was capable of causing genetic malformation, possibly sterility and possibly cancer.

In December 1967 the United States Public Health Service announced that the radiation danger found in General Electric's color sets could well be an industry-wide problem. The potential for biological damage was "quite low," according to Surgeon-General William H. Stewart. As usual, the "speciocentric" viewpoint prevailed —so long as the levels were not too high, there was no danger. No mention was made of the discovery that various low-level radiations acting simultaneously can produce other effects. Other levels—such as electromagnetic levels of radar, radio, and so on—might be equally "low." But taken together, they could add up to a very high over-all level.

X-rays are produced in *all* television sets, but they are supposed to be contained by tubes and casing. The Public Health Service has, since the time of the original revelation of the problem, discovered harmful radiation coming not only from shunt regulator tubes, but from some rectifier tubes as well. Moreover, a survey showed radiation "leaking" from color sets manufactured by Admiral, RCA, Philco, Westinghouse, Zenith, and even "modified" General Electric sets. In 1966 the National Center for Radiological Health tested black-and-white sets as well, but only for front-forward radiation from the picture tube. Nathan Dreskin, in an article in the March 2 edition of *Star Weekly,* quotes a spokesman from the Center as saying: "We know there's a hazard in some color television sets, but that's not to say there's no problem in black-and-white sets. We simply don't know." Dreskin continues: "In this electronic age we're being exposed to more and more radiation. There is really no such thing as a safe level of radiation. As one radiation expert told me, 'Any and all radiation carries a possible risk of injury, not only to genes but to bodily tissues as well. We can't really talk with certainty about safety thresholds."

Reports of radioactive crabs off the west coast of the United States, reports of fish being radioactively contaminated near American bases at Okinawa and around Japan, and reports of seaweed and kelp being killed off on the Pacific coast of North America by pollutants (including radioactive wastes) cannot be dismissed as "isolated" problems. The problem of radiation, like the problem of atmospheric pollution, is rapidly becoming pervasive—quite probably even global. With reference to the problem of diminishing resources and the need to convert eventually to atomic energy, it can be seen that the question of pollution will not be resolved by getting rid of chemical wastes only to replace them with radioactive wastes.

The question of radiation can be discussed at great length. It is not the purpose of this book, however, to make a Cassandra-like prophecy concerning the dangers of radiation. As far as my present thesis is concerned, heightened radiation levels are only one facet of environmental collapse. As such, they work synergistically with all of the other factors—factors which range from overpopulation and depletion of natural resources to pesticide poisoning and disruption of the oxygen-carbon balance. So far, then, I have been describing the collapse of our natural environment under the impact, mainly, of population and technology. We now move on to explore some of the further repercussions of environmental collapse. It is a matter, as we shall see, of widening our perspective, nothing more. We move now—and we need not move very far—from the problem of radiation to the closely related problem of nuclear weaponry. This may be viewed as being a reflection of the collapse of the "spiritual" or "moral" environment and, certainly, it is a factor in the collapse of the "psychological environment."

10

Defense
Socialism

At the dawn of the 1970s the United States was reported to have the equivalent of well over 100 billion tons of TNT in her nuclear stockpile. Between the two of them, the United States and the Soviet Union have stockpiled enough nuclear weapons to apply the equivalent of seventy tons of TNT against every man, woman, and child living on earth. The United States has some 1000 Minutemen Intercontinental Missiles (ICBMs), 697 long-range bombers, and 41 nuclear submarines capable of launching 656 ballistic missiles. Russia is thought to have 720 ICBMs, over 700 medium- and intermediate-range missiles, and about 155 strategic bombers. France already has 62 Mirage 4-A aircraft, each carrying a 60 kiloton atomic bomb, and a French missile base, which was set up in 1969 near the fashionable Côte d'Azur, is fitted out with 27 nuclear-tipped missiles. On June 17, 1967, China exploded her first hydrogen bomb. Today she is believed to have a modest ICBM force capable of striking at North America, and is already working on launching submarines. Britain is in the process of readying four Polaris-launching submarines to back up her force of V-bombers. And other nations—Canada, Czechoslovakia, East and West Germany, India, Israel, Japan, Pakistan, Spain, and Sweden—are now producing plutonium, which, given unstable enough conditions, could be syphoned from peaceful atomic power stations into weapon-making. And there are those who suggest that Israel has already taken that step.

There are several dimensions to the problem of the existence of nuclear stockpiles. The problem is not, as the negotiators in Geneva would have us believe, simply one of avoiding proliferation. Nor is it, as others would have us believe, simply a matter of preventing these weapons from some day being used. They *are* being used every day, in much the same way that capital is used even when it is not being invested or otherwise directly involved in any given transactions. Nuclear stockpiles function in much the same way as the gold supplies at Fort Knox. They are now as much a part of existing political frameworks as the gold supply is a part of the world's financial and economic structure.

In *Disarmament and the Economy* Kenneth Boulding notes that the "world war industry" accounts for roughly one tenth of the output of the world's total economy. John Kenneth Galbraith adds, in *The New Industrial State,* that the modern industrial state has come to depend on military spending. Annual outlay for defense in the United States jumped from three quarters of a billion dollars in the 1930s to $78 billion in 1972. Contrary to the cliché that "big business" opposes government intrusion, Galbraith points out that this increase—like all other increases in federal spending—"has been with the strong approval of the industrial system." He continues: "If a large public sector of the economy, supported by personal and corporate income taxation, is the fulcrum for the regulation of demand, plainly military expenditures are the pivot upon which the fulcrum rests. Additionally, they provide underwriting for advanced technology and, therewith, security for the planning of the industrial system in areas that would otherwise be excluded by cost and risk. And, to repeat, these expenditures are strongly supported by businessmen."

Galbraith says "there has been a tendency to minimize or ignore the role of military expenditures in the regulation of [consumer] demand. . . . That weaponry in the higher megaton ranges of destructive power has an organic relation to the performance of the economic system leads to unpleasant introspection. . . . Military expenditures are what now make the public sector [of the economy] large. Without them, the federal government would be rather less than half its present size. . . . Modern military and related procurement and policy are, in fact, extensively adapted to the needs of the industrial system." Few mature corporations in the United States do not enjoy an incestuous relationship with the federal government. Further, as Galbraith notes, they "identify" themselves closely with the goals of the various armed services. This should not be surprising, since they are dependent, for the underwriting of research and technological expansion, on the services which they serve. As a general rule, the more highly developed, complex, sophisticated, and, of course, costly a corporation becomes, the closer its relationship to the government.

"In its more simplistic outline in the last twenty years," Galbraith continues, "the relation of the Cold War to the needs of the industrial system has been remarkably close. . . . A drastic reduction in weapons competition following a general release from the commitment to the Cold War (disarmament, in a word) would be sharply in conflict with the needs of the industrial system." Dr. Ralph E. Lapp, a member of the Manhattan Project and author of *The Weapons Culture,* put the matter more bluntly. "The United States," he writes, "is becoming a weapons culture. The health of our entire economy has come to depend on the making of arms. The machinery of defense, lubricated by politics and technology, has become a juggernaut in our society. Pressures exerted by the giant corporations that compose our military-industrial apparatus are felt in the Pentagon, in the White House, and in Congress. Congressmen are re-elected depending on their success in winning defense contracts for their constituencies."

Such mature corporations as North American Rockwell, General Dynamics, and McDonnell Douglas exist, he said, "almost entirely on government arms contracts. Without this money, many of them would go bankrupt, and places like Southern California or the state of Washington would become economic disaster areas." In the past seven years some forty companies each did more than one billion dollars' worth of business with the government. In all, calculates Dr. Lapp, *well over a trillion dollars has been spent by the United States on national defense since the Second World War.* "No nation can devote so much of its ingenuity, manpower, and resources to the works of war without being deeply changed in the process. Our commitment to weapons-making has distorted the free enterprise system of our economy into a kind of 'defense socialism,' a system in which the welfare of the country is permanently tied to the continued growth of military technology and the continued stockpiling of military hardware."

As we shall see later, military spending is not so much a cause as it is a symptom of deep change in what is still nostalgically known as the "free enterprise system." Others have noticed the shift too. Galbraith refers to it as a large factor in the development of "technostructures." Professor Murray L. Weidenbaum, a former Boeing employee, refers to the most highly organized corporations as "the seminationalized branch of the economy." The aerospace industry in particular, adds Dr. Lapp, has become "a kind of national industrial welfare program."

At this point we should pause to bring the weapons situation into broader perspective. Population increase creates the need for more jobs. Defense contracts, it can be seen, are a large factor in the satisfying of this need. Without them, millions of people in the United States would be out of work. The weapons industry, it must be remembered, does not concern itself entirely with arming soldiers for combat overseas. It also serves paramilitary internal organizations, National Guardsmen, police, and, of course, ordinary citizens.

Then, too, not only does the population increase create a need for new jobs—as well as further pollution, intensified stripping of resources, and so on—it also creates problems of overcrowding in urban centers, which, as we shall see shortly, produces a rise in the crime rate. This serves not only to stimulate the demand for larger police organizations, but also increases the demand for weapons development at the local level. Further research into specialized "home-front" weaponry (Mace, for example) is called for. Further recruitment of police officers results. In turn, as the level of authoritarianism rises, it causes a further breakdown in the system of mutual trust and values upon which social organization is dependent. This results in yet more crime and further social breakdown and, again, forces a further boosting of local weapons stockpiling and police and military recruitment.

All along the line, in the process of manufacturing more weapons—whether they be atomic warheads or Mace—more munitions factories and whatnot come into existence and the level of pollution rises. The rate at which resources are gobbled up increases. More water is poisoned. More soil is saturated with chemical pollutants. The amount of radiation, particularly in the case of nuclear weaponry, reaches higher and higher levels. But so do the number of radar traps and a host of minor sources of microwave "pollution." These may not appear to amount to much, but they have been shown to have a cumulative effect. It may not be anywhere near as great as the increase in strontium 90 or cobalt 60 levels which were caused by the testing of nuclear weapons or the use of nuclear submarines, but it does constitute a prolonged low-level exposure similar to the type of exposure that produces lethargy, irritability, and ill-health in rats.

So far, we have been dealing with the more or less mechanical aspects of defense socialism. Corporations need to develop weapons in order to expand their own technological base and thus stimulate their own growth. But the word "weapons" covers a lot of ground. Obviously it no longer refers simply to a gun or a bomb. Nowadays the DEW line is a weapon, radar is a weapon, and satellites are weapons. Whereas some satellites may be straightforward "spy in the sky" devices, others—such as the Apollo moonships—are what McLuhan calls "iconic" weapons, a part of the propaganda war effort. The "thin" antiballistic missile defense system, almost entirely electronic in nature, is likewise a weapon. And computers, clearly, are now the most crucial weapons in the whole sophisticated arsenal of the modern military machine. Without them, there is no NORAD, no ICBMs, no ABM system, no spaceships or satellites, and no modern arms strategy based on games theory. Electronic eavesdropping devices, lasers, radios, telecommunications of all kinds, including the hot line and television, are all—in the context of military-industrial development—weapons.

The massive National Aeronautics and Space Administration complexes—capable of mobilizing 350,000 scientists, engineers, and specialized workers, and capable also of gobbling up $24 billion just to get a few men to the moon—is yet another dimension of defense socialism, bringing industry and government into almost total integration and extending the definition of "weapon" even further. As the definition extends itself, it embraces larger and larger portions of the population. Not only is the scientific elite of the country brought into its ambit, but so are the best of its communications technicians, educators, researchers, economists, psychologists, astronomers, meteorologists, sociologists, and so forth. War is no longer seen as the "opposite" of peace.

As the definition of "weapon" expands, it reaches deep into the behavior patterns not only of scientists and economists, but of the population as a whole. McLuhan notes, in *War and Peace in the Global Village,* that the United States is now in the midst of its first television war. "The television war has meant the end of the dichotomy between civilian and military. The public is now participant in every phase of the war, and the main actions of the war are now being fought in the American home itself." In the sense that the American economy has become a kind of war dance, the main participants being the government, and the most highly developed segment of the industrial sector, the public at large—consumers, workers, advertisers, stockholders, educators, and so on—all become "warriors."

As noted earlier, this phenomenon should not be viewed as being peculiar to America. Not only do other industrialized nations have "defense establishments"—i.e., huge defense budgets that function (like the defense budget in the United States) as "balance wheels" in the economy—but they also have increasingly large corporations in their midst. And by token of the same economic laws which force American firms to seek newer and more elaborate ways of getting the government to underwrite research costs, these other corporations have incestuous two-way relationships with their own governments. Further, most countries do not pay so much lip service to the "ideal" of free enterprise, and therefore the intercourse between government and industry is viewed less puritanically in these countries than it is in the United States. Finally, the output of American corporations abroad is five or six times larger than the goods exported directly from the United States. In the same way as its own citizens are increasingly drawn into the war dance, iconic or not, so too are more and more consumers, scientists, politicians, workers, and advertisers in other countries. As an increasingly large proportion of troops, supplies, resources, and weaponry is deployed in the strategic software arena of the Cold War, that part of the battle which has moved into the American living room through television and advertising moves similarly into British, French, Dutch, Israeli, Canadian, Italian, and Japanese living rooms as well.

Anthropologist M. F. Ashley Montagu argues that "from any dominance of biologically or inherited predetermined reactions that may prevail in the behavior of other animals, man has moved into a zone of adaptation in which his behavior is dominated by learned responses." Montagu continues, in *Man and Aggression,* that "it is within the dimension of culture, the learned, man-made part of the environment, that man grows, develops, and has his being as a behaving organism." Erich Fromm refers to what he calls the "pathology of normalcy." In *The Sane Society* he writes: "We find that the countries in Europe which are among the most democratic, peaceful, and prosperous ones, and the United States, the most prosperous country in the world, show the most severe symptoms of mental disturbance. The aim of the whole socioeconomic development of the Western world is that of the materially comfortable life, relatively equal distribution of wealth, stable democracy, and peace, and the very countries which come closest to this aim show the most severe signs of mental unbalance!"

We will discuss the pathology of normalcy in some detail later, along with McLuhan's and Montagu's conception of civilization as the mother of war. For the moment it is enough that we perceive that the development of "weapons cultures" in the highly industrialized nations—particularly in the United States and Russia—does not proceed without profoundly affecting the individuals, who are a part of cultures. Increasingly, their "learned responses" become adapted to the needs of the military-industrial welfare system. They grow and develop within an environment which is based more and more on the potential for destruction. That they are "brutalized" psychologically cannot be denied—as suggested by the severe signs of mental unbalance. McLuhan views the resulting behavior as being "spastic."

Erich Fromm notes that in observing the quality of thinking of man in highly industrialized societies, "it is striking to see how his intelligence has developed and how his reason has deteriorated. . . . Even from the nineteenth century to our day, there seems to have occurred an observable increase in stupidity, if by this we mean the opposite to reason, rather than to intelligence." Fromm speaks also of the "lack of realism" demonstrated by modern men. "To speak of our realism is almost like a paranoid distortion. What realists, who are playing with weapons which may lead to the destruction of all modern civilization, if not the earth itself! If an individual were found doing just that, he would be locked up immediately, and if he prided himself on his realism, the psychiatrists would consider this an additional and rather serious symptom of a diseased mind."

Milton J. Rosenberg, professor of social psychology at the University of Chicago, has noted "one of the most depressing open secrets of our time: our conceptual and military cold warriors, despite their elegant application of systems theory, have attained to a level of intellectual incompetence matched only by their hubristic excess." This judgment cannot be taken as limiting itself strictly to high-ranking military personnel. As we have already seen, the relationship between industry, government, the military, and many sections of the academic and scientific estates is so pronounced that an observation about one segment automatically applies itself to the others.

Moreover, the millions of specialists, executives, managers, workers, and so on, who are dependent for their economic welfare on the smooth functioning of the existing arms-oriented welfare system—all, to varying degrees, identify themselves with the goals of their respective organizations. They, too, are therefore guilty of "intellectual incompetence," a "deteriorated" ability to reason, and a "lack of reason." As the culture increasingly sustains itself on weapons development, the "learned responses" of its citizens increasingly amount to an adoption of the implicit goals of weaponry. This collapse of the ability to reason and to behave rationally is a central feature of environmental collapse.

The dimensions of environmental collapse, however, have not yet been exhausted. We have been speaking mainly of the brutalization of nature and, briefly, of some aspects of the brutalization of ourselves in the context of weaponry and the development of a weapons culture, partly as a result of overpopulation, technology, and economic adjustments to these factors. Let us now look more closely at our psychological environment. It can be said that up to a certain point in history, man's psychological environment was mainly a reflection of his physical environment. Indeed, to a considerable degree, this still remains the case. Now, however, as the physical environment for most individuals becomes increasingly man-made, it may be said that the reflection is reversed and that it is the physical environment which reflects the psychological realm. This can be seen more clearly in the context of the process generally referred to as alienation.

11

The
Shattered
Mirror

As suggested earlier, the world may be accurately described as a "global ghetto," with only a few ornate mansions thrusting up here and there among the tenements. Only 18 countries out of 124 can be said to be even relatively affluent. The great famine has begun, but its ravages are being felt almost exclusively in the ghetto. The princes and princesses of the affluent society expect to consume more, not less, in the future. On the other hand, hunger, lack of shelter, lack of adequate medical facilities, gross overcrowding, and so on are the price that people pay for living outside the highly industrialized nations. In the world of today, not more than one person out of seven can be said to enjoy physical well-being.

It can be shown, however, that among those who make up the affluent society, physical well-being is bought at a very high price. "Indeed," write Eric and Mary Josephson in *Man Alone,* "ever since the great technological and political revolutions of the late eighteenth century, with their shattering impact on a rigid social order and their promise of individual freedom, one of the most disturbing phenomena of Western culture has been man's sense of estrangement from the world he himself has made or inherited—in a word, man's alienation from himself and others." We have already looked at some of the other "prices" of a high level of industrialization. From the point of view of the individual, however, the price of physical well-being purchased on the industrialization plan is most plainly seen in the phenomenon of alienation, which might be described as a very high rate of compound interest. "Alienation as we find it in modern society," writes Erich Fromm, "is almost total; it pervades the relationship of man to his work, to the things he consumes, to his fellows and to himself." Echoing Fromm's sentiments, Eric and Mary Josephson have this to say about the frequency of occurrence of alienation:

> In modern terms, "alienation" has been used by philosophers, psychologists, and sociologists to refer to an extraordinary variety of psychosocial disorders, including loss of self, anxiety states, anomie, despair, depersonalization, rootlessness, apathy, social disorganization, loneliness, atomization, powerlessness, meaninglessness, isolation, pessimism, and the loss of beliefs or values. Among the social groups who have been described as alienated in varying degree . . . are women, industrial workers, white-collar workers, migrant workers, artists, suicides, the mentally disturbed, addicts, the aged, the young generation as a whole, juvenile delinquents in particular, voters, non-voters, consumers, the audiences of mass media, sex deviants, victims of prejudice and discrimination, the prejudiced, bureaucrats, political radicals, the physically handicapped, immigrants, exiles, vagabonds, and recluses. This is by no means a complete listing, yet even allowing for duplication, it includes a sizable majority of persons living in any advanced industrial society such as ours. Obviously, we are dealing with a word that lends itself to many different meanings. To deal with all of them we would truly need an encyclopedia of the social sciences.

Social psychologists Charles H. Cooley and George H. Mead argue that a person acquires a sense of self and identity through his interaction with others. Mead calls it "taking the role of another," while Cooley calls it a process of acquiring a "looking-glass self." Considering the evidence of the pervasiveness of alienation, a highly industrialized society may be described as one in which the mirror of the self tends to be shattered. Looking into this shattered mirror in search of our identities, we see only bits and pieces, fragments and wreckage.

Alienation, moreover, is nothing new. Back in the 1920s Carl

Jung wrote: "About a third of my patients are suffering from no clinically definable neurosis, but from the senselessness and emptiness of their lives. It seems to me, however, that this can well be described as the general neurosis of our time." Before Jung, Karl Marx had seized on the theme. And Marx, in turn, had borrowed the idea of alienation from Hegel—who described it, in *The Philosophy of History,* as being the "spirit" experiencing "a mighty conflict with itself."

Medieval Europe was not without its own experience of alienation. In *Man Alone,* the authors quote the fifteenth-century French poet Eustache Deschamps as writing: "I know no more where I belong." "Is this not," ask the Josephsons, "the alienated lament of all ages?" Similar experiences of alienation were recorded at the time of the Peloponnesian War in Greece, in the Egypt of four thousand years ago, and on Assyrian tablets dating back to 2800 B.C. However, as the Josephsons note, with the collapse of the medieval system, the likelihood of alienation increased appreciably. The Industrial Revolution, with its division of labor, made alienation less a peripheral phenomenon and more the central experience of life. Now we are into a second Industrial Revolution, one of the main features of which is the fact that nearly all "major purposeful activities" will be carried out by large systems. Not only has human energy been replaced by mechanical energy, but human thought is rapidly being replaced by the thinking done by machines. Not only are we alienated from physical processes; we are alienated as well from the crucial decision-making processes.

In short, together with the rapid acceleration of population increase, technological innovation, accumulation of data, and the proliferation of organizational controls, we see also an acceleration in the processes which are generally identified as the causes of alienation. In terms of psychological well-being, alienation is definitely a form of environmental collapse. In fact, it is not so much a sickness as a reaction to our developed mechanisms of social organization, a good indication of the degree to which they violate our basic psychobiological needs.

As we shall see shortly, the acceleration of the processes which cause alienation is rapidly nearing the upper limits of tolerance. And by tolerance I do not mean an arbitrary intellectual or moralistic definition of tolerance. I mean the fundamental psychosocial tolerance level beyond which homeostatic adjustment processes are triggered. This tolerance level, like various biological reactions, is governed by the principle which was introduced briefly at the beginning of this book—that of self-regulated revolution. At the outset I suggested that total revolution might not be possible until total warfare became impractical. Likewise, it might not be activated until alienation itself also became total, or at least nearly so.

There are strong indications that alienation is indeed approaching the upper limits of tolerance. It is the theme of this book that large, rapidly expanding segments of society have reached this upper limit and that homeostatic processes have been activated. What is referred to as the "generation gap" is one way of describing this process. "Turning on," "involvement," and "commitment" are others. They all refer to the same thing. Alienation is the symptom; turning on is the reaction of the psychobiological self. It is not very different, at bottom, from the tendency of the body to reject foreign tissue.

However, before this process can be appreciated, the depths of alienation—the response to our increasingly intolerable environment—must be explored. Probably the best analysis of alienation is the one offered by Erich Fromm. He speaks, in *The Sane Society,* of "socially patterned defects." If an individual shares a mental and emotional illness with many others, "he is not aware of it as a defect, and his security is not threatened by the experience of being different, of being an outcast, as it were. . . . As a matter of fact, his very defect may have been raised to a virtue by his culture, and thus may give him an enhanced feeling of achievement." Thus, the typical reaction of the alienated person to his own condition, Fromm writes, is to conform. "He feels secure in being as similar as possible to his fellow man. . . . To be different, to find himself in a minority, are the dangers which threaten his sense of security; hence a craving for limitless conformity.

"The alienated person," he concludes, "cannot be healthy. . . . If the modern age has been rightly called the age of anxiety, it is primarily because of this anxiety engendered by the lack of self. . . . The person who can only experience the outer world photographically, but is out of touch with his inner world, with himself, is the alienated person. Schizophrenia and alienation are complementary. In both forms of sickness, one pole of human experience is lacking."

Marshall McLuhan has managed to say much the same thing in quite different language and with a very different frame of reference. In *Understanding Media* he writes: "Physiologically there are abundant reasons for an extension of ourselves involving us in a state of numbness. . . . Man is impelled to extend various parts of his body by a kind of autoamputation. In the physical stress of superstimulation of various kinds, the central nervous system acts to protect itself by a strategy of amputation or isolation of the offending organ, sense, or function." Amplification of a separate or isolated function through technology "is bearable by the nervous system only through numbness or blocking of perception."

Men become fascinated by extensions of themselves, just as Narcissus was fascinated by his own reflection—an extension of himself by means of a mirror. Narcissus "adapted to his extension of himself and [became] a closed system." The "extension of himself" is a form of self-amputation induced by irritating pressures on the central nervous system. As a counterirritant, "the image produces a generalized numbness or shock that declines recognition. Self-amputation forbids self-recognition." McLuhan notes that a person suddenly deprived of loved ones—this is "an extreme instance of amputation of the self"—falls into a state of shock. "Shock induces a generalized numbness or an increased threshold to all types of perception. The victim seems immune to pain or sense. Battle shock created by violent noise has been adapted for dental use in the device known as *audiac*. The patient puts on headphones and turns a dial raising the noise level to the point that he feels no pain from the drill. The selection of a *single* sense for intense stimulus, or of a single extended, isolated or 'amputed' sense in technology, is in part the reason for the numbing effect that technology as such has on its makers and users. For the central nervous system rallies a response of general numbness to the challenge of specialized irritation."

Numbness, therefore, is McLuhan's word for alienation, and it may go a long way to explaining the ability, noted in the last section, of "normal" people to sharpen the knife blades of war-makers, thus making themselves accomplices in the crime of premeditated genocide. Further, as Fromm notes, through the process of cultur-ally patterned defects, no one is able any longer to see that his be-havior is insane, since everyone is insane and there is no evident standard of mental health against which to measure himself. Viewed as numbness—a defensive response activated by the central nervous system, like an anesthetic—alienation can be better under-stood as a symptom of the deep violation of our basic psychobiolog-ical nature.

The anesthetic function of alienation is to maintain some sort of equilibrium in the face of an increasingly deranged social situation. One has only to look at what happens when the "anesthetic" wears off to see how functional it has become in the social sense. The youngsters who for a while were storming the administration build-ings on campuses all over the world were individuals whose experi-ence of alienation had passed the tolerance level. Without the anes-thetic sensation of alienation to "calm them down"—in much the same way that nicotine dulls the nerves—they began to go wild. In the face of the suicidal—which is to say, pathological—direction in which their society is moving, theirs is the only "sane" reaction.

Insofar as alienation is concerned, it is difficult to divorce it from its most common context—namely, the modern urban center. While alienation is, in large measure, a form of psychological-industrial fallout and, at the same time, a reaction to bureaucratization and the development of larger systems, it is also overwhelmingly a prod-uct of urbanization. We turn now to the "lethal behavioral sinks" —the cities.

12

The Urban Titanics

History now takes place on the stage of the city. So far in this book I have been stressing synergistic effects and the interrelatedness of the problems which we have created for ourselves. All of these problems—overpopulation, pollution, exhaustion of resources, communal pathology, poverty, poisoning, alienation—come together in the cities. Further, it can be seen that the rapid acceleration of population increase, technological advance, and all of the other forces of change that have stimulated each other into high gear are all at work—as they are nowhere else—in the sprawling urban labyrinths. Cities are semiconductor material. Their inhabitants are all stuck together like tar babies. Ecological systems, economic systems, political systems, social systems, communications systems, transportation systems, education systems, systems of thought—like photographs or blueprints or nervous systems superimposed one on top of the other, they add up to what Constantinos Doxiadis calls the "ecumenopolis."

The rapid implosion of the world's population into cities cannot be dissociated from twentieth-century technology which, as Lewis Mumford notes, permitted "the removal of limits." While there have been large cities in the past—though none like the modern "megalopolis" (which means simply "big city")—too much of the total effort of earlier societies had to be spent on agriculture, with the result that no city or group of cities could contain more than a fraction of the total population of any given area. Today, in the United States, only 10 per cent of the population need concern itself with food production. Even in Russia, which is prevented by its ideological restrictions from making the same progress in agriculture as it has in weaponry and space exploration, only 45 per cent of the population stays on the farm. By contrast, until the Industrial Revolution, roughly 80 per cent of the population of every society had to till the soil. As Kenneth Boulding remarks, "we can now spare about 90 per cent of all people to produce bathtubs, automobiles, H-bombs, and all the other conveniences of life." Western Europe and Japan are rapidly approaching the United States in methods of food production. Partly as a result, European and Japanese cities—although for the most part spared the agonies of race conflicts—are nevertheless experiencing their own urban crises.

The very use of the term "urban crisis," now almost synonymous with megalopolis, implies, as Robert W. Glasgow suggests, "that urban society is at some critical turning point." The process set in motion by industrialization—the great exodus from the country into the city—cannot at this point be turned off or easily reversed. Arthur J. R. Smith, chairman of the Economic Council of Canada, noted in early 1969 that "the processes of increased concentration have tended to become self-sustaining. In other words, one of the most potent effects of large urban agglomeration is that it is apparently everywhere tending to encourage still greater agglomeration."

That urban society is, indeed, at some critical turning point can be seen by projecting population trends ahead a few years. In the United States alone, where New York City's John Lindsay summed up his municipal priorities in the word "survival," some one hundred million more people are expected to be born into or move into urban areas in the next twenty-five years. Lyndon Johnson remarked, with more than a trace of alarm, that "fifty years from now . . . there will be four hundred million Americans, four fifths of them in urban areas. In the remainder of this century . . . we will have to build homes, highways, and facilities equal to all those built since this country was first settled. In the next forty years we must rebuild the entire urban United States."

As bad as the situation is in the industrialized nations, at least they have a huge technological base on which to build. They can, if they have to, mobilize money, machines, and computers to tackle the problems of urban readjustment. The underdeveloped nations do not have even these resources to draw upon. And it is not just the specter of starvation which haunts the already overcrowded cities of the underdeveloped nations. Like their industrialized counterparts, they are faced with the psychological and behavioral consequences of overcrowding, and these consequences may prove to be far more disastrous. After all, people who have starved to death present only the problem of disposing of their bodies. It is the living who, if driven mad, will tear down everything around them.

In *The Hidden Dimension* Edward T. Hall says that "if what is known about animals where they are crowded or moved to an unfamiliar biotope is at all relevant to mankind, we are now facing some terrible consequences in our urban sinks. Studies of ethology and comparative proxemics should alert us to the dangers ahead as our rural populations pour into urban centers." An "active, swelling behavioral sink," he notes, gives rise to pathological conditions. In an industrialized society where there is plenty of evidence that the *norm* already is, or at least is verging on, pathological behavior, further pathology "may well destroy us by making our cities uninhabitable."

The National Commission on the Causes and Prevention of Crime has confirmed, at least partially, Professor Hall's prediction about "terrible consequences in our urban sinks." The commission, appointed while Senator Robert Kennedy was dying in a Los Angeles hospital, reported that "the basis of social order is threatened." It found, among other things, that "violent crime is at an all-time high. Rates for crimes of violence per 100,000 of the population are up 57 per cent over the levels of 1960. . . . More and more Americans are buying firearms for the purpose of self-defense. After more than a decade of relative stability, the annual sales of new firearms have more than doubled since 1963. . . . Sales of handguns—most of which do not lend themselves to sporting use —increased 400 per cent between 1963 and 1968. There are indications that this increase is largely due to continuing disorders and

widespread fear of crime." Nothing that has happened in the inter-
vening five years has in any way changed the Commission's findings.

In *Man in the Web of Life* John Storer notes that "for all our exploding population, the growth of juvenile delinquency and crime is
exploding even faster. Juvenile delinquency, rioting, and destructive
violence have appeared in all the technical societies, whether
Anglo-Saxon, Latin, Japanese, or Russian. . . . Society has always
had its revolts against authority, but today's riots and delinquency
have taken on a new appearance." Storer notes that the crime rate
is increasing at five times the rate of population growth, "and the
greatest rise was among teenagers. This rise has continued and the
tendency has been worldwide. There are obviously many causes that
contributed to this startling rise, but one fact seems especially significant. The crime rate in the bigger cities was much higher than
for the smaller ones. . . . This does not mean just an increase in
numbers; it is the *rate,* or number for each 1000 people. In cities
with a population over a quarter million, the rate was seven times
that of the rural areas. In cities with over a million people, the rate
jumped to four times that for all other cities and nineteen times that
of the rural areas." With the ratio of rural and urban populations
having been reversed in the past fifty years, the meaning of this
crime explosion for all technologically advanced nations can be easily appreciated.

Edward Hall refers us to studies carried out at the Penrose Laboratory of the Philadelphia Zoo, in which pathologists R. L. Snyder
and H. L. Ratcliffe examined the causes of death of some 16,000
birds and mammals over a twenty-five-year period. They found that
many animals suffer stress from overcrowding and that this stress
manifests itself among animals and birds in the same way that it
does among human beings. They develop high blood pressure and
other circulatory and heart diseases. Dr. Hans Selye has shown that
overcrowding leads to enlargement of the adrenal glands.

In another study, at the National Institute of Mental Health at
Bethesda, Maryland, and also at the Jackson Memorial Laboratory
at Bar Harbor, Maine, it was found that crowding beyond a certain
point produced psychological and physiological stress in laboratory
mice. Males began to fight, became more active and restless, and females showed a sharp decline in their ability to reproduce. Further,

they took to killing and eating their young. John B. Calhoun of the National Institute of Mental Health summed up the findings of the study by saying: "We have seen that a fairly psychologically and behaviorally stable animal . . . can be altered into an unstable one merely by increasing the size of the group. A look at some of our human problems of social unrest, juvenile delinquency, and political upheaval suggests very strongly that man is not immune to some of the same social pressures as mice. . . ." In *Man in the Web of Life* Storer adds: "The rapid growth of world tensions suggests that long before the world reaches the limits of its potential food supply it may reach the limits of man's tolerance for the environment that is being built by himself and his crowding fellows."

Calhoun's final and significant conclusion was that crowding beyond a certain density led to a "behavioral sink," which means simply that sex behavior was perverted, reproduction was affected, nest-building was disrupted (signifying a breakdown in family structure), and *all* forms of pathology were aggravated. Sadism and homosexuality became endemic. Tail-biting among males became common. Kidneys, livers, and adrenal glands were all enlarged, and tumors became commonplace in the reproductive organs of females.

Calhoun's investigations amount to the first concrete step in the direction of the research suggested by Freud into the pathology of civilized communities. Certainly they would support Freud's contention that the development of civilization (the urban side of it, at any rate) increasingly contradicts the needs of human beings. Moreover, Calhoun's findings support the statement made by Ashley Montagu in *The Human Revolution:* "The fact is that as man has advanced in civilization he has become increasingly, not less, violent and warlike. The violence that has been attributed to his original nature has, in fact, been acquired predominantly within the relatively recent period of man's cultural evolution. In our own time, most of us have grown so accustomed to the life of 'each for himself' that it is difficult for us to understand that for the greater part of man's history every man of necessity lived a life of involvement in the welfare of his fellows." Which prompted McLuhan to describe civilization as being "the mother of war."

In *The City in History* Lewis Mumford makes the same point. He says that the development of cities wrought a basic change in human relationships. Primitive villages were basically family units, intimate communities made up of a "watchful . . . deeply concerned group." Under such circumstances, there was no need for codified rules of conduct or for laws—which, together, constitute what we call "morality." But with the formation of cities, the "we" of the small intimate clan "becomes a buzzing swarm of I's." The mixing together of different peoples, clans, tribes, and so on, brings lawlessness and violence in exactly the same way that it does among rat colonies which are forced into contact in the laboratory. In the course of human history, laws were brought into existence to iron out some of the confusion and conflict. The laws themselves— emerging about 3500 B.C. in Mesopotamia—were violent. But in order to cope with the situation, they had to be. Thus, they included burning to death, mutilation, drowning, and other forms of torture.

Mumford argues that, rather than being a holdover from the jungle past, these new forms of organized and sanctioned violence were a characteristic peculiar to urban culture. Only as urban cultures became more sophisticated were more effective means of social organization developed. Brute force, after all, was a clumsy tool. Religion was much more efficient. Ultimately, we see the gradual refining of social controls reaching its zenith on Madison Avenue in the twentieth century—just at the time, ironically, when urban culture finally outgrows itself and begins to collapse.

Returning to the studies of the effects of overcrowding on animals, we find that in creatures such as lemmings and some species of deer it leads to an automatic increase in the death rate—either, as in the case of the deer, through adrenal failure or, in the case of the lemmings, through mass suicide. These reactions, of course, are the result of homeostatic processes, and in nature they serve to alleviate the conditions of overcrowding which triggered them—thus arresting the process of social decomposition. Apart from adrenal failure and mass suicide, other homeostatic influences are famine, disease, and the multiplication of natural enemies.

While it is true that only in laboratory situations does overcrowding lead to conditions such as those described above, it is also true that today's cities can be fairly described as "laboratory settings." Through technology, medicine, increased food production, and social organization, we have so far managed to sidestep the effects of the homeostatic mechanisms which prevent overcrowding among lower animals. However, the operative words here are "so far," and it is a much qualified "so far."

For the most part, what we have succeeded in doing is constructing an artificial ecosystem, one in which an ecological balance—even a man-made one—must be maintained. But evidently this balance can be maintained only up to a point. Nature is "managed" by strict biological laws. Civilization is managed by man-made laws. The crucial difference is that biological laws are simply abstract formulations of the reality of biological phenomena, whereas most man-made laws are expressions of cold-blooded ideologies and are indicative of a general ignorance of the real biological nature of human beings. And until such time as we replace ideological laws with laws that more closely approximate biological realities, we will never be able to achieve the balance that is achieved in such a decentralized and stable fashion in nature.

Studies of mice, deer, and lemmings, it may be argued, do not prove anything about human nature—to suggest that the mechanisms which operate in the animal world have an exact parallel in the world of men is to indulge one's anthropomorphic bias. Conversely, one may argue that to deny categorically a possible relationship is to ignore all of the evidence that has been accumulated by science. In *The Hidden Dimension* Hall reports that similar studies have been made on human beings—and the results confirm the fact that we too are affected in exactly the same way as the animals which have already been studied. Hall describes the studies in the following terms:

> The Chombard de Lauwes, a French husband-and-wife team who combine the skills of sociology and psychology, [have] produced some of the first statistical data on the consequences of crowding in urban housing. With typical French thoroughness, the Chombard de Lauwes collected measurable data on every conceivable aspect of the family life of the French worker. At first, they recorded and computed crowding in terms of the number of residents per dwelling unit. This index revealed very little and the Chombard de Lauwes then decided to use a new index to establish crowding—*the number of square meters per person per unit*. The results of the index were startling. When the space available was below eight to ten square meters per person, social and physical pathologies doubled! Illness, crime, and crowding were definitely linked.

The danger of overcrowding can be clearly seen when we look only a few decades into the future, at which time the size, complexity, and problems of the cities will be increased to incredible proportions. As the President's Task Force on Suburban Problems stated in early 1969, the rapidly growing crisis in the cities is already extending itself deep into the suburbs, which "face a quiet, slowly building crisis." The report of the task force pointed out that 40 per cent of the nation's poor now live in the suburbs, that crime, decay, and pollution are growing in the suburbs at the same rate as they are in the cities, that the "cultural dehydration" of suburban life has led to an alarming rise in vandalism, drug offenses, and larceny among children, and that such basic services as police protection, sewage and waste disposal, and transportation are collapsing at a surprising rate.

Moreover, the problems of the behavioral sink—even when as many factors as pollution, overcrowding, drugs, and so on have been considered—cannot be fully appreciated until the impact of new technologies is taken into account. Taken together, they add up to a global crisis the proportions of which are without precedent in human history.

By now, we have reached the point in our survey of the features of environmental collapse to see that it is about to force a drastic, rapid, and profound change. The number and the magnitude of the dangers that we face should now be clear. Moreover, the repeated failure of specialists to solve problems in one area—for example, pollution—should now be understandable. Nothing short of a complete overhaul will have any real effect on present conditions. Either the Phoenix is building its funeral pyre or the dance of Shiva has begun, and conditions would seem to indicate the stirrings of Shiva, not the Phoenix.

However, as the reader will have gathered, the picture has so far been one-sided. In almost every crisis to which I have referred, there are opposite (if not yet equal) reactions setting in. Part II of this book will deal primarily with these reactions. It has been necessary, first of all, to establish the over-all context in which these reactions are emerging. Like the problems of environmental collapse which have elicited these reactions, the reactions themselves cannot be understood as separate events. They are part of an unfolding process—a trough following a wave or a wave following a trough, whichever way you choose to look at it.

Thus far, we have been discussing the collapse of civilization, Western civilization in particular, but not Western civilization alone. The division between "Eastern" and "Western" civilizations is more apparent than real. As a social process, the development of civilizations—whether in Asia or in Europe—has tended to follow the basic patterns noted by Toynbee. The trimmings have been different, but the matrix—as embodied in social institutions and as defined by their goals—remains, for all practical purposes, the same.

Before we move on to a description of the responses which have been generated as a result of environmental collapse, we must look at the roots of the civilization which is now crumbling around us. The reader who finds this statement—that civilization is crumbling—to be an exaggeration or a distortion of the facts is asked to go back to the preceding sections and to prove that the processes which I have been describing are not real. Moreover, I would ask him to demonstrate that, in terms of their cumulative effect and in terms of their global scale, they are not without precedent in the whole of human history.

Richard Kostelanetz writes, in *Beyond Left & Right,* that "the prerequisite for a relevant radical thought today is a profound sense of our historical uniqueness. Only thinking that transcends the old pieties and categories—that is clearly beyond both 'right' and 'left'—can discover the new sources of malaise and formulate ideas that will nourish the roots of our future common experience." So far in this book I have been attempting to reveal the "new sources of malaise." In the next part I will try to show how new ideas are already being formulated and, to varying degrees, acted upon. But first we must understand the one characteristic cause that is common to every dimension of decay, collapse, and disintegration that we have so far been discussing. The problems, as I have stressed, are so closely interrelated that they cannot be isolated without distorting their nature. More than that, however, they can *all*—separately or together—be traced to one behavioral trait which has been a constant characteristic of civilization throughout history. And it is precisely this characteristic that is now bringing civilization to an end. I am referring here to organized anarchy.

13

The
Organization
Anarchists

The common definition of anarchy, like the common definition of revolution, is purely political. *The Concise Oxford Dictionary* defines anarchy as the "absence of government; disorder; confusion." The word stems from the Greek term *"anarkhos,"* meaning "without ruler."

A competent biologist would immediately see, in this definition, a serious contradiction. Nature is without a ruler, at least in any sense that we know it. Yet when we speak of the balance of nature, we are referring to the homeostatic ecological tension which exists throughout nature and which keeps the amount of oxygen and carbon in the atmosphere in perfect balance, thus allowing the continued growth of plants and animals. Earlier, I referred to the "management" of nature, meaning that the animal community is self-governed by strict biological laws. In nature, there is an "absence of government," although at the same time there is no "disorder" or "confusion" in nature. Instead, there is a pattern of genetic determinism and an over-all order so precise and so persuasive that the science of ecology has just begun to explore it. To the Greeks, whose knowledge of ecology was negligible, the absence of a ruler may indeed have meant the same thing as lawlessness, disorder, and chaos—if for no other reason than that as civilized human beings they found that they were incapable of organizing communities without visible centralized control. In *African Genesis* Robert Ardrey suggests that "hunger and individual survival extend an invitation to anarchy. So also does sex, if we view it (as we must) as a behavioral compulsion, and not with the hindsight of its biological consequences. Other instincts, however, immediately command order: care of the young, establishment and defense of territory, social survival, dominance. We may therefore speculate that at some early moment in the evolvement of living things, natural selection found in duality of purpose a superior endowment for the creatures in its charge. The individual creature must survive; but so must his group, his population, his race, his species. And so the anarchistic instincts favor the demands of the individual creature, the instincts of order, the demands of his kind."

In the context of the group or community, the urge for self-survival can readily be seen as being anarchic. If every individual were truly "in it for himself" and for no one else, no group composed of such individuals could long survive. In *The Descent of Man* Darwin noted that "no tribe could hold together if murder, robbery, or treachery were common." Moreover, no tribe could long survive unless it was able to coordinate its efforts. Since primitive times, our most basic weapon of survival as a species has been the ability to pool our resources. Human organizational ability was more than a match for any animal, no matter how large or fast that animal may have been. Science and technology are extensions of this basic organizational strength. The computer, in this context, can be seen as the very tool that we have been looking for all along—an "organizing machine" which extends and magnifies our ability to organize in the same way that a rifle or missile extends our puny abilities to claw or strike. The computer, however, is even more central to our basic character than either the gun or the bomb. "Communal aggression," as such, is merely an extension of "communal organization." Without the organized community, organized aggression is impossible. Organization remains the key. The evidence suggests that aggression (on a communal or group basis) is, more than anything else, a way of intensifying and consolidating organizational strength within the community.

At the one pole of human duality, we have the anarchic self-survival impulses of the individual; at the other, the organizational impulse for group survival. At the end of the history of civilization, as at its beginning, we see that the conflict between the two becomes more pronounced than at any stage in between. In the process, however, through the gift of organizational genius, we have created hundreds of thousands of organizations to serve our needs. And, like the gods which we created at earlier periods, we have endowed our institutions and organizations with basic human characteristics. Institutions, like tribes, have corporate personalities or a corporation "self." Composed of many individuals, each institution nevertheless ends up reflecting a "common" stance, one which is peculiar to the group that it represents. Institutions, finally, are individual entities, just like their human creators, and the urge for self-survival is built into them. However, in few institutions is the impulse for group survival—meaning the survival of other institutions as well—built in to any such degree.

Our institutions reflect, for the most part, the anarchic side of our natures. And by "institution," I mean the governments of Japan, India, the United States, Russia, and the Netherlands as much as I mean the Elks Club, General Motors, the Catholic Church, Dow Chemical, and the National Rifle Association. Each is strongly motivated in the direction of its own self-aggrandizement, its self-survival, its self-image, its own profit, its own welfare, and its own victories. Charity, in all cases, begins at home.

Communism as an institution—no less than Catholicism, Protestantism, capitalism, Black Power, or the Republican or Conservative parties—are all basically anarchic, insofar as they are "in it for themselves." It is a paradox—though not a contradiction—that through the very success of our organizational abilities and impulses, we have managed to create so many immense anarchic organizations. In our need to find ways to assure group survival, we have created individual corporate Frankensteins which now threaten our survival to an extent that it has never been threatened before.

This is what C. Wright Mills means when he says that *"organized irresponsibility* . . . is a leading characteristic of modern industrial societies everywhere." He is speaking specifically of bureaucratic institutions, "concentrations of power" whose goal it is to manipulate or coerce. There is no difference, in this sense, between governmental and economic bureaucracies.

Today there are some 124 basically anarchic national institutions on the face of the earth. Each is concerned primarily with its own survival. At the same time, each national institution—particularly within the democratic nations, although it remains the case within totalitarian nations as well—contains hundreds and thousands of equally anarchic organizations and corporations, some concerned with making money, others with religion, others with defending various vested interests or else attacking them. Trade unions and chambers of commerce alike are basically anarchic. So too are rate-payers' associations, school boards, municipal councils, provincial and state governments, and so on. What some writers take to be the basically "aggressive" behavior of these organizations is nothing more than a defensive or offensive manifestation of their individual impulse toward self-survival.

It can be seen now, in view of the process discussed so far in this book, that the net effect of widespread anarchic interaction has been to bring *all* institutions, organizations, corporations, and governments to the brink of extinction. Pollution is a direct result of unchecked anarchic industrial self-survival. The coal company, iron firm, chemical company, or rubber manufacturer which causes the pollution in the first place does so because the men who run the firm are concerned with their own economic survival and not with the survival of competing firms or of people in the surrounding areas. Resources are gobbled up, stripped away, and processed in the same way, the companies involved responding to increased demand and the desire to increase their own profits—rather than being primarily concerned with the survival of the industry as a whole or, more abstractly, the population as a whole. Pesticide poisoning of the land and the food we eat (and, finally, of us) can be traced further than the need for stepped-up food production. It can be traced to the profit-oriented, or self-oriented, behavior of pesticide manufacturers.

The problem of drugs can be traced in the same way to the anarchic behavior of drug companies, no matter how neatly rationalized their efforts might be. War may be described simply as the result of dealings between conflicting anarchic nations. And, at this historic moment, when some of those nations are armed with deadly nuclear weapons, we live on a planetary stage which is cluttered with some

124 anarchists. And as natural resources dwindle, the competition between them—traditionally enough to break down whatever reservations they might have had to fight with one another—is bound to increase. How thirsty—really thirsty—would the United States have to get before it decided to take water from Canada, whether or not the Canadians approved?

At bottom, we find again the problem of overpopulation. There are, as Kenneth Boulding points out, many reasons for nations' not wanting to institute effective population control measures, including the "unwillingness of many countries to seem to weaken their relative position in the world." But beyond the self-interest issue which strangles rational international relations, we find the problem of sexual anarchists who are more concerned with their own gratification than anything else. In the same vein, it can be seen that the Catholic Church, in refusing to support birth control measures, is —despite its tortured rationalizations to the contrary—more concerned with losing power and authority than it is with the welfare of the millions of starving, disease-ridden children who are doomed to an intolerable existence in slums as a result of their parents' having obeyed the Church.

As noted earlier, competition (which is the behavior of anarchists) has become a culturally patterned defect. The successful competitor is admired and is encouraged to perform new feats of self-aggrandizement. Further expansion, further profit, and further exploitation are the trademarks of a successful and envied corporation, government, or individual. It is only beginning to dawn on a few individuals and groups that if organized corporate anarchy is allowed to go unchecked much longer, we will all perish. The "murder, robbery, and treachery" referred to by Darwin are endemic in our economic, political, religious, and social behavior today. As Boulding put it, "we are all engulfed in a profound and appallingly dangerous misallocation of our intellectual resources." It might also be added that the same misallocation applies to our emotional, spiritual, economic, political, and technological resources as well.

Let us now turn to the *antianarchic* processes which are now appearing spontaneously—in the homeostatic, self-regulatory manner explained earlier—at almost every level of our existence, from the political and economic spheres to the religious, psychological and characterological. Not all are recent developments, and none represents a complete break with the past. For the most part, these are processes which are being forced into existence by the need for adjustment to changing circumstances. At the moment these developments are all in the initial or at least early stages. As the rate of collapse increases, however, we may expect to see them forced more and more into the open.

The real revolution in our time is the struggle against organized and institutionalized anarchy. In an article in *The Nation* Robert and Leona Rienow wrote: "The tragedy of our times is that we have institutionalized the agents of appetite and victimized the advocates of deeper satisfactions. We stand sullenly frozen in the consequences of our folly—the doctrine of ever more people demanding ever more things—while our leader, standing before Congress, recites our phenomenal growth statistics and laments 'Why are you not happy?' " The Rienows refer to "the agents of appetite." Others put it less delicately, blaming the contemporary dilemma on greed, a lust for power or money, self-interest, even, as Bonaro W. Overstreet suggests in *Understanding Fear,* on "the fact that millions upon millions of people today are simultaneously dominated by fear." Both capitalism and communism are blamed because, as systems, both put the corporate or ideological self ahead of general global welfare. Whether industrialists, politicians, racists, or advocates of one religious system are identified as being the guilty parties, the fact remains that each is an anarchist. He is not recognized as such simply because he is attached to an institution or organization of some sort. The reality has not yet surfaced in the minds of many of us that it is the *organizations* which are the real anarchists. And the agents of these organizations, although they proclaim themselves to be—and, further, believe themselves to be—the advocates of order, consistently fail to place the general welfare of the local, national, or global community ahead of the welfare of their own organization. General Bullmoose is as much the personification of the agents of anarchy as is the Pope.

It is one of the crueler paradoxes of our time that many of the revolutionaries whose objective is to break down the system of organized anarchy which prevails throughout civilization are themselves feared and hated because they have been labeled "anarchists." The fact is, however, that in seeking an integrated and more organically ordered world, they are the enemies of organized anarchy. Yet by adopting a misleading and politically defined label, they too think of themselves as being anarchists. In doing so, they succeed, if nothing else, in compounding the confusion that already exists.

The forces, movements, trends, developments, and innovations which are described in the remainder of this book represent not so much an abrupt dislocation of historic trends as simply a continuation of cyclical trends which have persisted throughout history. Social organization has always served to minimize conflict and anarchic impulses within communities, either channeling them into group activities—for instance, the building of cities, temples, spaceships, or gross national product—or directing them outward against a real or imagined enemy.

If war has seemed to be either the basic social system or at least a crucial dimension of the process of civilizing peoples, this should not be surprising, since wars and the formation of armies have always served the needs of social organization. In Caesar's clanking legions, Napoleon's inspired foot soldiers, and Hitler's goose-stepping hordes, we see the process of social organization reaching its apex. However, at no period in history have the forces for integration, cooperation, and brotherhood been entirely submerged. The theme of all great religions—although eventually obscured by the institutionalized forms into which they evolved—has remained constant.

Moreover, civilization itself began as a tightened form of social organization, replacing the looser forms to be found in primitive societies. The earliest civilizations, taking shape in Mesopotamia, ancient Egypt, and the Indus valley in India, all shared this characteristic. It manifested itself, for example, in the building of large-scale irrigation systems which could not be built by any single family or tribe. Richard Carrington tells us the early civilized cultivators "had to consult together and decide how the layout of the irrigation works could best be designed to meet their common needs. They then had to carry out the actual labor of construction in conjunction, and later to agree on the proportion of water to be allotted to each family in relation to the total amount available. This principle of cooperative effort for the good of the whole community instead of certain privileged individuals is fundamental to civilized society."

It can be seen, however, that the principle of cooperation was understood only ethnocentrically. It functioned within each society or community, but the concept of a "community of societies" or of a global society made up of many different ethnic or racial groups never took root. In the rise of the modern megalopolis, with its many wards or municipalities, we see the cooperative concept taking a giant step forward. The early cooperative efforts to build irrigation systems, so essential to the development of civilizations, is a primitive form of large-scale integration. Increasingly complex modes of organization force further integration, coordination, and cooperation.

To date, however, the principle has spilled only rather superficially over border lines and is still inward-turned, as it is in the case of institutions and organizations of every kind. The pattern is clear enough. Anarchic individuals, driven by population pressures (among other things), are forced to learn to cooperate. In consequence, they create civilizations, "the most highly evolved technique so far discovered by any living organism to ensure the survival of the species, and at the same time to allow it to attain new levels of awareness." But having taken this giant evolutionary step, they ultimately succeed in creating anarchic societies and organizations. The next step, as crucial as the transition from primitive society to civilization, is clear. Conceivably, until we had achieved the global village, the forces of integration could never emerge from the shadow of organized anarchy. But they are beginning to emerge today, thus triggering a global conflict—with the by-now overwhelmingly dominant forces of organized anarchy clearly aligned on one side, only because there is no other choice at this point.

The agonizing and bloody transition from competitive, self-oriented behavior to new global forms of cooperative, integrated behavior does not represent an overthrowing of existing orders so much as an accentuation of behavioral patterns which existed even before the advent of civilization. The forces for change described in the preceding sections press inexorably against the tendencies to competition and anarchy. They force us—in many cases, kicking and screaming all the way—into more cooperative patterns of behavior. In *A Million Years of Man* Richard Carrington concludes:

> The lessons of human history show beyond any possibility of doubt that cooperative effort is the only valid survival technique remaining

to our species. As we have seen countless times . . . "adapt or perish" is a fundamental law of nature. When evolution was still proceeding at the physical level, adaptations for survival were likewise mainly physical. But . . . in [the] new psychosocial phase of evolution, the development of cooperative mind became the main technique of survival, and, in spite of the new penetrations now being made into what we may call psychospiritual awareness, it still remains so. Unless man learns to cooperate with his fellows, his local dominance on this particular evolutionary center in the universe is liable to cease.

We turn now from our examination of the disaster caused by organized anarchy to an examination of the response.

Large-Scale Integration

Unlike the simple society, the modern industrial society is highly differentiated and therefore requires great integration in order to function. . . . Thus, geometric increase in the complexity and organization of modern life will necessitate corresponding, even if not directly proportional, increases in the scope and complexity of human and organizational controls. One need not assume the triumph of the police mentality, or the intrusion of the motivation that denigrates human dignity, to foresee this. Each restriction will have its valid and attractive rationale, which may even be libertarian. . . . Rules governing mutual adjustment will inevitably be very stringent, and there will be a strong emphasis on adjustment (other-directed orientations) in place of individualism.

—Anthony J. Wiener
Faustian Progress

14

In Search
of the
Organic

We turn now to specific examples of large-scale integration. These are processes which are basically existential, homeostatic, organic, and gestaltian. One may look for cause-and-effect connections between these developments and various aspects of environmental collapse. In many cases it will be possible to make such causal connections—to show, for instance, that what John Kenneth Galbraith calls "technostructures" have emerged in response to the increased complexity of modern industry. Such a connection is valid in particular instances. But in the overview, causality becomes a cumbersome tool. It imposes on us the demand to untangle all the knots and to trace the connections between all events. This makes for an interesting exercise in scholarship, but it denies us access to an understanding of synergistic effects. Even after all the possible cause-and-effect sequences have been tracked down, all relationships duly noted, and the sequential events fitted into their proper places, we are still no closer to comprehension, simply because we have not allowed that the whole may be more than the sum of its parts, that several different processes—interacting one upon the other, one upon all, and all upon one—may produce an effect, or several effects, which do not appear to be specifically related.

Carl Jung's concept of "synchronicity," which stresses the peculiar interdependence of objective events and which he called an "acausal connecting principle," allows us more conceptual freedom. It is also more existential, since it concerns itself not with *why,* but with *what* is going on. Events evolve one out of the other, some out of many, many out of a few. One may choose to select two or more aspects of environmental collapse as being causal factors in the evolution of one or more instances of large-scale integration. It may be shown, for instance, that characterological change in urban centers (a dimension of large-scale integration) is the *result* of the interaction of several aspects of environmental deterioration—overcrowding, alienation, loss of primal community, technological innovation, and even the intrusion of electronic forms of communication. But once we have established such causal relationships, the tendency is to stop there—to choose, in effect, to set a limit on the number of factors which may be included in any equation of social change. Thus, we surrender to the demands of the method of analysis and set arbitrary limits solely to make the analysis workable.

Having recourse to the concept of synchronicity, we are free to acknowledge the workability of an analysis that sets *no* limits on the relationships of events. Thus, we are able to see things in the following terms. The environment changes; change produces other changes, which in turn set in motion still further changes; all of these make waves, and the waves overlap; the direction of events is altered, and the events themselves are transformed; new sets of responses are worked out to deal with new pressures, and these responses create yet other pressures, which have effects of their own on the effects which produced them in the first place. Environmental collapse, as suggested earlier, can be understood only as a synergistic effect. Similarly, large-scale integration is a synergistic effect, or, more accurately, a variety of synergistic effects having an over-all—and, again, synergistic—effect of their own.

It is evident by now that our total environment is undergoing profound and rapid change. It is in relationship to this environmental alteration that the processes of large-scale integration will be viewed. Interactions are obviously taking place. Homeostatic adjustments are being made. New sets of responses—to new situations—are being spontaneously worked out. If many of these responses do not appear to make sense—for example, the roughly simultaneous decision of millions of students to drop out of school—it is only because many of us have chosen not to view this action within a larger context. Seen against the background of environmental collapse, the dropout phenomenon is not as senseless as many of us would like to believe it to be. It represents a rejection—as significant as the "decision" of the body to reject foreign tissue—of standards and behavioral patterns that have become unbalanced, even cancerous, and whose effect is to threaten further the social organism.

Most of the processes thus far described and offered as examples of organizational anarchy can be seen to be nonorganic. That is, they involve an artificial separation of functions. They increase division rather than unity. Conflict is the unharmonious meshing of parts. They stimulate further conflict.

Large-scale integration represents organic processes. These are processes which are spontaneous, as opposed to structured, which are reactions more than conscious decisions. As will be shown, they tend to be existential. They are also gestaltian.

"Gestalt" is the German word for "whole." It means roughly the same thing as the word "Tao." In the English language, the only word we have that approaches this concept is "synergy." Thus, "gestaltian," "Taoistic," and "synergistic" are, practically speaking, synonymous words. They involve a recognition of synchronicity. Modern science has, of course, reached the point where cause-and-effect is no longer paramount. Led by the physicist, today's scientist is back to the pre-Socratic idea that everything is in a state of flux, that the world is a continuous on-going process. For example, in *Quantum Physics* David Bohm notes that "the world cannot [any longer] be analyzed correctly into distinct parts; instead, it must be regarded as an indivisible unit." This evolution of Western science is, in itself, a further manifestation of large-scale integration. Moreover, such awareness underlines the fact that all aspects of large-scale integration involve, to varying degrees, an implicit recognition that boundaries and divisions are *artificial*. They have no existence except in the minds of those who create and preserve them.

Large-scale integration is a process which acts to break through the organizational barriers which perpetuate conflict and competition. Whether the barrier is departmental, ideological, or racial, the *effect* of large-scale integration is to remove the barrier—or at least to reduce its effectiveness—by forcing a higher definition of the real functions of the parts. In other words, there is no suggestion here that large-scale integration involves a leveling or homogenizing of functions. Rather, it serves to emphasize *actual* differences, as opposed to *arbitrary* differences. We might consider, as an example, the so-called "parts" of the human body. Each part is clearly defined in terms of its function. But although the function of the heart, for example, is well defined, the heart itself is able to function only so long as the other parts of the body carry out *their* functions. In short, the functions of the various organs in any given organism are integrated. Similarly, human societies are composed of integrated processes, "parts" whose functions are highly defined. And so long as these parts continue to function harmoniously—the family in relation to the state, the schools in relation to the economy, the personality in relationship to the environment—there is no imbalance.

However, as the preceding section was intended to show, severe imbalances have been imposed on the social organism, and this is particularly true in the highly industrialized nations. The homeostatic response is to attempt to restore the society, through the vehicle of the individual, to some semblance of balance—in short, to reintegrate the functions of the parts in relation to actual needs. In the example of alienation, we see a clear psychobiological need to reintegrate the community; in the example of abuse of the physical environment, we see a similar need to reintegrate economic and political functions with the actual biotope; and so on.

Further, since many of the ways in which we abuse our physical environment and our own psyches are the result of having adopted speciocentric viewpoints, it can be seen that the need arises at this point to develop a *new* viewpoint—one that recognizes the interdependence of things, of functions, of processes. And with the rise of an "ecological consciousness," a humanistic psychology, and a greatly heightened appreciation of Oriental philosophy and religion, to say nothing of the application of computers to a wide variety of problems, we see the needed viewpoint emerging. Furthermore, to the extent that they stimulate a consciousness of the "wholeness" of things, psychotropic drugs can also be seen as a form of homeostatic response.

It can easily be seen that most of the conflicts that divide us today are of a more elemental nature than those that divided us not long ago. Which is to say, they are more highly defined. This is a point that will be developed later, in the section on convergence. For the moment, it is enough that we note that the developments referred to as dimensions of large-scale integration tend to be organic, as opposed to nonorganic, and that they involve ever-increasing precision in definition of functions, roles, needs, and aims.

Now let us begin our survey of the evolution of large-scale integration with one of its most central features—namely, social character.

15

Revolt of the Other - Directed

The process of large-scale integration was already well under way in 1948, when David Riesman, Nathan Glazer, and Reuel Denney sat down to write *The Lonely Crowd: A Study of the Changing American Character*. The axis of their study was well laid. Later, writers like McLuhan would attempt to pry open the lid of the mass psyche by using a television antenna; some would apply the tools of the economist; and in other cases the ego would be used as a jackhammer. Yet Riesman's sociological dipstick remained one of the best indicators available. It revealed a revolution—only beginning then—which promised to be at least as disruptive as the one which brought the Middle Ages to an agonized, tumultuous end and triggered the Renaissance, the Reformation, the Counter Reformation, the Industrial Revolution, and, finally, the political revolutions of the seventeenth, eighteenth, and nineteenth centuries.

While recognizing the role of media, technology, and economics in the shaping of this new revolution, Riesman and his colleagues did not attribute more than peripheral importance to them. Rather, they linked their findings to population curves. As a catalyst of change, population should not be underestimated in importance. But—like others who have applied a specialized viewpoint—

Riesman constructed too simple a model. Attempting to explain the modern revolution in terms of population shifts alone is like attempting to explain the functioning of a jet engine by providing a detailed description of the generator and nothing else.

Riesman takes note, to begin with, of Erich Fromm's observation about the link between character training and society: "In order that any society may function well, its members must acquire the kind of character which makes them *want* to act in the way they *have* to act as members of the society or of a special class within it. They have to *desire* what objectively is *necessary* for them to do. *Outer force* is replaced by *inner compulsion,* and by the particular kind of human energy which is channeled into character traits." It is a long jump, Riesman admits, from economic and historic necessities to systems of child training, but "the satisfaction of the largest 'needs' of society is prepared, in some half-mysterious way, by its most intimate practices." In other words, there is an organic relationship between historic imperatives, developments in industry and government, and the life of the individual.

Riesman defines three types of social character: tradition-directed, inner-directed, and other-directed. Primitive, medieval, and feudal societies were dominated by tradition-directed people who learned to deal with life by means of adaptation rather than innovation. For tradition-oriented people, institutionalized roles are available—even for those who are deviants. Behavior is guided and directed by the rigid structure of tradition. Society, in short, is a series of square holes, and individuals are made to fit. Tradition-directed societies—sometimes called folk societies, status societies, or *Gemeinschaften*—are characterized by "relative slowness of change, their dependence on family and kin organizations, and—in comparison with later epochs—their tight web of values."

Riesman argues that this type of society remains in a phase of "high growth potential" in which a population explosion is held back only by a high death rate. Then comes a period of "transitional growth" in which there is a drop in the death rate. Population rises. "The imbalance of births and deaths puts pressure on the society's customary ways." Relatively rapid change is now brought about—improved communications, sanitation, methods of agriculture, and so on. Expansion takes place in technology, production of goods, numbers of people, exploration, colonization, and imperialism. Capital is quickly accumulated and personal mobility increases.

Strict and self-evident, tradition-direction can no longer cope with the situation. The individual needs a greater degree of flexibility in order to deal with ever-changing requirements. The mechanism he acquires in place of tradition is what Riesman calls a "psychological gyroscope." The source of direction for the individual becomes *inner*—"in the sense that it is implanted early in life by the elders and directed toward generalized but nonetheless inescapably destined goals." The gyroscope, once planted, gives the individual a detailed set of behavioral instructions, called values. These values serve to keep him on course for the rest of his life. Metaphorically, one might say that in the stage of tradition-direction, the individual is, like an unhatched chick, kept secure within the eggshell of society. When the shell breaks, he is forced into unfamiliar terrain and needs cultural guidance, similar to the genetic guidance with which the chick is provided. What Riesman calls inner-direction is manifested in the Protestant ethic—which, it must be stressed, is only *one* visible manifestation of it.

Following the period of transitional population growth, the birth rate, according to Riesman, begins to follow the death rate downward. People find themselves in "a centralized and bureaucratized society and a world shrunken and agitated by the contact— accelerated by industrialization—of races, nations, and cultures. The hard enduringness and enterprise of the inner-directed types are somewhat less necessary under these new conditions. Increasingly, *other people* are the problem, not the material environment. And as people mix more widely and become more sensitive to each other . . . gyroscopic control is no longer sufficiently flexible, and a new psychological mechanism is called for."

At this point, other-directed individuals begin to appear in ever-increasing numbers. Initially, they emerge in the upper middle class of North American cities. These are people for whom "relations with the outer world and with oneself are mediated by the flow of mass communication." They require "more 'socialized' behavior both for success and for marital and personal adaptation. Connected with such changes are changes in the family and in child-rearing practices." Riesman continues:

In the smaller families of urban life, and with the spread of "permissive" child care to ever wider strata of the population, there is a relaxation of older patterns of discipline. Under these newer patterns, the peer-group (the group of one's associates of the same age and class) becomes much more important to the child. . . .

What is common to all the other-directed people is that their contemporaries are the source of direction for the individual—either those known to him or those with whom he is indirectly acquainted, through friends and through the mass media. This source is, of course, "internalized" in the sense that dependence on it for guidance in life is implanted early. The goals toward which the other-directed person strives shift with that guidance: it is only the process of striving itself and the process of paying close attention to the signals from others that remain unaltered throughout life. This mode of keeping in touch with others permits a close behavioral conformity, not through drill in behavior itself, as in the tradition-directed character, but rather through an exceptional sensitivity to the actions and wishes of others.

Later, referring to "the insatiable force of this psychological need for approval," Riesman adds: "While all people want and need to be liked by some of the people some of the time, it is only the modern other-directed types who make this their chief source of direction and chief area of sensitivity." And further: "The other-directed person, though he has his eye very much on the Joneses, aims to keep up with them not so much in external details as in the quality of his inner experience. That is, his great sensitivity keeps him in touch with others on many more levels than the externals of appearance and propriety."

In time, we shall see how mass media lend themselves admirably to keeping in touch on many levels. Moreover, it will be seen how nothing explains the ever-increasing popularity of drugs—particularly marijuana—so much as the rise of other-directedness. The other-directed "turn on" to each other as a matter of course. Any device, such as marijuana, which assists the process is not only welcome, but is in many cases viewed as being almost essential. Like underarm deodorant in a time of artifically conditioned awareness of body odors, marijuana is much in demand. Likewise, any other mechanism which facilitates the sharing of common experience—

for example, the mass media—rises steadily on the scale of cultural importance.

Like the tradition-directed person, the other-directed person lives in a group milieu. Only the inner-directed person, who lives in the transitional period between two different stages of group orientation, can afford to go it alone. "Rugged individualism," in a word, is only a kind of stopgap behavioral measure, developed to cope with the exigencies of a temporary situation. The meaning of W. I. Thomas's remark—"individualism is only a stage of transition between two types of social organization"—now becomes clear.

Riesman makes an important qualification to his own thesis. He points out that it is a mistake to assume that societies always manage to produce the kind of social organization and character types which they need in order to survive. "Such an assumption, raising the image of a separate body, 'society,' making certain demands on people and testing out various processes, would introduce an unwarranted teleology into social change. What seems to happen is that by sheer 'accident' any of a number of ways of insuring characterological conformity may exist in a given society. . . . We must not overestimate the role of character in the social process. . . . We are [also] forced to take account of the possibility that people may be compelled to behave in one way although their character structure presses them to behave in the opposite way. Society may change more rapidly than character, or vice versa. *Indeed, this disparity between socially required behavior and characterologically compatible behavior is one of the great levers of change* [my italics]."

Riesman sees many of the tensions in North American society —tensions which have multipled many times over since his book was written and which have acquired, in the process, glib labels such as "the generation gap"—as being rooted in a characterological, rather than an ideological, struggle between the generally younger other-directed people and the often older inner-directed types. As for the reasons for the characterological struggle, "when the basic physical plant of a society is felt to be built, or rather, when the building can be routinized by management planning, there begins to be room at the top for the other-directed person who can see the subtle opportunities given in the human setting. Though material abundance becomes technologically possible, people continue to work—and do make-work—at a pace more in keeping with the earlier era of transitional growth: mobility drives are still imbedded in their character. *But the product in demand is neither a staple nor a machine; it is a personality."*

The role of the teacher, as well as that of the parent, changes considerably during the stage of other-directedness. Parents, for instance, "have their sources of direction in the mass media. For their uneasiness as to how to bring up children, they turn increasingly to books, magazines, government pamphlets, and radio programs. These tell the anxious mother to accept her children. She learns there are no problem children, only problem parents, and she learns to look into her own psyche whenever she is moved to deny the children anything, including an uninterrupted flow of affection." In short, "more is staked on every single child than in the earlier epochs when many children were not raised to maturity." As for the teacher, his or her role in this situation "is often that of opinion leader. She is the one who spreads the messages concerning taste that come from the progressive urban centers. She conveys to the children that what matters is not their industry and learning as such, but their adjustment in the group, their cooperation, their [carefully stylized and limited] initiative and leadership."

Riesman notes a "curious resemblance" between the role of the teacher in the modern school and the role of the industrial relations department in a modern factory. The teacher and the industrial relations expert are increasingly concerned with teaching cooperation. Thus, like the factory worker, the other-directed child is trained to "take his place in a society in which the concern of the group is less with what it produces than with its internal group relations." Moreover, the child is taught by his parents as well as his teachers that "he should be part of a crowd and *must* have fun." (This attitude, of course, not only lends itself to the lessening of friction in an increasingly crowded environment, but also serves well the needs of the industrial system—a matter which we will examine later.)

In this context, "invisible differences" between one's own child and the children of others are suppressed, since they cast doubt on the adjustment of the parents themselves. "Overt vanity" becomes a crime as terrible as dishonesty was in other times. Training in consumer tastes replaces training in etiquette (a highly tradition-oriented business). Just as the inner-directed person poured his energy into production, the other-directed person—reflecting the shift from a scarcity consciousness to what is called a psychology of abundance—pours his energy into consumption. As one begins to compete for approval, overt competitiveness must be repressed. *"There has been an enormous ideological shift,"* Riesman notes, *"favoring submission to the group,* a shift whose decisiveness is concealed by the persistence of the older ideological patterns. The peer group becomes the measure of all things; the individual has few defenses the group cannot batter down."

Let us touch now on a few other crucial features of other-direction. Riesman notes that in business and politics leadership becomes more and more amorphous. In business, "if one is successful in one's craft, one is forced to leave it." The successful reporter becomes a deskman, columnist, or editor. The doctor becomes the administrator of a clinic or hospital. The professor becomes a dean or president. The factory superintendent becomes a holding-company executive. The "craft skills" of all these successful types must be shed and replaced by "manipulative skills." They must work less with things and more with people. "Indeed," writes Riesman, "a society increasingly dependent on manipulation of people is almost as destructive of the craft-oriented professional and businessman as a society in the earlier stages of industrialization is destructive of the handicraft-oriented peasant and artisan. . . . The industrial process advances by building into machines and smooth-flowing organizations the skills which were once built, by a long characterological and apprenticeship process, into men." Of course, many areas remain where organization requires an inner-directed man "who can say 'no' without going through an elaborate song and dance." But mainly this occurs in areas in which technological problems have not yet been overcome.

Riesman also makes another distinction between inner- and other-directed men. The inner-directed man can always take a compass reading on some star of the past, a hero who provides the model for his own behavior. The other-directed man, on the other hand, "moves in the midst of a veritable Milky Way of almost but not quite indistinguishable contemporaries." There is no Canopus—a great scientist, businessman, general, statesman—who provides a frame of reference relevant to his own other-directed behavior, since he is seeking "the respect, the affection, of an amorphous and shifting, though contemporary, jury of peers." Riesman writes: "To say that the judgments of peer-groupers are matters of taste, not of morality or even opportunism, is not to say that any particular child (or adult) can afford to ignore these judgments. On the contrary, he is, as never before, at their mercy. If the peer-group were—and we continue to deal here with the urban middle classes only—a wild, torturing, obviously vicious group, the individual child might still feel moral indignation as a defense against its commands. But like adult authorities in the other-directed socialization process, the peer-group is friendly and tolerant. It stresses fair play. Its conditions for entry seem reasonable and well meaning. . . . The child (and again, the adult) is therefore exposed to trial by jury without any defenses . . . from the side of its own morality. . . . *All the morality is the group's.*"

At this point, we might note that what has since come to be called the "new morality" is, in part, an other-directed group morality, as opposed to an inner-directed morality in which values were locked within a fixed frame of reference early in life and remained firmly in place from that time on. The latter, of course, was highly authoritarian and the former may be described as being humanistic—if we may strip the latter word of the pieties which are normally attached to its usage. There is a difference here between the meaning of "humanistic" in an inner-directed epoch and its meaning in the present, increasingly other-directed period. Formerly, it had strong moralistic overtones. Now, in the context of group morality, it has a psychological base, fully articulated in the rise of the "humanistic psychology" movement.

The arrangement of the words here is slightly misleading. "Humanistic psychology," for all its fine ideological overtones, applies to what can more accurately be called "psychological humanism," as opposed to "moralistic humanism." In short, we are talking now about an ideology that has become *functional* due to changing characterological patterns. In previous eras, since it went against the characterological grain, it remained, for the most part, "pie in the sky." Now it has a psychological niche to fill, mainly with the personalities of the other-directed. Visions are seldom harvested until ripe. And they are not ripe until there is good psychological and characterological soil for them to grow in. With the rise of other-directedness, the word "humanistic" takes root in the need for peer-group approval and in an ever-increasing sensitivity toward others and, more important, toward their judgment of one's self. Humanistic attitudes, previously relegated to do-gooders and moralists, are now embraced by the other-directed crowd, since these attitudes closely approximate their own psychological needs for ways in which to relate and be related to. In a series of interviews with young people, Riesman and his colleagues asked them what they thought was their best trait. Most were hard-pressed for an answer, but finally decided that it was their "ability to get along well with everybody." Other than that, a "sense of humor" was felt to be very important, since it oils the machinery of group interaction and allows the group to function all the more harmoniously.

Riesman sees certain positive sides to this development. He takes note of the refusal of young people to commit themselves to long-range goals. "We are not," as I was told in Haight-Ashbury in the summer of 1967, "a goal-oriented generation." Posterity, in fact, becomes a four-letter word—first, because it implies vanity (which is criminal among the other-directed), and second, because it reflects the values of the earlier inner-directed period. "The uncertainty of life in our day is certainly a factor" in this refusal to accept long-range goals, writes Riesman. But more important, "the seemingly sure commitment of many inner-directed youths was based on an unquestioning acceptance of parental orders and parental ranking of occupations. The other-directed youth of today often asks more of a job than that it satisfy conventional status and pecuniary requirements; he is not content with the authoritarian rankings of earlier generations."

At this point Riesman pauses to attempt to redress the balance in any comparison between inner- and other-directed people. Inner-directed people would seem to be of sterner and more intrepid stuff. Yet they are also more limited. There is nothing wrong, Riesman notes, with being concerned with others. "We must ask anyone who opposes the manipulation of men in modern industry whether he prefers to return to their brutalization, as in the early days of the industrial revolution. In my scheme of values, persuasion, even manipulative persuasion, is to be preferred to force." The other-directed person is subject to stresses and strains which, while they are less hard-edged and less physically demanding than the problems faced by the inner-directed man, are nevertheless as difficult—if not more so—to cope with.

Turning to politics, Riesman draws attention to a shift in the mode of political decision-making from dominance by a ruling class to power dispersal among many marginally competing pressure groups:

> There has been, in the last fifty years, a change in the configuration of power in America, in which a single hierarchy with a ruling class at its head has been replaced by a number of veto groups among which power is dispersed. . . . A clear-cut power structure helped to create the clarity of goals of the inner-directed; an amorphous power structure helps to create the consumer orientation of the other-directed.
>
> We have entered a social and political phase in which power is dispersed among veto groups. These groups are too many and too diverse to be led by moralizing; what they want is too various to be moralized and too intangible to be bought off for cash alone; and what is called political leadership consists, as we could see in Roosevelt's case, in the tolerant ability to manipulate coalitions. This means that men who at an earlier historical period were political leaders are now busy with the other-directed occupation of studying the feedback from all the others—their constituencies, their correspondents, and friends and enemies within influential pressure groups. . . . Of course, political figures in all ages have been dependent on their following, and opportunism and manipulation are not a twentieth-century discovery. The inner-directed leader, however, was quite conscious of discrepancies between his views and those of others: if he shifted course, it was still *his* course. . . . He did not need to have everybody love him, but only those who matter for his fortunes. . . .
>
> Today we have substituted for . . . leadership a series of groups, each of which has struggled for and finally attained a power to stop things conceivably inimical to its interests and, within far narrower limits, to start things. . . . The various groups, large and small . . . have in many instances succeeded in maneuvering themselves into a position in which they are able to neutralize those who might attack them. . . . The only leaders of national scope left in the United States today are those who can placate the veto groups. The only followers left in the United States today are those unorganized and sometimes disorganized unfortunates who have not yet invented their group. . . .
>
> In the amorphous power structure created by the veto groups, it is

hard to distinguish the rulers from the ruled, those to be aided from those to be opposed, those on your side from those on the other side. . . . By their very nature, the veto groups exist as defense groups, not as leadership groups. . . . I am talking, of course, about the national scene. The smaller the constituency, of course, the smaller the number of veto groups and the greater the chance that some of them will be dominant. . . . The veto groups, taken together, constitute a new buffer region between the old, altered, and thinning extremes of those who were once leaders and led.

Riesman concludes: "The chiefs have lost the power, *but the followers have not gained it.*"

Finally, Riesman turns to definitions of the terms "adjusted," "anomic," and "autonomous." This is an important section in his book. The adjusted, he argues, are the typical tradition-, inner-, or other-directed—"those who will respond in their character structure to the demands of their society or social class at its particular stage on the curve of population. Such people fit the culture as though they were made for it, as in fact they are. . . . The adjusted are those who reflect their society, or their class within the society, with the least distortion."

Then there are the anomic and the autonomous, who do not conform. The word "anomic" is derived from *"anomique,"* meaning "ungoverned" or "ruleless." In Riesman's usage, however, the term is virtually synonymous with "maladjusted," except that an anomic person, as opposed to a merely maladjusted person, can sometimes have a high value in society—as in the case of artists. The autonomous are those who "on the whole are capable of conforming to the behavioral norms of their society—a capacity the anomics usually lack—but are free to choose whether to conform or not." He mentions the fact that the test of an individual's degree of adjustment is not so much whether his overt behavior obeys social norms, but whether his character structure does. "Nonconformity in behavior does not necessarily mean nonconformity in character structure. . . ."

While inner-directed and other-directed people can be accommodated within a totalitarian structure—the former fitting naturally into it and the latter being responsive to persuasion on what might be called an organic although no less totalitarian basis—it is the autonomous person against whom modern totalitarianism must wage total war. Increasingly, as totalitarianism in various guises becomes the simple response to the pressures for change summarized at the beginning of this book, it *is* the autonomous person who comes under attack. "For," as Riesman notes, "the autonomous person's acceptance of social and political authority is always conditional: he can cooperate with others in action while maintaining the right of private judgment. There can be no recognition whatever of such a right under totalitarianism—one reason why in the Soviet Union artistic works and scientific theories are so relentlessly scrutinized for 'deviationism,' lest they conceal the seeds of unconscious privacy and independence of perception. Fortunately for us, the enemies of autonomy in the modern democracies are less total and relentless. However, as Erich Fromm has insisted in *Escape from Freedom,* the diffuse and anonymous authority of the modern democracies is less favorable to autonomy than one might assume."

The autonomous person today is confronted—not directly, but indirectly—by invisible assassins. It is difficult for him to define his enemy. "An autonomous person today must work constantly to detach himself from shadowy entanglements with this top level of other-direction (meaning the inability of his peers to understand savage emotions, the friends who pardon, understand, and are amused by everything)." Even in 1950, groups of autonomous people could be found, particularly in Bohemia. Frequently, they were not as free or autonomous as they appeared to be. "On the contrary, they are often zealously tuned in to the signals of a group that finds the meaning of life, quite unproblematically, in an illusion of attacking an allegedly dominant and punishing majority of . . . chiefs." It is an easy matter for a member of a nonconformist group, who is conforming to the so-called nonconformity of the group, to "degenerate into other-directed play-acting."

In an era that is dependent on other-direction, Riesman says, a "heightened self-consciousness, above all else, constitutes the insignia of the autonomous. The characterological struggle that holds the center of the stage today is that between other-direction and inner-direction, as against a background in which tradition-direction gradually disappears from the planet. Now we already discern on the horizon a new polarization between those who cling to compulsive adjustment via other-directedness and those who strive to overcome this milieu by autonomy." Rather than expecting the imminent polarization between other-direction and autonomy to become a savage struggle—as has the struggle between inner-direction and other-direction since the time of his writing—he suspects "at least the possibility of an organic development of autonomy out of other-direction." This is his best insight.

In this summary of Riesman's classic, we have been looking at what I call "characterological large-scale integration." The social effect of other-direction, after all, is to shift the emphasis from single components (individuals) to whole arrays of circuits (groups), all of which are functioning in the same piece of semiconductor material (the urban environment). A greatly heightened sensitivity—a characteristic of the recent breakthroughs in computer technology —keeps individuals in touch with one another at many more levels than the purely superficial levels of appearance and belongings. Rugged individualism recedes, like the valve of the old radio, into history. It is replaced by complex interactions. Crude tradition- or inner-directed social behavior is refined and new dimensions of responsiveness are introduced. As the old power pyramid crumbles into a gravel heap of veto groups, the rule of social organization becomes manipulation, cooperation, and coordination—rather than authoritarianism.

In addition to representing characterological large-scale integration, the rapid evolution of other-direction and the strong signs of at least the possibility of autonomy coming up fast on its heels further represent a deeply antianarchic movement. Anarchic personalities are ill-adapted to a group milieu. Anarchic impulses, in turn, are severely constrained by the pressures of peer-group morality and the need for approval. The heroes of Ayn Rand's novels can clearly be seen to be first-degree anarchists. They may stand out "in violent integrity against the pressure for group adjustment," but their integrity is strictly of the charity-begins-at-home variety. Besides which, the whole process of other-direction, like the process of large-scale integration, gives every sign of being nothing more than a transitional stage, a kind of damping down of the violently anarchic behavior patterns of the inner-directed.

So far as I know, no similar study of changing urban character has been carried out in any of the other highly industrialized or post-industrial nations. However, Riesman has noted that the shift in political decision-making from dominance by a ruling class to power dispersal among many marginally competing pressure groups may be one of the causal factors in the rise of other-direction. If this is, indeed, the case, there is reason to believe that other-direction is becoming the characterological norm in other highly industrialized societies as well. In totalitarian societies, this may be considerably less the case. On the other hand, other forces could be considered causal factors as well: a reduction in the size of families, rapid implosion of populations into urban centers, a shift from authoritarian to manipulative social organization, plus the "ecumenical impact" (as Richard Kostelanetz puts it) of certain pervasive technologies, the increased interaction between various ethnic and racial groups in the urban sinks, the effects of specialization and high levels of differentiation in the industrial sector, and the near-universal rise of "technoplanning" and "technostructures" in all highly industrialized countries. Further, the role of media, particularly electronic media, should not be overlooked. The breakdown in the political decision-making process may well be, as Riesman suggests, one of the main triggering mechanisms in the rise of other-direction. But the other factors are critical as well. And if such is the case (as it certainly appears to be), then it is fairly safe to assume that other-direction is rapidly becoming the basic character type to be found in other industrialized and urbanized nations, regardless of ideological stances. And finally, Riesman fails to note that in the United States there is considerably more ideological resistance to the rise of other-direction than would be the case in socialist and communist countries, where, in fact, political revolutions against the most overt forms of inner-directed behavior have already been carried out.

We turn now to the field of economics, where developments strikingly parallel to those taking place in the area of social character have been observed. That there is a strong relationship between the two goes without saying. I will not venture to suggest which had greater influence on the other. It would be too simple to say that character is entirely molded by economic necessity, or that economics follows character in the development of a given society. It would not be outrageous, on the other hand, to suggest that the influences run both ways and, in turn, are related to other developments.

16

Gestalt
Economics

There are approximately 100,000 industrial complexes in the world today—including both private corporations and state undertakings. It hardly needs to be pointed out that these complexes exert an enormous influence on the lives of all of us. And insofar as they embody economic forces—a cumulative effect of social, technological, political, and environmental forces interacting simultaneously —they may exert not only an enormous but possibly a *decisive* influence. For example, the educational system in any given country functions, in large part, according to the needs of the industrial sector. And it is in the vast labyrinth of the industrial sector that a real and fundamental revolution—disguised both by token ideological statements to the contrary and by nostalgia—has been taking place.

Even in 1956 C. Wright Mills was able to observe quite casually in *The Power Elite* that the competitive, autonomous economic market had ceased to make the decisions that shape the economy of America. "There is simply too much at stake for that sort of slipshod method to be the going rule." The corporate revolution, Mills noted, "has transformed property from a tool of the workman into an elaborate instrument by which his work is controlled and a profit extracted from it. The small entrepreneur is no longer the key to the economic life of America." And, he added, while "Americans like to think of themselves as the most individualistic people in the world . . . among them the impersonal corporation has proceeded the farthest and now reaches into every area and detail of daily life. . . . The story of the American economy since the Civil War is thus the story of the creation and consolidation of this corporate world of centralized property." It is also the story of large-scale integration and of incipient convergence. In 1968 the number of corporate acquisitions rose to a record 4462 in the United States, which was ten times as many as there had been in 1950. As *Time* magazine noted in March 1969, the "expanding take-overs of hundreds of companies could transform the entire structure of the U.S. economy." In January 1973 *Forbes*'s report on the state of American industry covered a total of 780 companies—to qualify a company had to have sales of at least $200 million—whose combined stock market value was $755 billion.

The greatest fear among conservative businessmen is that mergers between large companies "tend to reduce competition." Yet it can be seen that the trend toward corporate convergence follows a logical sequence. Up until two hundred years ago, power was definitely associated with the land. Then it shifted gradually to capital. G. William Miller, the head of Textron Inc., one of the major conglomerates in the United States, argues that the great advantage of corporate conglomerations is that they can shift capital in great amounts. In short, capital is being used more effectively, and its power is undergoing another historic shift to "mobility," possibly as pivotal as the shift from land-based power to capital-based power. *Time* magazine, in suggesting that large-scale take-overs could "transform the entire structure of the U.S. economy," fails to allow that the structure has already been transformed and that the acquiring of shares, securities, and so on, merely *deepens* the process of integration. The only thing that take-overs transform is the list of shareholders. The economic pieces—already interlocked and integrated by tacit price-fixing "understandings," control of both supplies and market, and diversification—are merely in the process of being legally wedded after years of living in sin.

Admittedly, what happens in the United States does not necessarily set a pattern for what happens in other industrialized nations, but the broad outlines hold. And the net effect of these changes is approximately the same. The techniques applied by IBM, AT&T, or DuPont are the same as those applied by the governments of Japan and Israel.

Let us turn now to an examination of the topography of what John Kenneth Galbraith calls "the new industrial state." He notes, to begin with, that changes in the economic system "have been much discussed. But to view them in isolation from each other, the usual practice, is to greatly minimize their effects." This is the same insight which guided our discussion of environmental collapse in Part I of this book. And it applies no less meaningfully to Galbraith's analysis of the economic system and to the further points to be made in this book. The changes, he writes, "are related to each other as cause to consequence. All are part of a yet larger matrix of change. In its effect on economic society, this matrix has been more than the sum of its parts."

Nearly all of the consequences of technology, he writes in *The New Industrial State,* derive from the need to divide and subdivide tasks "and from the further need to bring knowledge to bear on these fractions and from the final need to combine the finished elements of the task into the finished product as a whole." Technology, which he defines as "the systematic application of scientific or other organized knowledge to practical tasks," can be seen to be a highly defined form of large-scale integration. The drift of his argument is that technology, under all circumstances, leads to planning. "In its higher manifestations it may put the problems of planning beyond the reach of the industrial firm. Technological compulsions, and not ideology or political wile, will require the firm to seek the help and protection of the state. This is a consequence of advanced technology of no small interest."

Economic planning, says Galbraith, "involves, inevitably, the control of individual behavior." Actually, this is untrue. As he later on points out himself, what it really involves is control of aggregate demand—which is to say, control of great masses of individuals through market research, advertising campaigns, and so on. While the aggregate or whole is thus manipulated, each individual is free to opt out at any time. To this extent, economic planning is not totalitarian, since it works, as does a physicist, with statistics, mass behavior, and swarms.

It is important to distinguish between "aggregate control" and "control of the individual." Galbraith commits a serious error when he fails to make that distinction. Economic planning through control of aggregate demand means, at bottom, that the welfare of the country is not dependent on control of the individual. Even the most totalitarian state, once it has learned the techniques of economic planning, can afford to let the individual alone. From the point of view of social organization, which is to say, social control, *it does not matter what the individual does.* He is not likely to affect market behavior and he therefore does not have to be silenced. In short, society can permit individuals to liberate themselves without the stability of the whole social structure being threatened.

Getting back onto surer ground, Galbraith points out that the "market economy . . . has ceased to be reliable. Technology, with its companion commitment of time and capital, means that the needs of the consumer must be anticipated—by months or years." In place of the raw, uncontrolled market, Galbraith notes, what emerges in response to the need for planning is "vertical integration." The planning unit takes over the outlet or source of supply. This is an elementary safeguard, because the firm, now certain of its own sources, has succeeded in controlling yet another potentially unreliable area. Even in cases where the sources of supply are not taken over, they can be controlled. "This consists in *reducing or eliminating the independence of action of those to whom the planning unit sells or from whom it buys* [my italics]."

Size is a key factor here. An outfit like General Motors is so large that many of its suppliers are dependent on it for survival. "This induces a highly cooperative posture." Thus, there develops a "mutual security system" based on the common interest of not rocking the boat. Price control becomes a reality, particularly as the number of "competing" organizations dwindles. "Each . . . shares the common interest in secure and certain prices. . . . Thus do size and small numbers of competitors lead to market regulation." Large firms can further reduce uncertainty for themselves by "entering into contracts specifying prices and amounts to be provided or bought for substantial periods of time." In the world of large firms, it follows, "there can be a matrix of contracts by which each firm eliminates market uncertainty for other firms and, in turn, gives to them some of its own."

In socialist or communist nations prices are managed largely by the state. In Western countries prices are managed just as extensively—although through more elaborate mechanisms—by large firms. What destroys the market is not socialism, but advanced technology "and the specialization of men and process which this requires and the resulting commitment of time and capital. . . . The modern large corporation and the modern apparatus of social-ist-planning are variant accommodations to the same need."

Going into an analysis of capital and power, Galbraith writes that in the classical economic tradition, technology was always as-sumed to be stable. As we have already seen, this is far from being the case today. For as long as it was, however, "a meager supply of capital was matched by an equally meager opportunity for its use." As technology began to surge forward, the opportunities for the employment of capital likewise accelerated. The great shift from ag-ricultural wealth to industrial wealth began. The exodus from the farm to the factory got under way, and power slipped from the hands of the landed gentry into the hands of the industrialists who controlled capital. A further shift is now taking place. Power, Gal-braith acknowledges, is shifting from capital to organized intelli-gence, if for no other reason than that "power goes to the factor [of production] which is hardest to obtain or hardest to replace." Sav-ings (meaning a supply of capital) having been assured by planning, the crucial production factor is now the organizational ability to apply technology. Which brings us to "the new locus of power in the business enterprise and in society"—the rise of what Galbraith calls the "technostructure."

Before going into his description of technostructure, it is worth noting that it is not, as it might seem from Galbraith's analysis, the mutant child of industry alone. General James M. Gavin, who was responsible for the planning of the airborne assault on D Day, has pointed out that the techniques of management which were first employed by the military in the Second World War were "new— new both in scope and diversity and in their pioneering use of the latest scientific advice and equipment, such as systems analysis, op-erational research, data control." Privately, General Gavin tells us, he labeled this new concept in management techniques "technoplan-ning." Later, reading Galbraith's book, he realized that "techno-planning" had emerged almost simultaneously at the dead center of the economy, even though he had assumed it to be a characteristic peculiar to modern military operations.

Nor is technoplanning limited to military and industrial organization. Architect and town-planner Constantinos A. Doxiadis has coined the word "ekistics" to refer to "the total science of human communities." Ekistics is Doxiadis's word for technoplanning. The concept can further be seen to be deeply rooted in new agricultural techniques, such as farm management, management of natural resources, and efforts to maintain ecological balances. (As will be seen later, technoplanning, the main response to the problems which are posed by environmental collapse, is one of the most highly developed forms of large-scale integration.) Moreover, it is evident that technoplanning is increasingly becoming the essential fact of life in highly industrialized nations. To the extent that technoplanning, in crude or sophisticated forms, is becoming the mainspring of industrialized civilization, the trend is irreversible. Finally, the central point about technoplanning is that it has just barely begun. As Gavin points out, it was a "new technique" little more than two decades ago. Thus, the technostructures referred to by Galbraith are only the tip of the iceberg. They are prototypal. They are not the end product of any evolution, economic or otherwise, but the beginning of an entirely new kind of organized approach to existence.

Since Galbraith has analyzed them in the industrial sector more thoroughly than anyone has yet analyzed their counterparts elsewhere, his analysis casts considerable light on the future as well as the present. We would therefore do well to consider the following:

It is not to individuals but to organizations that power in the business enterprise and power in society has passed. And modern economic society can only be understood as an effort, wholly successful, to synthesize by organization a group personality far superior for its purposes to a natural person and with the added advantage of immortality. The need for such a group personality begins with the circumstance that in modern industry a large number of decisions, and *all* that are important, draw on information possessed by more than one man. Typically, they draw on the specialized scientific and technical knowledge, the accumulated information or experience and the artistic or intuitive sense of many persons. And this is guided by further information which is assembled, analyzed, and interpreted by professionals using highly technical equipment. The final decision will be informed only as it draws systematically on all those whose information is relevant.

Group decision-making extends deeply into business enterprise. When power is exercised by a group, "not only does it pass into the organization, but it passes irrevocably." A decision which requires the combined information of a group cannot safely be reversed by an individual. He will have to get the judgment of other specialists. This returns the power once more to organization. Therefore, "group decision, unless acted upon by another group, tends to be absolute."

Nothing so characterizes the economic forms of large-scale integration as their scale. In 1971 the five largest industrial corporations in the United States had combined assets in excess of $75 billion. They possessed more than 12 per cent of all assets used in manufacturing. The fifty largest corporations in the country possessed more than one third of all assets used in manufacturing. Between them, the five hundred largest had well over two thirds. In all, there were some two thousand corporations with assets in excess of $10 million each, and they accounted for 80 per cent of all the resources used in manufacturing. Three industrial corporations —Ford Motor Company, Standard Oil of New Jersey, and General Motors—have more gross income each year than all of the farms in the country. The gross revenue of each firm far exceeded that of any single state. The revenues of General Motors, in 1972, were one-fifth of those of the federal government.

It is within these corporate giants that the technostructure has developed. And lest anyone imagine that the technostructure is only an experimental and passing phase in economic development, one has only to realize that large corporations *rarely lose money*. "In 1957," writes Galbraith, "a year of mild recession in the United States, not one of the one hundred largest industrial corporations failed to return a profit. Only one of the largest two hundred finished the year in the red." More recent figures tend to back up Galbraith's contention that "a developed technostructure is able to protect its profits by planning." In the process, the profit-and-loss system—which is supposed, in American business liturgy, to be the main economic incentive—recedes into the background, shed like a skin. Of the big corporations analyzed by *Forbes* in its January 1,

1973, issue, fifty—or just 7 per cent—showed a loss for 1972. But among the corporate giants—*Forbes*'s top 200 by stock market valuation—only *one* showed a loss. The bigger you are, the harder to fall.

At the same time, the great anarchic entrepreneur—Rockefeller, Harriman, Guggenheim, DuPont, Chrysler, Hilton, Hartford, and so on—becomes a legendary figure of the past, as remote from the realities of the modern economic world as Davy Crockett is from the realities of urban existence. "The great entrepreneur must, in fact, be compared in life with the male *Apis mallifera*. He accomplishes his act of conception at the price of his own extinction." In his wake are legions of organization men, galaxies of groups and committees. Yet "individualism is the note that 'sounds through the business creed like the pitch in a Byzantine choir,' " despite the new reality of organization and the technostructure, which requires "not indifference but sensitivity to others, not individualism but accommodation to organization, not competition but intimate and continuing cooperation," which are "the prime requirements of group action." This is realized by the younger generation of executives. "Interdependence is recognized."

Expanding his argument to embrace the motivational apparatus of the technostructure, Galbraith makes another important point which brings the development of new social characteristics—such as other-direction—closely into line with economic developments. "Urbanization and compulsion," he notes, "go poorly together." Just as the ascendancy of peer-groups makes authoritarian compulsion difficult, if not impossible—thus forcing the refinement of brutalization into manipulation—so too does the rise of group decision-making in the modern corporation weaken the authority of the memo from the head office. Further, a large number of the individual's needs must be satisfied by the organization, since purely monetary compulsion is receding (like the importance of capital itself) into the background.

"The organization man has been the subject of much sorrow," writes Galbraith. "But all who weep should recall that he surrenders to organization because organization does more for him than he can do for himself." Having said all this, he acknowledges that in any discussion of the lessening importance of monetary reward it must be remembered that it is "an extremely important stimulus to individual members of the technostructure up to a point. If they are not paid this acceptable and expected salary, they will not work. But once this requirement is met, the offer of more money to an engineer, scientist, or executive brings little or no more effort. Other motivation takes over." Primarily, this involves identification with the goals of the technostructure.

In short, the area in which the technostructure is most vulnerable —by virtue of its dependence on highly qualified and specialized manpower—is the area where financial reward is least effective as a means of attracting and holding the necessary talent. The technostructure is therefore *forced* to concern itself with finding other ways of attracting the people it needs. Galbraith argues that "a secure level of earnings and a maximum rate of growth consistent with the provision of revenues for the requisite investment are the prime goals of the technostructure. Technological virtuosity and a rising dividend rate are secondary. . . . After these ends are achieved, there is further opportunity for a variety of other and lesser goals" —among them: "building a better community; improved education; an effective attack on heart ailments, emphysema, alcoholism, hard chancre, or any other crippling disease."

Nearly all economists, he writes, "dismiss pursuit of such goals as irrelevant window dressing. *This is an error* [my italics]. So long as their subordinate role is clearly recognized, including the limitations imposed by cost, they are a perfectly plausible expression of the goals of the individual members of the technostructure and, thus, collectively of the mature corporation. What has been called the 'social corporation' is a logical manifestation of the mature corporation and the motivation of its members." The individual will identify himself with the goals of the corporation, Galbraith argues, "only if the corporation is identified with, as the individual sees it, some significant social goals." The individual "serves organization . . . because of the possibility of accommodating its goals more closely to his own. . . . The corporation, thus, becomes an instrument for attributing social purpose to the goals of those who comprise it."

The point was made earlier that, as the technological base associated with modern weapons-making expands, and as the economy comes more and more to be a form of defense socialism, an ever-increasing number of people spend their days sharpening knife blades. While what I said earlier about a deteriorated ability to reason and relate remains true, Galbraith points to a further dimension of the psychological processes involved. The need for "significant social goals" surfaces here, since employees must be able to identify with the firm. "The manufacture of an exotic missile fuel, or a better trigger for a nuclear warhead, attracts the loyalty of [the firm's] members because their organization is seen to be serving importantly the cause of freedom."

This, then, is the central point concerning corporate behavior: "What an organization will seek from society will be a reflection of what members seek from the organization. If men principally want money from a corporation, the corporation will be primarily concerned with extracting money from society. If they are interested in economic security or personal prestige, the corporation can hardly fail to reflect this in the kind of business it conducts." In the age of the great entrepreneur, the organization was profit-oriented and operated as barbarically as any Hun involved in the sacking of Rome. The organization in that period was a collection of anarchists and, of course, behaved anarchically. This still remains the case. But as the bulk of production is handled more and more by mature corporations whose main feature is the technostructure and whose key personnel are concerned more with security and the avoidance of risk than mere profit-making, we see—for the first time—social goals emerging as a reality.

This is dismissed (particularly by the Left) as "the logical extension of the pervasive liberal doctrine of pragmatic America and the 'end of ideology.'" As David Horowitz and Reese Erlich put it in the November 30, 1968, issue of *Ramparts:* "The mythology of salvation through the application of technology by the Great Partnership between government and private corporations has not only survived, it has risen to a new intensity of apocalyptic promise," The article argued that the large modern corporation has gathered about itself the full mystique of modernity: advanced technology, the "systems engineering" approach (a product of military contracting), electronics, and space. Erlich and Horowitz note that Litton Industries, one of the fastest-growing corporations in the United States, has become a blend of "enormous social welfare industry" and "multi-billion-dollar defense contractor." Litton Industries "is the perfect example of the new corporation extending itself beyond the limits that have divided the private oligarchies of business from the realms of responsibility traditionally reserved to government." Erlich and Horowitz support the position of Dr. Ralph Lapp, described earlier in this book, about America's having become a weapons culture: "Fully 70 per cent of all research and development being done in the United States today (about $16 billion worth) is paid for by the federal government, whereas a little more than twenty years ago it supported almost none at all." And according to Roy Ash, number two man at Litton, "almost all new products have their first application in military uses." The *Ramparts* writers are so outraged by this, coupled with the anarchic behavior of outfits like Litton, that they refuse to see that the creative social energies of such corporations *can* be harnessed, just as the energies of individuals *within* these superstructures have been harnessed.

Writers on the Left who are outraged by such attitudes fall into the same trap as their opponents. In other words, they fail to accept the fact that corporations—the most sophisticated and effective social tool ever devised—might learn, at the dawn of *post*-civilization, to cooperate, just as individuals learned to cooperate at the dawn of civilization. There is no reason to expect that such a move would be the result of a conscious or ideological decision, any more than it was when families in Mesopotamia learned to work together to build irrigation systems 6000 years ago. Individuals, at that stage, were acting every bit as much in their own interests as corporations are today. However, it was definitely in their own interest to cooperate and to pool their resources, however much they may have secretly despised their neighbors.

Anarchic behavior, it may be said, is not overcome by political slogans but by *need*. The thrust of my argument is that the need—made clear, it is hoped, in Part I—is now as real as it could ever be. The application of a systems approach by a corporation to basic problems—regardless of whether or not the corporation acquired its skills by manufacturing weapons and providing napalm—violates nothing but the values of its critics. Marshall McLuhan once remarked that "anybody who spends his time screaming about values in our modern world is not a serious character. . . . When your old world is collapsing and every thing is changing at a furious pitch, to start announcing your preferences for old values is not the act of a serious person. This is frivolous, fatuous. . . . Moral bitterness is a basic technique for endowing the idiot with dignity. . . . The moralist typically substitutes anger for perception."

In short, moral indignation over the anarchic behavior of corporations prevents many otherwise perceptive people from seeing the value of these "organizational tools." It does not cross their minds that corporations are not inhabited by people from another planet. Corporations are operated by people who are other-directed, and perhaps in many cases even autonomous. These people will surface eventually, and they need not surface in the head office or executive suite, since—as Galbraith shows us—power has sunk deep into the organization. Increasingly, the corporations come to be other-directed, seeking from society that which their members seek. And this will mean—already *does* mean—that approval, among other things, will be needed. It is partly in response to this need that "social goals" become significant dimensions of corporate consciousness. Further, as environmental collapse proceeds to the point where it becomes a highly evident threat, the response of such corporations will be reflexive. The anarchic urge for self-survival, if nothing else, will goad them into action. In the process, they will have to learn, as individuals have done, to cooperate and build together.

By now, technoplanning and its most institutionalized form—the technostructure—are plainly visible on the social landscape. Both the act and the institution are advanced forms of large-scale integration. They cannot be reversed, since they stem from ancient imperatives of growth and civilization. The irrigation dams referred to earlier were primitive forms of large-scale integration. Today the vastly accelerated complexity of society has led to further and further integration, coordination, and cooperation, reaching a break boundary about the time of the Second World War. At that point, in terms of economics and military organization, the complexity became too great for mere planning. Technoplanning—involving systems analysis, computers, feedback loops, and so on—became necessary to cope with the complexity of organization which was then evident to executives and the military. That the complexity was less obvious to politicians accounts in large part for the chaos in large urban centers. It is no coincidence that just at the time when armies and corporations were becoming fantastically efficient, cities and governments—having failed to integrate themselves on a large scale —began to collapse.

Corporations and the military can be seen to have responded to a need to organize themselves more efficiently. More centralized and manageable than cities or nations, they could more easily adapt to the new techniques of large-scale organization. However, they also function in a far more specialized fashion than the larger entities. It was therefore much easier for them to make the transition. The need, however, for civic, national, and international administrations to make a similar adaptation—in view of the related problems of environmental collapse—is now clear.

The parallels between changes in social character and changes in organizational character are more than striking. They represent an interaction and, at the same time, a mutual and almost identical response to the same problems of increased complexity, presenting itself in the form of urbanization, population increase, and technology. To dismiss these parallels as being somehow coincidental or of nothing more than passing interest is to miss sight of two central features of the great modern revolution.

At the apex of the history of Western civilization stood the great "individual." In capitalist societies he was interchangeable with the great entrepreneur. Suddenly, in the course of roughly three decades, the great entrepreneur vanishes and is replaced by nameless teams of men. More slowly, the "rugged individual" vanishes into the late movies and children's comic books. In his place stands the sensitive, other-directed group man, a man whose horizons are wider than any mere physical horizons could ever have been and whose environment is people, not the "raw land." Further, the rugged individual and the great entrepreneur die out (like the dinosaurs) at the very point at which a continuation of their anarchic behavior becomes suicidal. Were it to continue much longer—which it *is* doing, although the handwriting (much of it in the form of graffiti) is on the wall—anarchic behavior would result inevitably in the extinction of human life—either through nuclear war, slow poisoning, genetic disruption, or strangulation through a tilting of the oxygen-carbon balance.

17

La Technique

Roughly midway between the publication of *The Lonely Crowd* and *The New Industrial State*, we see the publication in France of Jacques Ellul's *La Technique*, translated as *The Technological Society*. At first the book received little attention. Later, thinkers such as Robert Theobald were to describe it as "one of the most important books of the second half of the twentieth century." Among other things, it provides us with the necessary link between the social phenomenon of other-direction and the economic and military phenomenon of technostructures. Further, it extends the rather narrow horizons of Galbraith's insight and provides a mechanism for the emergence of other-direction.

Ellul defines technique as *"the totality of methods rationally arrived at and having absolute efficiency* (for a given stage of development) in *every* field of human activity." Although he makes no reference to Riesman's studies and predates Galbraith's, Ellul manages to identify the essence of technoplanning, notes the degree to which social character is forced to adapt to technological developments, and, at the same time, clearly perceives the self-regulatory nature of the revolution which is upon us. He offers the widest possible description of large-scale integration, examines its mechanisms, and underlines the fact of convergence. His argument is so thorough—and so similar in its largest outlines to the argument presented in this book—that I would gladly consign my own book to the garbage can were it not for the fact that Ellul—like Aldous Huxley—fails completely to allow for the possibility of the emergence of new levels of awareness. He views the developments that he is describing with the same revulsion that Huxley demonstrated in *Brave New World*. He is both repelled and frightened by the strange new forms of existence taking shape around him. His is, finally, a brilliant nineteenth-century mind.

In his discussion of the rise of technostructures, Galbraith stresses the fact that the "first requisite for survival by the technostructure is that it preserve the autonomy on which its decision-making power depends." Power remains securely within the technostructure only so long as "earnings are large enough to make accustomed payments to the stockholders and provide a supply of savings for reinvestment. If earnings are less than this level, it will be necessary to appeal to outside suppliers of capital. These, in turn, can ask questions and impose conditions and thus abridge the autonomy of the technostructure." The efficiency of the technostructure is impaired by outside interference (which is not subject to the collective group decision-making apparatus) as surely as the performance of a machine is impaired by the throwing of a monkey wrench.

I have already referred to General Gavin's point that technoplanning "spontaneously" became a feature of modern military operations at the same time that it was becoming the central feature of large corporate operations. Ellul makes it clear that both of these developments stem from the emergence of technique as the central fact of modern life. Further, he argues that these do not develop as part of any Machiavellian scheme, but in response to the "laws of development" of technique. As Robert K. Merton puts it in his introduction to Ellul's book, because of technique, our civilization is "committed to the quest for continually improved means to carelessly examined ends. Indeed, technique transforms ends into means." The most obvious visible form of technique is planning. But planning becomes the tool not of human goals, but of the goals of technique. Human goals, inspired by ideals associated with human needs, tend strongly to get lost in the technological shuffle.

The *means*—technique—become, in all cases, more important than the ends. And even the ends become *better techniques*. This is readily apparent in any examination of economics or modern military structures. A new weapon, rocket, spaceship, or antiballistic missile system *must* be developed. It is always developed for good reasons, reasons that make sense technologically, and always in response to other technological developments. Thus, technology engenders itself, becoming, as Ellul puts it, "self-augmenting."

Ellul does not use the word which Galbraith coined, "technostructures," but his thesis goes deeper than Galbraith's. Galbraith, in talking about technostructures in the economic sphere, is merely talking about one tip of the iceberg, the main body of which is technique—the ensemble, or gestalt, or total effect of all separate techniques interacting with one another to orchestrate a technological symphony with no conductor or score. And it is a symphony, moreover, that cannot be turned off at just any point. Individual techniques may be abandoned or rejected or reversed, but the whole orchestra continues to play, more and more loudly, simply because each part remains the best and most efficient way of doing things. The maddening part of it all—and to Ellul, the threatening part—is that the net effect of all these "best" ways of doing things may in fact be the worst way. He is talking, of course, about a synergistic effect, comparable to the synergistic effects of pollution, drugs, pesticides, radiation, and so on. Taken by itself, a given pesticide may represent, despite certain side effects, the best way of boosting agricultural production. Taken by itself, a given drug (again, despite certain side effects) may represent the best way of combating specific diseases. Taken by itself, a certain economic technique may represent the best way of boosting the over-all standard of living. But understood in terms of their cumulative effect, drugs, pesticides, and economic methods may all amount, in the long run, to a general collapse of standards of physical and mental well-being, and, specifically, to an erosion of man's ability to steer his own course and to gain the strength that comes from the experience of responsibility which is implicit in decision-making.

Today it is everywhere apparent that something is drastically wrong with society. The synergistic or cumulative effect can easily be seen by a quick glance at the headlines. But each "cause" of the general malaise turns out, upon examination, to be a "good thing."

And, as with a healthy tooth, there is no rational reason for extracting it. Besides which, Ellul argues, the removal of specific causes—the rejection, for instance, of a given technique—cannot possibly affect the over-all ensemble of techniques. Techniques *always* produce unpredictable secondary effects, and in order to deal with these effects, more techniques—more "best ways" of dealing with specific problems—must be brought into play. These may solve the problems that were created by the secondary effects. But they, in turn, give birth to a whole litter of other secondary effects, each of which demands a further application of other techniques, thus guaranteeing the creation of more unpredictable secondary effects, which require *more* techniques, producing that many more problems and therefore requiring that many more techniques—*ad infinitum.* This is why, Ellul argues, "technical progress tends to act, not according to an arithmetic, but according to a geometric progression." It is, quite literally, the progression of cancer. It is self-regulated because no one person, group, organization, country, or even international agency controls the process. It augments itself.

The great congealing crises of our time—overpopulation, depletion of natural resources, pollution of land, sea, and air, poisoning of our own bodies, extinction of various species essential to the ecological balance, draining away of water reserves, radiation, the cataclysmic creation of behavioral sinks in the big cities, and so on—can all be seen to be related not only to one another, but also to technology. They are, to varying degrees, the secondary effects of techniques which were applied because they were the "best way" of doing things. The separate rational, efficient, logical techniques, acting synergistically, have succeeded in creating an over-all situation which is irrational, illogical, and inefficient. As a result, we are now on the brink of extinction. We may not have time to halt the tailspin. On the other hand, we may—but only through the rigorous application of literally millions of other techniques to solve the problems that have been created by techniques in the first place. The solution to every different problem of environmental collapse is basically the same. Regardless of its specific characteristics, it involves, at bottom, the introduction of more controls, more organization, more coordination, more integration, and more cooperation. At this stage we have backed ourselves into a corner in which we have no choice but to disregard all the checks on the development of techniques—the libertarian and traditional resistance to controls—and literally let the technological monster out of its cage to protect us from the very forces which it has unleashed against us from *within* its cage.

In short, the take-over of human affairs by technique has just begun. The threat of environmental collapse guarantees that it is about to take a quantum jump ahead, out of absolute necessity. What the results of this jump will be are unpredictable. Massive interference in nature has so far succeeded in creating a thin illusion of affluence and mastery while, at the same time, stirring up an environmental storm of unparalleled ferocity. At this stage, we need an even more massive interference to protect us from the consequences of the first interference. The secondary effects of this next great interference could, conceivably, be far worse. But again, we have no more choice than does a chess player who has been backed into a corner. (It is true that we now have "chess machines"—i.e., computers—which will make us far better players, but their ability has not been conclusively tested.)

Technique, as Ellul points out, is not only the basis for modern military operations and industrial behavior, it is also rapidly becoming the basis for political, administrative, educational, and police behavior as well. The equivalent of technostructures are now taking shape everywhere, coalescing in the heart of government policies, within schools, universities, police organizations, and political parties. It does not require a lengthy argument to persuade us that the characteristics of the technostructure—the collapse of the power to make decisions into the corporate body, the diminishing role of the individual, the application of systems analysis, modern managerial techniques, and so on—are all coming to be the characteristics of political organizations as much as of large corporations.

The distinction between "consumer" and "voter" is increasingly blurred. Both are subject to management through the principles of control of aggregate demand. Hal Evry, of Public Relations Center in Los Angeles, has succeeded in electing thirty-five out of thirty-nine candidates to the state senate by using a Burroughs 300 and an IBM 1401 computer to determine—in exactly the same way that a large corporation determines—the "wants" of the public. For a cost of $60,000, he all but guarantees to elect his customers. Of course, there is nothing new about public relations firms being hired to merchandise candidates for public office, but the similarity of techniques between electioneering and marketeering is not always appreciated. Political organizations are increasingly dependent on a technostructure composed of groups of specialists and the techniques of planning.

In education, the self-regulatory aspects of educational "change" can be as easily seen. Increasingly, administration comes to be the central problem. To the extent that school systems are financed by the state, they are dependent for their functioning on the decisions of specialists and groups of specialists. Group decision-making replaces individual initiative at the administrative level. "After the general direction given by initiators (like Decroly or Montessori), it is the findings of thousands of educators which ceaselessly nourish the improvement of technique. In fact, education systems are completely transformed as a result of practice—without anyone's being quite aware of it."

The self-augmentation of technique can here be seen at work, and, as in the other cases of self-augmentation, the individual increasingly has a smaller role to play, is less able to affect the "whole," and, particularly, is less able to "reverse" the main forward thrust of technique. The best way is always used, and when it turns out *not* to be the best way, it is jettisoned and another technique is applied in its place. Sooner or later, the right technique is found. In the meantime, the concern comes more and more to be with technique—i.e., the means—and less and less with any overall goal, except such goals as will be most consistent with the combination of right techniques. Increasingly, school systems come to demand autonomy, simply because developing technostructures, like the technostructures referred to by Galbraith, base their decision-making powers on autonomy. Outside interference, by politicians or taxpayers, are monkey wrenches thrown into the educational technostructure, and the pressure mounts from within the technostructure to secure greater degrees of autonomy. (This, of course, is already the case in political organizations, which had more fertile autonomous ground to grow in.)

The same phenomenon can now be seen in police organizations. They too are rapidly developing technostructures of their own. *"Terror,"* Ellul points out, "is replaced by *efficiency."* The tools of the police technostructure are "fingerprint files, record of firearms, application of statistical methods which allow the police to obtain in a minimum of time the most varied kinds of information and to know from day to day the current state of criminality in all its forms." Other elements include the use of punch-card mechanical index systems, which offer "four hundred possible combinations and permit investigations to begin with any element of the crime: hour of commission, nature, objects stolen, weapons used, etc." Another key aspect of police technoplanning involves the use of suspect files "which show whether the police ever suspected any individual for any reason or at any time whatsoever, even though no legal document or procedure ever existed against him. . . . This means that any citizen who, once in his life, had anything to do with the police, even for noncriminal reasons, is put under observation—a fact which ought to affect, speaking conservatively, half the adult male population."

Since the time of Ellul's writing, computers have been put to work by police in some American cities to locate potential trouble spots and predict riots and disturbances. It is only a question of refining the technique to bring it to the point where smaller, more individual disturbances can be pinpointed with a very high degree of probable success. And, increasingly, police administrations demand more autonomy to guarantee the unimpaired functioning of *their* technostructure. In late 1969 a police superintendent in San Francisco told me that "we are just now beginning to define ourselves." Definition, we shall see, is essential to the creating of a technostructure.

Ellul points out that the need for autonomy is one of the main characteristics of technique. In the case of the police, they "must be independent if they are to become efficient. They must form a closed, autonomous organization in order to operate by the most direct and efficient means and not be shackled by secondary considerations. . . . It matters little whether police action is legal, if it is efficient. The rules obeyed by a technical organization are no longer rules of justice or injustice. They are 'laws' purely in the technical sense." What Ellul says here about the police is exactly the same as what Galbraith says about large corporations. "Technique's own internal necessities," he adds, "are determinative. Technique has become a reality in itself, self-sufficient, with its special laws and its own government administrations."

Galbraith has remarked that the development of the technostructure in industry has done away with the need for genius. Ellul notes that this is the central characteristic of technique everywhere. He quotes Robert Jungk to the effect that "considered from the modern technical point of view, man is a useless appendage." Eliminate the individual, adds Ellul, "and excellent results ensue. . . . Freeing man from toil is in itself an ideal. Beyond this, every intervention of man, however educated or used to machinery he may be, is a source of error and unpredictability. The combination of man and technique is a happy one *only if man has no responsibility* [my italics]." This is increasingly the case as technoplanning comes to dominate political considerations. Technique, in terms of politics, "is still in its childhood," Ellul notes. But referring back to the use of computers to elect candidates to office, we have only to see that public relations experts insist that the "perfect campaign" is one in which the candidate says nothing at all, to see that this same principle is at work. Technique works if the candidate has no responsibility for his campaign and says nothing for which he might be held responsible.

It will be evident by now that an inner-directed social character is not consistent with the needs of technique, technoplanning, technostructures, or whatever label we care to use. Group decision-making requires cogs that mesh well. An other-directed social character is flexible and plastic. Unlike a rigid and unbending inner-directed personality, it is perfectly adapted to a milieu in which technique dominates. Ellul would argue, I'm sure, that other-direction represents, more than anything else, an adaptation of social character to the requirements of technique.

It is necessary now to show how the related problems of environmental collapse specifically require the development of technostructures—or the application of technique—in virtually every sphere of existence. Let us begin with the problem of overpopulation.

Considering the cultural and institutional resistance to population control, the earth's population will likely triple and possibly quadruple itself before it is stabilized. Sooner or later, by human engineering or natural "environmental resistance," it *will* be stabilized (or else eliminated altogether). This is obvious enough. What it means is that technoplanning will have to be applied to birth and that the number of births will have to be controlled just as the number of sales are controlled today—with considerable accuracy—by large corporations. Moreover, control of parents will have to be as thorough as control of the consumer is rapidly becoming. Advertising techniques will increasingly be applied by the state to ensure not only the proper attitude toward cornflakes and new cars, but also the proper attitude toward family planning and birth control. Police techniques, educational techniques, and all the social mechanisms for control of attitudes will be integrated into a computer-orchestrated program of social planning. The control of population, itself, will therefore *force* large-scale integration.

There is no way around it, since anarchic individual sexual impulses—and deeper, more profoundly biological impulses toward fecundity and reproduction—will have to be brought under control. In other words, if we faced no problem today except overpopulation, we could still be certain that sooner or later we would face the necessity—and it is not simply a technological necessity—of large-scale integration of individual and corporate needs with regard to reproduction. Tentative steps in this direction have already been taken on a small scale, with pressures being put on governments of countries with population problems to deal with them seriously. Boulding has noted "the total unwillingness of mankind to face up to what is perhaps its most serious long-run problem." This unwillingness means, quite simply, that controls will have to be imposed. They will not be any the less "controls" even if they take the shape of advertising campaigns, psychological manipulation, group pressures, and so on. The simple fact is that if manipulative controls fail to work, more crudely totalitarian ones—such as forcible injection of anti-pregnancy vaccines and financial penalties, even forced abortions and imprisonment for delinquent fathers—will have to be applied. Since this will be done for the good of humanity as a whole, and, more specifically, for the good of one's countrymen and kin, there will be no humanitarian argument that can be effectively raised against it. Individuals who would defy such a system of organization will come to be seen as irrational and antisocial. They will be criminals.

The problems of pollution, likewise, can be seen by themselves to be a source of enormous pressure for large-scale integration. Air pollution crosses state, provincial, and national boundaries at will.

The Swedes cannot solve their air-pollution problems without working out some sort of agreement with the Germans and the French. The Germans and the French, in turn, must cooperate with each other, with the Swedes, the British, the Russians, and so on. The proportions of atmospheric pollution have become global, and the solutions must also be global. Already, as indicated earlier, international action is now being planned. Agreements, while not yet even at the negotiation stage, are nevertheless inevitable. Conceivably, it will take an "oxygen famine" before governments react. But already the cry for curbs on the sources of pollution is growing rapidly in volume.

Here—far more obviously than in the case of overpopulation—the observation that technology creates problems which can only be solved by further technology becomes apparent. The solutions to pollution of the rivers, the air, and the land are *all* technological. The "freedom" of various industries to poison the air will be curbed. Presumably, in the case of large corporations, the danger to their technostructures' autonomy will be recognized and a concern with "neighborhood effects" will correspondingly increase. At this point, the already far-advanced integration of industry and state will become more pronounced. When political seats start to be washed away in a tide of sewage, one may rest assured that government will suddenly become responsive to pollution problems. A complex web of interconnected pieces of legislation—tied together by some large general bans, prohibitions, and imperatives—will be superimposed one on top of the other. The net effect will be to control not only corporate pollution, but individual sources of pollution as well. The wise investor today would get in fast on the electric toilet market, as well as the markets for various types of filters, fans, and so on. Garbage disposal techniques will multiply, and of course the new techniques will cause further secondary effects, and the response, again—a spastic, pathetic reflex by this time—will be the implementation of more and more compulsory techniques.

It is the *compulsory* nature of these techniques that needs to be understood, because technology has now reached the point where the very problems that it creates guarantee that its further application will be institutionalized, reinforced by statute, enshrined by legislation, and, in general, made mandatory—always, of course, in the best interests of the population as a whole. The process at this stage—in the face of the dimensions of the environmental counterattack—is *not reversible*. Quite literally, through the unrestrained application of technology, we have collectively succeeded in creating a new enemy—a global threat to all of humanity. The enemy is attacking. Martial law must be declared. And since the techniques that we will be forced to use to defend ourselves are certain to make the enemy stronger in many respects, *martial law will never be lifted*. Traditional ideals about freedom, democracy, and libertarianism, in short, are about to be consigned to the museum, along with Plato's *Republic*.

This is the real meaning of environmental collapse. As R. D. Lawrence put it (apparently without realizing what he was saying) in *The Poison Makers:* "Governmental action [with regard to pollution] is still sluggish, like the writhing of some giant kraken inching into wakefulness deep within the bowels of the sea." When the giant kraken awakes—and all of us who are warning about pollution are helping to probe him into wakefulness—his tentacles will coil around us all. Conceivably, such anarchic impulses as the desire to smoke cigarettes will, at some point, be prohibited—along with the right to burn whatever fuel we like, to dispose of refuse in our own incinerators, to burn leaves, and to litter beaches. These, of course, are only minor examples of the ways in which we will all be affected. More explicitly, the type of food we eat, the water we drink, the plants we grow, and even the air we breathe will increasingly be determined by the imperatives of technological necessity.

For instance, Ellul points out that in 1960 the World Congress for the Study of Nutrition "considered the problem of how modern nutrition is vitiated by the use of chemical products which are themselves significant contributory causes of the so-called diseases of civilization (cancer, cardiovascular illnesses, etc.). But the congress's studies indicate that the solution can no longer be a return to a 'natural' nutrition. On the contrary, a further step must be taken which involves *completely* artificial alimentation, so-called rational alimentation. It will not be enough merely to control grains, meat, butter, and so forth. *The stage at which this would have been feasible has been passed* [my italics]." In short, we will have very little choice as to what foods we eat. Farm-management techniques will be integrated with synthetic food-production techniques, and as population grows and newer and more efficient food-production techniques are developed, the older techniques which gave us natural foods will be abandoned. Land use will be brought under control, populations will be relocated, and so forth.

The tremendous amount of phosphate pollution from fertilizers and animal waste may preclude the *efficient* use of land—taking pollution and water problems into consideration—for the pasturing of huge herds of animals. Our plates will come to be filled with synthetic meats. Clearly, water is going to be more and more in demand in the course of developing nuclear sources of power to replace vanishing fossil fuels. Most agricultural methods demand an enormous amount of water. As the competition for water increases, those industries which are able to make the least rational demand for it will gradually give way to the others—such as nuclear power installations—which can. Also, as pollution controls are applied, the "staggering output" of waste from livestock and poultry— thirty-three million tons annually in Ontario alone—guarantee that once more efficient methods of food production are found, the old, less efficient methods will have to be jettisoned. Technology, in all these instances, requires further technology, and each application makes the outcome more certain. The concerns of the individual come to have less and less weight, as the concern for the *population as a whole* becomes the main consideration. J. de Castro, writing in *The Geography of Hunger,* notes that "the new techniques of soil cultivation presuppose more and more powerful state control, with its police power, its ideology, and its propaganda machinery." This is the price that we must pay for survival. Ellul then goes on to say:

> William Vogt, surveying the same problem, is still more precise: in order to avoid famine, resulting from the systematic destruction of the topsoil, we must apply the latest technical methods. But conservation will not be put into practice spontaneously by individuals; yet, these methods must be applied globally or they will not amount to anything. Who can do this? Vogt, like all good Americans, asserts that he detests the authoritarian police state. However, he agrees that only state controls can possibly produce the desired results. He extols the efforts made by the liberal administration of the United States, in this respect, but he agrees that the United States continues "to lose ground literally and figuratively" simply because the methods of American agricultural administration are not authoritarian enough.
>
> What measures are to be recommended? The various soils must be

classified as to possible ways to cultivate them without destroying them. Authoritarian methods must be applied (a) to evacuate the population and to prevent it from working the imperiled soil; and (b) to grow only certain products on certain types of soil. The peasant can no longer be allowed freedom in these respects.

Ellul says that "all experts on agricultural questions are in fact in fundamental agreement" that "only strict planning on a world scale can solve the problems of agriculture"—which means that we "will be obliged to apply extremely rigorous administrative and police techniques."

In terms of administrative functions, the emergence of techno-structures in agriculture is guaranteed. So far, only large corporations and the military have given birth to them. But the problem of overpopulation, coupled with the problems of pollution and deple-tion of natural resources, will necessitate the application of the same methods which proved so efficient in the economic and mili-tary spheres. The methods, after all, are simply the ensemble of techniques orchestrated by a group decision-making apparatus—which is to say, a technostructure. Agricultural planning, popula-tion planning, and pollution-control planning involve the same basic techniques. Emerging, as they will, from the deep body of govern-ment, they will quickly assume technostructural forms. Computers will be used, systems analysis, operations research, data control, and so on—the full arsenal of technoplanning. The administrative agencies in charge of the various fields will thus inevitably develop technostructures, and they will quickly come to demand autonomy. The decision-making process, so far as a central governmental ad-ministration is concerned, will crumble yet further into the gravel heap of veto groups and autonomous bodies. Power will be further dispersed and decentralized and made subject to the internal needs of the different agencies involved.

In short, all the physical dimensions of environmental collapse force into existence a whole new social landscape, composed in the main of technostructures of various kinds. In every case, as Ellul says, "what can really be foreseen more or less clearly is the need of state intervention to control the effects of technical applications." The torrent of technology is washing away the libertarian landscape of familiar social concepts and replacing them with 1984-like "min-istries." And so far, what we have been experiencing is comparable to nothing more than some very steady "leaks" which have to date succeeded in filling up the social basins of economic and military organizations. As yet, the technological leakage has been more or less held back by a dam of traditions and institutionalized values, preventing many of the other realms of life from being flooded. Environmental collapse amounts to an earthquake which will smash the dam and unleash a technological flood that is certain to wash the remains of our culture down the drain.

Ellul is very specific on this point. Moreover, his thinking is consistent with that of a good number of others, including Kenneth Boulding, Arnold Toynbee, Galbraith, and McLuhan, to mention only a few. "Our technique, which is destroying all other civilizations, is more than a simple mechanism; it is a whole civilization in itself." Under the impact of technique, "communities break up into their component parts. But no new communities form." The existing cultures of the world "are being ringed by a band of steel." The breadth of the revolution which we are experiencing comes down to this: "Without exception in the course of history, *technique belonged to a civilization* and was merely a single element among a host of nontechnical activities. Today, *technique has taken over the whole of civilization.*" It is the "post-civilization" referred to by Boulding, the "world order" referred to by Toynbee, and it is a technical civilization which augments itself at every turn in the way just explained.

Few thinkers have been so explicit about the way in which technical civilization is taking shape. Ellul notes that "technique integrates everything." He is fully aware that the mechanism of this transformation from existing civilizations to post-civilization is what I call large-scale integration. Further, he perceives that its goal is "total integration," which is the state of completed convergence. At the time at which he was writing, the computer technique of large-scale integration had not been developed. His book was published in 1954, a year before the first integrated circuit had appeared. I am certain that he would see in these recent technological developments apt metaphors for what he was talking about. While not knowing about these specific developments, and thus being unable to differentiate between different types and levels of integration, he nevertheless was able to point out that "the technique of the present has no common measure with that of the past." He was talking, of course, about the quantum difference between planning and technoplanning, between a transistor, an integrated circuit, and large-scale integration. He refers to "the new integration," thanks to which "there is to be no more social maladjustment or neurosis." The efforts of psychologists, sociologists, and teachers—"the psychotechnicians in general"—are all geared in this direction: "Man is to be smoothed out, like a pair of pants under a steam iron."

"Technique, on the most significant levels, integrates the anarchic and antisocial impulses of the human being into society." The great power of technique, he argues, is that it "diffuses the revolt of the few and thus appeases the need of the millions for revolt." Social movements, such as surrealism, youth hostels, revolutionary political parties, political anarchism, have all failed to stem the tide of technology precisely because, "seeing his discontent expressed far better than he could express it," the potential rebel "is satisfied vicariously with an official revolt and ceases to criticize." Rebellious writers such as Henry Miller, James Baldwin, and Norman Mailer —assisted in bringing their discontent and outrage to millions by various techniques (including advertising)—succeed in performing "the sociological function of integration." The result is that "miniature fireworks issue from the magic bottle, but not revolt." In other words, Ellul is saying that neither literature nor art, neither dropping out nor political action can do battle with technique, since technical necessity forces the adoption of technical methods in the battle, thus converting the opposition to the cause, even when they are most violently opposed. The ensemble of techniques is added to by the strident notes of protest, which are sounded through technological means, whether they are printing presses, radios, television sets, or even organized demonstrations. Each step moves irresistibly in the direction of the technological society.

> Technical means are so important, so difficult to achieve and to manage, that it is easier to have them if there is a group, a movement, an association. Such movements are based on authentic impulses and valid feelings, and do allow a few individuals access to modes of expression which otherwise would have been closed to them. [The phenomenon of the underground press which has emerged in the last few years is a perfect example, and the whole trend toward communal art reinforces the point.] But their essential function is to act as vicarious intermediaries to integrate into the

technical society these same impulses and feelings which are possessed by millions of other men. . . . The basic human impulses are unpredictable in their complex social consequences. But thanks to "movements" which integrate and control them, they are powerless to harm the technical society, of which henceforth they form an integral part.

We can refer back to the point, made near the beginning of this book, that an old-style revolutionary take-over is no longer possible in a highly industrialized or post-industrial society. Revolutionary movements cannot succeed because of the technological necessities of the functioning of society. Moreover, as Ellul makes clear, these movements have the effect of serving their enemy. One has only to glance at the hippie movement to see that its only success was to integrate itself into society, to provide an outlet for pressures, drives, frustrations, and anarchic impulses which might otherwise end up being directed more destructively at society as a whole. Black Power, Yippie, Red Power, and radical student movements are similarly doomed to serve the system which they so despise. Even when they attempt to organize a guerrilla-style assault on the bastions of society, they serve only to strengthen the degree of social integration. They articulate the feelings of many, thus sparing them the frustration of not experiencing their rebellion.

Vicariously experienced rebellion articulated through revolutionary movements functions, in the long run, in the same way as Hollywood spectaculars. For every performer there are a thousand passive observers whose own potential for rebellion is diminished each time that they witness the revolutionary or romantic vision being enacted on the movie screen. Further, as we shall see shortly, thanks to television, the degree of involvement experienced by an audience is so great that in many respects they *were* there, they *did* participate. When the youthful rebels were chanting, at the peak of the 1968 Democratic Convention in Chicago, "The whole world is watching," they were, more or less, correct. What they apparently did not appreciate was that the whole world was not only watching, but was actually *there*. This being the case, there was no need for the whole world to be there in the flesh. Empathy and vicarious outrage or excitement or rebellion assured that the next time around, the proportion of audience to actors would not be profoundly altered.

Similarly, every time that the underground press levels a broadside at the establishment, the pent-up frustrations of the individual members of the mass media—including those who might finally be driven to act on their own if the situation became intolerable—are sublimated or vicariously released. There is less need for personal rebellion because someone else is acting it out. There is a strong parallel between this phenomenon and the techniques of "psychodrama," in which other members of a group act out the rages and confusions of a participant who then becomes a passive witness to the drama of his own conflicts. Therapeutically, it works. The effect is to integrate the individual more thoroughly with society. He is able, after all, to see the insides of others, to watch their psyches perform in the nude. He is afterward more sensitive to the needs and fears of others, and is, in turn, more aware of his own needs and fears in relation to those of others. He becomes, as a result, less antisocial and more sensitive, more empathetic, and so on.

"All revolutionary movements," writes Ellul, "are [now] burlesques of the real thing." The real thing, after all, is no longer possible. "But this must not be imputed to the activities of Machiavellian wire-pullers. The phenomenon appears naturally in the interaction of human techniques with social movements that seek to express basic human instincts. Our analysis could be repeated for pacifism, communism, and all of the multifarious movements designed to secure peace or social justice. They all fall into the same pattern and fulfill the same function. Some are indeed more authentic and 'truer' than others because they better express human revolt; they are more successful in pulling the teeth of aggressive instincts and in integrating them into the technical society. (If I have not mentioned religions, it is because they no longer express revolt; they have long since, in their intellectual and social forms, undergone integration.)"

This is Ellul's parting shot:

> With the final integration of the instinctive and the spiritual by means of these human techniques, the edifice of the technical society will be completed. It will not be a universal concentration camp, for it will be guilty of no atrocity. It will not seem insane, for everything will be ordered, and the strains of human passion will be lost among the chromium gleam. We shall have nothing more to lose, and nothing to win. Our deepest instincts and our most secret passions will be

analyzed, published, and exploited. We shall be rewarded with everything our hearts ever desired. And the supreme luxury of the society of technical necessity will be to grant the bonus of useless revolt and of an acquiescent smile.

Although Ellul says that it will not be a concentration camp, he means this in its dramatic form. Elsewhere, he argues that the goal of the technological society is, indeed, a concentration camp—but only in terms of its administrative functions. We have already seen —in Galbraith's analysis of technoplanning in the economic sphere —that collectively we must be brought under control in order for the technostructure to function properly. The same applies, of course, to all other technostructures, particularly the one that is developing within police organizations. "The techniques of police, which are developing at an extremely rapid tempo, have as their necessary end the transformation of the entire nation into a concentration camp. This is no perverse decision on the part of some party or government. To be sure of apprehending criminals, it is necessary that *everyone* be supervised." The Nazi's use of concentration camps, he argues, has warped our perspectives. "The concentration camp is based on two ideas which derive directly from the technical conception of the police: preventive detention (which completes prevention) and re-education. It is not because the use of these terms has not corresponded to reality that we feel it necessary to refuse to see in the concentration camp a very advanced form of the system. Nor is it because the so-called methods of re-education have, on the whole, been methods of destruction that we feel we must consider such a concept of 're-education' an odious joke. The further we advance, the more will the police be considered responsible for the re-education of social misfits, a goal that is part of the very order which they are charged with protecting. We are experiencing at present the justification of this development."

And of course, the experience of environmental collapse in the cities today makes the justification that much easier. Police organizations are in a far better position to demand the necessary autonomy to strengthen their technostructure when it is blatantly evident that crime rates are climbing, that riots must be anticipated, and so on. They can draw support in the form of funds in exactly the same way as technostructures within industry secure funds for research on the basis of "national defense." The same principles are at work.

The nation is threatened by an enemy, therefore defense research is necessary and funds to underwrite technological research cannot be refused. In the same way, as cities are threatened, police are assured the necessary financing to underwrite the expensive technological base upon which a technostructure is dependent for its growth. The experience of environmental collapse which is triggering the unleashing of a technological take-over elsewhere can be seen to be at work in the same way with respect to the evolution of police techniques. And the controls, correspondingly, will be greater. The individual, again, will have less and less say in the matter.

The role of other-direction should be clear in all this. The other-directed, group-oriented individual is far less likely to effectively resist this trend than the earlier inner-directed type would have been. Moreover, since each new technique is applied for a perfectly rational, logical, and even humanitarian reason—control of pollution or overcrowding, prevention of crime, or raising the standard of living—there is no sound reason for him to *want* to resist. Furthermore, the other-directed person is far more vulnerable to manipulation through the medium of his peer-groups and far more susceptible to psychological pressures which can now be brought to bear, thanks to technique, with unparalleled efficiency.

Also, technique is the enemy of anarchy, including—if so applied—organized anarchy. The organization anarchists, as much as individual anarchists, are in the process of being brought to heel by the rise of technostructures and the application of technique or technoplanning, which, by definition, imposes order where formerly there was only randomness. The emerging social character of other-direction reinforces the limitations on anarchic, individualistic behavior. Taken together, the two developments—if indeed, they can be seen to be separate—amount to an antianarchic force of unprecedented strength and mobility. Group-man is much less "in it for himself" than his individualistic predecessor, and a corporation —or government or institution—whose central feature is the technostructure is far more inhibited in its self-interested pursuits than were earlier forms of organization. And, as pointed out, these "new" forms of organization and institution are being forced into existence at a very rapid rate. They appear to be quite capable of dealing—if given enough time—with even the most pressing aspects of environmental collapse. Environmental collapse, in fact, may be seen to be the midwife in the delivery of a new civilization, one based on cooperation, coordination, integration, and control.

In its full proportions it is a terrifying outlook. Human beings, quite literally, will cease to be relevant. We will be free—as the members of no other society were free—to do as we please, within some very rigid confines. Ellul is saying, in effect, that man is in the process of being domesticated. In the pasture he will be allowed to chew where he likes, think what he likes, and say what he likes, but his freedom will be as meaningless as the freedom of cattle. He is telling us that *Brave New World* is rapidly becoming a reality. The "freedom" of the full-blown technological society will lack one major ingredient: the capacity seriously to challenge or attempt to alter the existing order, even though it may prove to be spiritually corrupt, intellectually sterile, and morally outrageous. We are apparently a long way on the road to that destination, and, thanks to our inability or refusal to control our individual and collective anarchic impulses, we have created a nightmarish environmental situation in which we have *no choice* but to take the plunge, since the alternative—continuation of the way we have been behaving— guarantees our destruction.

Ellul is appalled by the prospect. And he is not alone. The "politics of despair," suicidal radical social movements now in their infancy, and the "theater of the absurd" are all, to varying degrees, reflections of the same sense of helplessness and hopelessness in the face of the emerging shape of society. It is difficult, in fact, to find a voice—which is not the voice of a thoroughgoing technician— which contains any note of optimism.

Difficult, but not impossible. The fact is that Ellul, like many others, refuses to acknowledge (or else is unaware of) one of the best definitions of civilization ever given. Richard Carrington has defined civilization as "the most highly evolved technique so far discovered by any living organism to ensure the survival of the species, and *at the same time to allow it to attain new levels of awareness.*" Admittedly, we are, if we are to survive at all, being forced into the pasture where we will be, for all intents and purposes, powerless to effect social change. The "system" appears well on its way to taking over the job of running our lives and civilization. The ship of civilization is well on its way to being guided by an automatic pilot. And we, the passengers, will be treated like prized cattle. However—and this is the point steadfastly overlooked by writers ranging from Aldous Huxley to Jacques Ellul—*we are not cattle*. We are much more complex and unpredictable. And further, our capabilities have not yet been tapped. The bulk of our brain remains in neutral, not having been put to use as yet. Those of us who do behave like cattle constitute, for the most part, the most retrogressive and backward elements in society. The "cattle" are not representative of the best and most advanced—particularly in terms of intellect and emotions—specimens of humanity. Finally, Ellul, as much as Huxley and a large number of "humanistic" writers, fails entirely to comprehend the possibility of "new levels of awareness." David Riesman foresees the distinct possibility of the organic development of an autonomous social character out of other-direction, and this is his best insight. Ellul—while being perfectly accurate in his assessment of the impact and the effects of technique—has no such insight to offer. It does not appear to occur to him that the destruction of civilization as we have known it, with all its cultural values and categories—its hang-ups, in short—might be not only necessary, but a good thing as well, possibly a necessary stage to break a bottleneck that has doomed every civilization in history to the ash can.

We turn now to an examination of a "technique" which, at least according to Marshall McLuhan, is qualitatively different from other techniques.

18

The Secret
Agents of
M.E.D.I.A.

Few things are more subversive than media. To understand this is
to begin to understand media and the gist of what Marshall McLuhan has been saying. In *War and Peace in the Global Village* he
quotes an AVCO advertisement:

WE ARE 25,000 PEOPLE
CHANGING THE WAY YOU LIVE

"The world of advertisements," he writes, "has for a century been a
frank declaration of war on the community of customers." And
while television and the computer were totally and invisibly under-
mining Western society from within, "typically, the FBI and the
CIA were looking in the rearview mirror for the revolutionary
agents who were threatening the identity of the country." *The Medium Is the Massage* begins on a similar note, using a quote from
Alfred North Whitehead: "The major advances in civilization are
processes that all but wreck the societies in which they occur."

"Societies," states McLuhan, "have always been shaped more by
the nature of the media by which men communicate than by the
content of the communication." By "medium," McLuhan means
any extension of ourselves. A medium can be a book, clothing, car,
plane, boat, light bulb, radio, television, typewriter, spaceship, or

city. Generally, McLuhan's basic concept is that the medium which a man uses will change him in relationship to his environment, rather than the reverse—which has always been assumed to be the case. A society which adopts print technology, for instance, will be drastically altered and will come to behave, think, and perceive in a manner quite different from the way in which it behaved, thought, and perceived in the past. And a society which adopts electronic communications techniques, such as radio or television, will be similarly affected.

Where some thinkers have concentrated on population pressure as an instrument of change, others concentrate on economic pressures, social pressures, or pressures from the physical environment, McLuhan concentrates on the pressures generated by media—or, more specifically, technologies. He has the edge on the other, more decidedly speciocentric writers in that he expands his definition of "medium" to embrace most of the other forces—money, for instance, becomes a medium. But in the end (as he freely admits) he winds up exaggerating those qualities which interest him. In an interview with Gerald Emanuel Stearn, reprinted in *McLuhan: Hot & Cool,* he quotes Wyndham Lewis as saying that "art is an expression of a colossal preference" for various rhythms, colors, structures, and pigmentation. "Exaggeration," says McLuhan, "in the sense of the hyperbole, is a major artistic device in all modes of art. . . . You can't build a building without huge exaggeration or preference for a certain kind of space."

Granted. On the other hand, as Galbraith points out, "good architecture is also mostly meaningless unless it is within a consistent framework. The Taj Mahal would lose much of its queenly elegance if surrounded by modern service stations." No doubt McLuhan's work amounts to an intellectual Taj Mahal; yet, unless viewed in a larger context, it loses much of its beauty. The point that I wish to make here is that McLuhan has made the same basic discoveries through an examination of media that Riesman, for instance, made through an examination of social character, Galbraith through an examination of the new industrial state, and others—to be referred to later—through similar examinations of other fields. Let us now set McLuhan's Taj Mahal with its TV antenna next to Galbraith's technostructure, Riesman's other-directed house of mirrors, and Ellul's luxurious concentration camp.

Like Riesman, McLuhan sees us moving back into a group milieu. Riesman noted that tradition-directed societies were made up
of groups, whereas inner-directed society was composed of individuals. And now we are entering an other-directed period where
groups once again are the central feature. McLuhan's argument follows in the same groove; tradition-directed societies were "tribal,"
inner-direction meant "detribalization," and other-direction means
"retribalization." Tribal man lived in a world of growth and organic interrelationships. He lived mythically and integrally. But "by
Plato's time, the written word had created a new environment that
had begun to detribalize man." With the development of the phonetic alphabet, "education by classified data" had begun and has remained the Western program ever since. The coming of print
technology—the Gutenberg revolution—in the sixteenth century
created individualism and nationalism. In place of the organic interrelationships of tribal man, we have the fragmented, uniform, continuous, and sequential awareness which characterizes literate Western man.

McLuhan points to the sixteenth century as the turning point in
the development of literacy and the detribalization of the West.
Riesman, in his quite different context, arrives at the same century
as being the one which "cut us off pretty decisively from the family
and clan-oriented traditional ways of life in which mankind has existed throughout most of history." Detribalization, or inner-direction, is therefore seen as being mainly a characteristic of the Western world during no more than the last four hundred years. (Ellul,
too, notes that "society was at a crossroads" in the sixteenth century. He also notes that "every intellectual had perforce to be a uni-
versalist.")

Riesman and McLuhan are also in agreement about the next
great shift from detribalization or inner-direction to retribalization
or other-direction. It was at roughly the time of the Second World
War, although the Electric Age began one hundred years ago. Its
effects, however, were not really felt until the television set reached
into every home in the late 1940s, the period when, in Riesman's
jargon, the rise of other-direction was "just beginning." This crucial
period—the 1940s—also saw, in the military and industrial
spheres, the real shift from planning to technoplanning, the extinction of the great entrepreneur, the collapse of the political and cor-

porate organization chart, and the birth of technostructures—all of which dovetail with retribalization and other-direction.

If other-direction can be understood as amounting to *characterological* large-scale integration, the larger dimensions of other-direction—i.e., retribalization—can be seen as *psychic* large-scale integration. The effect of electronic technologies, McLuhan argues, is to extend our central nervous system "to involve us in the whole of mankind and to incorporate the whole of mankind in us," forcing us to "participate, in depth, in the consequences of our every action." Integration, at this stage, could not be on a much larger scale. "Electric speed in bringing all social and political functions together in a sudden implosion has heightened human awareness of responsibility to an intense degree. It is this implosive factor that alters the position of the Negro, the teenager, and some other groups. They can no longer be *contained,* in the political sense of limited association. They are now *involved* in our lives, as we in theirs, thanks to the electric media." Shortly, we will see how this altered awareness gives rise to existentialism which has spilled—mainly since the 1940s—out of the ivory towers of universities into psychiatry, theology, literature, theater, art, politics, and education.

The dimensions of the revolution in human affairs wrought by print, resulting in the shift from tradition- to inner-directed (or detribalization), is difficult for most of us, raised in the literate grid of the West, to grasp. It can be better understood if we peer into the Middle Ages, as has Lewis Mumford. "The unattached person during the Middle Ages," he writes, "was one either condemned to exile or doomed to death: if alive, he immediately sought to attach himself, at least to a band of robbers. To exist, one had to belong to an association: a household, a manor, a monastery, a guild; *there was no security except in association, and no freedom that did not recognize the obligations of a corporate life. One lived and died in the style of one's class and corporation* [my italics]." In *The Long Revolution* Raymond Williams notes that in the Middle Ages the word "individual" meant "inseparable." Today the word "individual" is used to describe a separate entity, which reflects "a change in emphasis which enabled us to think of 'the individual' as a kind of absolute, without immediate reference . . . to the group of which he is a member." As Eric and Mary Josephson point out in *Man Alone:*

Williams suggests that this change took place in the late sixteenth and early seventeenth centuries; and since then we have come to speak of "the individual in his own right, whereas previously to describe the individual was to give an example of the group of which he was a member, and so to offer a particular description of that group and of the relationships within it." This semantic change reflected profound changes in the social order after the medieval period, particularly the break-up of the feudal caste system. When men found they could change their status and social mobility increased, the idea grew of being an individual apart from one's social role. Also important . . . was man's new detachment from and power over nature: When man (as subject) divorced himself from nature (as object) in order to understand and control it, individualism was given further impetus. . . . It is this historical emergence of the individual as we now know him, of man alone, that makes alienation so crucially a modern problem. . . . When the medieval system collapsed, the likelihood of alienation increased appreciably.

As mentioned earlier, "numbness" is McLuhan's word for alienation. He describes it as the process of autoamputation, a reaction of the central nervous system to the impact of new technologies. As tribal man becomes literate, "nearly all the emotional and corporate family feeling is eliminated from his relationship with his corporate group. He is emotionally free to separate from the tribe and to become a civilized individual, a man of visual organization who has uniform [or inner-directed] attitudes, habits, and rights with all other civilized individuals." But, as he notes in *The Gutenberg Galaxy,* "schizophrenia may be a necessary consequence of literacy." Erich Fromm and others have pointed out that alienation is neurosis and, in its most extreme forms, schizophrenia. And in fact the collapse of the medieval system—due largely, according to McLuhan, to the impact of print technology and the resulting spread of literacy—certainly did increase the instances of alienation, neurosis, and schizophrenia.

In *Madness and Civilization* Michel Foucault begins by noting that "at the end of the Middle Ages, leprosy disappeared from the Western world." The Renaissance marks the appearance not only of "the individual as we know him," of alienation as a central factor of social life, and of literate, inner-directed Western man, but also of "something new . . . the Ship of Fools, a strange 'drunken boat' that glides along the calm rivers of the Rhineland and the Flemish canals." The *Narrenschiff*, or Ship of Fools, was real. But it was also a literary composition, a great mythic theme of the time which was reflected in the painting of Hieronymus Bosch. "The dawn of madness on the horizon of the Renaissance," writes Foucault, "is first perceptible in the decay of Gothic symbolism; as if that world, whose network of spiritual meanings was so close-knit, had begun to unravel, showing faces whose meaning was no longer clear except in the forms of madness." In the sixteenth century "the classic experience of madness is born." The lazar houses and leprosariums which were emptied by the end of the Middle Ages are now replaced by the hospital of madness and the madhouse. By the seventeenth century "reason has become mobile"—mainly through print —and Nicolas Joubert declares himself the Prince of Fools. One out of every hundred residents of Paris found himself confined in a madhouse. There was, as Foucault says, "an absurd agitation in society."

Today more than half the hospital beds in the United States are occupied by mental patients. In Vancouver, British Columbia, Joikum Foikus declares himself the Town Fool. Madness, schizophrenia, neurosis, and alienation—all components of literacy— reach unprecedented levels. If it is true that 90 per cent of all the scientists who ever lived are living today, it is probably also true that 90 per cent of all the schizophrenics who ever lived are living today. Moreover, the technological revolutions triggered by print have pushed exploitation, not only of nature but of human beings, to the breaking point.

At the same time, we see individuals retreating into the warm embrace of the group. Galbraith remarks in *The New Industrial State* that today, unless he is associated with some organization or another, "the individual is a cipher. He cannot be placed in the scheme of things; no one knows how much attention, let alone respect, he deserves or whether he is worthy of any notice at all." On the other hand, "if he is with a well-known corporation—a good outfit—he obviously counts." Of course, the prestige of business organizations is declining, but other types of organization, including veto-groups, are multiplying. The similarity between Galbraith's comments on life in corporate America and Mumford's comments on life in the corporate Middle Ages is obvious. Mumford is describing the "tribal" state of being and Galbraith is describing "retribalization."

It is no coincidence, therefore, that the latest and most successful techniques of psychotherapy involve the use of groups. They deliberately try to re-create the preliterate sense of community which has been lost, to mold the "buzzing swarm of I's" back into a sense of "we." In other words, group therapy techniques consciously attempt to retribalize people at the same time that electronic media, unconsciously and accidentally, are effecting the same end.

Perhaps the homeostatic processes at work in this self-regulated revolution are now becoming clearer. In its broadest outlines it comes down to this. Until the end of the Middle Ages the individual was *part* of a group—a kind of conscious cell in a larger corporate body. A manuscript culture existed; but for the most part, literacy was *oral*. With the invention of the printing press, literacy became *visual*. Depth of involvement and of human relations was destroyed by the resulting mechanical technologies. The result, as Robert Nisbet says, is that "traditional primary relationships of men . . . became functionally irrelevant."

Mechanical technologists, as McLuhan notes, are fragmentary. "The power to translate knowledge into mechanical production by the breaking-up of any process into fragmented aspects to be placed in a lineal sequence of movable, yet uniform, parts was the formal essence of the printing press." Thus, as Lewis Mumford puts it, the effect of mechanization was to make it "more and more difficult to absorb and cope with any one part of the environment, to say nothing of dealing with it as a whole."

In the meantime, social order—based on organic relationships —was literally shattered. Specialization, the division of labor, and the resulting breakup of the once tightly knit web of kinship increasingly isolated and atomized the individual, leading to increased suicide rates, more homicide, more alcoholism, juvenile delinquency, insanity, and so on. Individual anarchic impulses, no longer held in check by rigid social order, were now released. Detribalized, inner-directed man is an anarchist who has, to a large extent, escaped the restraining embrace of the group. Lacking any real sense of involvement, commitment, or moral attachment to society, he becomes increasingly destructive, indifferent to others, greedy, and self-indulgent. He is the cancer cell which breaks away. In the mid-twentieth century, we see the results of his reckless self-inter-est. Environmental collapse, if McLuhan is right, is the ultimate re-sult of the Gutenberg revolution. For only a species which has no sense of solidarity could possibly wreck the environment in the way that literate Western man has done.

The individualism and "freedom" of literate inner-directed West-ern man can now be seen to have just about run its course. And at this point, environmental resistance sets in. Inner-directed man drowns in the great cities which his technologies have made possi-ble, and other-directed group man floats to the surface. The disequi-librium caused by print and mechanization is homeostatically can-celed out as society "rights" itself. The group, after a brief four-hundred-year period of breakup and disintegration, coalesces and integrates itself once more. Today Western society can be seen as a corporate body that has been knocked off balance by a series of heavy, numbing technological blows and that is now in the pro-cess of getting back on its feet. The count, however, has already reached "seven . . . eight . . . nine." The fight will be over very shortly—unless society can manage to lurch up from the mat.

McLuhan is optimistic. He believes that we are almost back on our feet. It is difficult to tell whether he realizes the *need* for us quickly to retribalize ourselves, since he seems almost blissfully un-aware of the snowballing effects of environmental collapse. Cer-tainly, while he makes the connection between Gutenberg and the assembly line, he does not appear to be acutely aware of the fact that the connection goes further—that the "gift of Gutenberg" was not only the assembly line, but cancer, emphysema, bronchitis, the extinction of many species of birds, the near extinction of the bison and blue whale, the pollution of every river and lake in North America, radiation, pesticides, and the cloud of poison that now girdles the earth. He *does* see the connection between literacy and violence in its traditional outlines. In *Understanding Media* he re-fers us to the Greek myth of Cadmus: "Reputedly, the king who in-troduced the phonetic letters into Greece sowed the dragon's teeth, and they sprang up armed men." This myth, he says, encapsulates a prolonged process in a flashing insight. "The alphabet meant power and authority and control of military structures at a distance." The power of letters "as agents of aggressive order and precision" leads to the establishment of military bureaucracies and empire-building. This is what he means when he remarks, in *War and Peace in the Global Village,* that "civilization is the mother of war." Literacy is its patron. Having made this connection, however, he does not seem to appreciate the further dimensions of environmental collapse.

The question that McLuhan appears to be trying to answer is the one that was phrased by Dr. Lamont C. Cole: "Can man domesticate himself?" Or, more precisely, can man domesticate himself *in time?* The processes described by McLuhan—as well as Ellul, Riesman, and Galbraith—are no more reversible than the ones that took place at the end of the Middle Ages. The tools for the domestication of man are clearly at hand. At this stage the Global Village is the only alternative to a global Buchenwald. But the deadline imposed by environmental collapse is as close as midnight on the Doomsday Clock posted by the Bulletin of Atomic Scientists, which had been fixed at 11:48 since 1963, but was advanced, in January 1968, to 11:53. In the seven minutes that we have left to live, can we make the jump from institutionalized anarchy, exploitive literate individualism, and suicidal inner-direction back to the restraining embrace of the group?

McLuhan is no more capable of answering this question than anyone else. However, the drift of his thesis (with not a few qualifications) would seem to be strongly positive. His basic idea, after all, is that the *structure* of a society is determined largely by the *media* of communication which that society uses—as opposed to the *content* of the communication. This is the meaning of his statement: "the medium is the message."

In *Technics and Civilization,* written back in 1934, Lewis Mumford, although unaware of the radically different effects of electronic technologies, nevertheless takes note of a drift in the direction of large-scale integration even without the stimulus of TV or computers:

> The machine imposes the necessity for collective effort and widens its range. To the extent that men have escaped the control of nature they must submit to the control of society. As a serial operation, every part must function smoothly and be geared to the right speed in order to ensure the effective working of the process as a whole. So in society at large there must be a close articulation between all its elements. Individual self-sufficiency is another way of saying techno-

logical crudeness: *as our technics become more refined it becomes impossible to work the machine without large-scale collective cooperation,* and in the long run a high technic is possible only on a basis of worldwide trade and intellectual intercourse. The machine has . . . intensified the need for collective effort and collective order. . . . To the extent that the collective discipline becomes effective and the various groups in society are worked into a nicely interlocking organization, special provisions must be made for isolated and anarchic elements that are not included in such a wide-reaching collectivism—elements that cannot without danger be repressed or ignored. But to abandon the social collectivism imposed by modern technics means to return to nature and be at the mercy of natural forces.

The great discovery of literate Western man was the manifold technique of learning to protect himself from the ravages of nature, to supply himself with food, clothing, and so on. Having made these basic discoveries, he now needs to be protected from the ravages of himself. And the only protection appears to be group consciousness or the tribal state of being, both of which are, like the computer, the "foes of disintegration and chaos." In their highest form—at the stage of large-scale integration—they are antianarchic.

The enormous importance of McLuhan's writings stems not from his observation that media—or technologies—play a large role in structuring society (since other writers, including Mumford, have made this point time and time again), but from the fact that he sees a crucial difference between electronic and mechanical technologies. Unlike Ellul, for instance, he does not believe that all techniques are fundamentally the same in their effect. While the idea that electronic techniques are identical in their effects to mechanical techniques leads inevitably to the conclusion that "henceforth, men will be able to act only in virtue of their commonest and lowest nature," McLuhan's line of thought leads in the opposite direction. Machine technology imposed linear patterns, thus causing fragmentation and alienation. "The essence of automation technology is just the opposite. It is integral and decentralist in depth, just as the machine was fragmentary, centralist, and superficial in its patterning of human relationships." Electronic technologies have the effect of transforming literate Western man "into a complex and depth-structured person emotionally aware of his total interdependence with the rest of human society." "Integral awareness" replaces linear detachment. As a result of the "electric speedup," the sensitivity and pliability of the human organism begins to be developed.

Before proceeding with the main argument of this book—that we are heading, of necessity, toward a global concentration camp, but that *this represents possibilities for genuine freedom and creativity for which there is no parallel in history*—it is necessary to offer McLuhan's best observation. The observation comes in the context of his concept of the "global village," which he insists is the completely retribalized world in which each individual is plugged into an electronic central nervous system.

When it was suggested to McLuhan that a global village might be a great homogeneous society in which the individual parts would be as interchangeable as standardized nuts and bolts, McLuhan replied: "There is more diversity, less conformity under a single roof in any family than there is with the thousands of families in the same city. The more you create village conditions, the more discontinuity and division and diversity. *The global village ensures maximal disagreement on all points.* It never occurred to me that uniformity and tranquillity were the properties of the global village. It has more spite and envy. *The spaces and times are pulled out from between people. A world in which people encounter each other in depth all the time.* The tribal-global village is far more divisive— full of fighting—than any nationalism ever was. *Village is fission, not fusion, in depth.* People leave small towns to *avoid* involvement. The big city *lined* them with its uniformity and impersonal milieu. . . . The village is not the place to find ideal peace and harmony. Exactly opposite. Nationalism came out of print and provided an extraordinary relief from global village conditions."

Seen against the background provided by Ellul, with supporting evidence from Galbraith and Riesman, McLuhan's observation would seem to be in complete conflict with the emerging realities. As large-scale integration progresses, social controls deepen and penetrate every last hiding place. A concentration camp built around the cornucopia of industrialization would seem to be in the offing, and the question that must be answered is not *how* this situation can be avoided—since the fact of abrupt, almost omnipotent environmental collapse makes it impossible to avoid this eventuality —but rather, will it amount to the dead-end of the ant heap or will it be a giant step in the direction of limitless development and exploration?

Before attempting to answer this question, less quantitative aspects of large-scale integration must be understood. I refer to group psychotherapeutic techniques and drugs, both of which complement the development of other-direction, are admirably suited to the effects of electronic media, perfectly in tune with the effects of automation, cybernation, computerization, and all "software" techniques, as well as being very much in line with the emergence of technostructures.

19

The Drug
Revolution

Drugs such as marijuana facilitate the process of large-scale integration. As much as other-direction and electronic media, drugs have the effect of intensifying human relationships. Moreover, the question of drug use cannot be viewed in isolation from these other developments any more than the question of pollution can be viewed in isolation from technology. Again, we see a complex organic relationship. "The fact is," writes McLuhan, "that getting 'turned on' is only very incidentally chemical and is, on an overwhelming scale, a fact of electric engineering. . . . The elders of the literate societies don't easily turn on because their sensibilities have hardened in a visual mold. But the pre-literates and semi-literates and non-literates of our own society not only 'turn *on*,' they also turn *against* the older, literate, and mechanical culture."

The parallel between the development of other-directed social character and the increased use of hallucinogenic drugs should be obvious. The other-directed person—the "TV child," as McLuhan would have it—requires depth relationships and has a heightened social awareness. The effects of marijuana, according to *The Cannabis Report* published by the British Home Office, are "a sense of heightened awareness: colors, sounds, and social intercourse appear more intense and meaningful." However, enough has been written about drugs to make it unnecessary for us to go into the subject at great length. It is enough, for the purposes of this book, to summarize the main points and to note the role played by drugs in the process of large-scale integration.

Undoubtedly, drug legislation will be revised in the future. The question is a matter of timing. The major studies of drug use that have so far been carried out—the Wootton Report in England, the seventy-year-old Indian Hemp Drugs Commission in India, and the 1944 New York Mayor's Committee on Marijuana—have all agreed (much to the disappointment of legislators who favor continued prohibition) that "the long-term consumption of cannabis in moderate doses has no harmful effects." The main argument against legalization—that it is addictive and leads inevitably to the use of hard drugs such as heroin—has been shown to be without substance. "Cannabis," according to the Wootton Report, "does not cause physical dependence, and withdrawal effects do not occur where its use is discontinued." If any sort of psychological dependence does develop—and this point is debatable—"it is of a different order from the intense psychological dependence which normally follows the use of hard drugs." The Wootton Report, in fact, argues that cigarettes and alcohol are far more dangerous than marijuana. In short, the arguments against the legalization of drugs are not rational. Rather, they are emotional, and are more rooted in a fear of existing values and concepts being upset than anything else.

These fears are well grounded. But the hope that the erosion of existing values can be stopped by the imprisonment of marijuana users represents nothing more than the convulsive reaction of a crumbling order. Television sets, large urban centers—in fact the whole thrust of modern technology—would have to be banned as well. No one is about to arrest television manufacturers or the full staff of IBM, or to ban the growth of cities—and these are the central causes of the erosion of existing values. The use of drugs is merely a footnote or, at most, an underlining of the point. McLuhan put it very well when he said: "All . . . legal restrictions [against marijuana and hallucinogenic drugs] are futile and will eventually wither away. You could as easily ban drugs in retribalized society as outlaw clocks in a mechanical culture. The young will continue turning on no matter how many of them are turned off into prisons, and such legal restrictions only reflect the cultural aggression and revenge of a dying culture against its successor."

In an article in the underground newspaper *The Georgia Straight,* in March 1969, writer Stan Persky said: "The cannabis laws are . . . crumbling. Eventually only the seeds and twigs will be left. Twenty years from now (assuming there's something left on earth to look back on) people will wonder what [it] was all about, why we perpetuated an era of tiny terror, why we violated constitutional safeguards against unreasonable search to look for a weed, and what was the point of sending kids to jail for puffing gentle cannabis." This opinion is shared by people other than the members of the underground press, and it is a reasonable assessment of the situation. There is more good reason for banning tobacco than there is for banning marijuana, since tobacco *is* demonstrably addictive and causes cancer. Tobacco, moreover, is a miserable pleasure at best. The reasons for the banning of marijuana are mainly cultural, as opposed to rational. And, in view of the revolutionary changes that are affecting our civilization, the cultural wave just breaking will leave marijuana sitting high and dry on the beach of legal sanction.

Steps have already been taken in this direction, and the Wootton Report in England is significant. "Our main aim," the report stated, "is to remove, for practical purposes, the prospect of imprisonment for possession of a small amount [of marijuana] and to demonstrate that the taking of the drug in moderation is a relatively minor offence. Thus, we would hope that juvenile experiments in taking cannabis would be recognized for what they are, and not treated as antisocial acts or evidence of unsatisfactory moral character." Far more than "moral character," the taking of drugs is indicative of social character—other-directed or autonomous social character in particular.

Marijuana has been called a "social drug." It functions in groups to break down feelings of personal isolation and to stimulate exchange between members of a group. It gives its users at least the illusion of tremendous rapport and communication at levels that are not normally accessible. Inhibitions against self-expression are reduced, if not altogether wiped out. As in a group-therapy situation, revelations about one's own fantasies are approved and tacitly encouraged. In the normal course of social events, on the other hand, such revelations are discouraged or dismissed. The effect of marijuana is to break down—not heighten—social barriers and the walls between individuals. McLuhan has accurately referred to the "group-oriented" or "tribal" characteristics of drug users. (This, of course, excludes users of hard drugs, who are a different social type.)

The increased popularity of hallucinogenic drugs cannot be separated from the increased use of legal drugs. As pointed out earlier, the use of legal drugs has swelled enormously in industrialized societies. The drug revolution did not start in the 1950s or the 1960s. It started in the 1920s. Apart from the cultural, social, and technological reasons for the increased use of drugs, the factor of simple sequence has to be considered. Attitudes do not change overnight. Radical changes in attitude take place because the over-all social climate changes. Deep-rooted inhibitions—such as the cultural inhibitions in Western society against drugs—wither slowly from within. They do not go down like the walls of Jericho.

Current attitudes, especially among the young, can be traced in part to the fact that the resistance of their parents to drugs has been decaying steadily since the 1920s, at which date the drug industry began its incredible period of growth. Drug sales in North America have increased more than 1200 per cent since 1920, and only fifty years later, in 1970, had attained a sales volume of $12 billion per year. Today adults consume barbiturates, sedatives, tranquilizers, antidepressants, reserpine, chlorpromazine, and things like Doriden, Valmid, and Librium—without thinking twice about it. Not surprisingly, the casual consumption of drugs by one generation has created a favorable climate for the unquestioning consumption of drugs by the next. Hallucinogenic drugs are not basically different from pep pills or tranquilizers, except that they offer more in terms of awareness and intercourse.

This point about awareness needs qualification. Aside from the writings of poets such as Allen Ginsberg—who acknowledges that he writes under the influence of various drugs—there is little concrete evidence that hallucinogens actually *do* heighten awareness. Of course, this is the old problem of trying to explain colors to a blind man. A new level of awareness can be comprehended only by someone who has experienced it. To the blind man, the concept of colors is necessarily meaningless. However, it is a striking feature of all descriptions of hallucinogenic drug experiences—from marijuana to LSD—that the user reports that *the awareness of interrelationships is greatly heightened.* It is primarily for this reason that drug-taking and an absorbing interest in Eastern mysticism come to be so closely associated. The concept of Tao, or the "oneness of the universe," is in near-perfect harmony with drug-induced levels of consciousness.

Descriptions of the LSD experience—and here I am referring to "pure" LSD—tend to converge on this one point: the sensation of *being in infinity,* of being a part of the universal whole. I have talked to several people who have taken pure LSD, and their descriptions are characterized by this recurring theme. Frank Ogden, former LSD therapist at the Hollywood Hospital in New Westminster, British Columbia, insists that the experience of "being reborn" is characteristic of all therapeutically valid LSD trips. And in the process of being reborn, one's sense of self has first to dissolve back into infinity before it can be reassembled. Even among marijuana users, the sensation of being aware of interrelationships is common. They tend to see "connections" where no relationship is apparent to nonusers. Such testimonies indicate a dissolving of the barriers to perception. Visions of unity—in earlier times limited only to seers and saints—now become commonplace experiences among the users of psychedelic drugs.

Modern psychology makes it clear that most failures to communicate or to express oneself or even to see oneself in relationship to others is not due to an inability to do so. Rather, it is due to the existence of psychological barriers, most of which are imposed by cultural conditioning. Psychology tends to support what evidence there is that these barriers are artificial and can be broken down. This would appear to be the main function of so-called hallucinogens. In other words, they do not create hallucinations so much as they tend to dissolve linear patterns of perception. This would account for the popularity among drug users of philosophers such as Alan Watts, who refers to our whole history of thinking as "an illusion." "However much we divide, count, sort, or classify . . . particular things and events, this is no more than a way of thinking about the world: it is never *actually* divided." We do not need, he adds, "a new religion or a new Bible. We need a new experience—a new feeling of what it is to be 'I.' " Drugs, he said in an interview in Vancouver in

1969, are illegal mainly because they give people a mystical experience that challenges the authoritarian structure of Western religion and society. Watts admits that he has used LSD. Most people, he says, are looking at creation through a narrow slit in a fence—a point that is perfectly in line with the fact that man's perceptions of the universe are restricted to a narrow band on the electromagnetic spectrum. Drugs such as marijuana, mescaline, and LSD can widen the slit.

I have already suggested that a consciousness of interrelationships is one of the central characteristics of the age which we are now approaching. The growing awareness of ecology is an example. The ecumenical movement in Western religions is another. The interdependence—now tacitly agreed upon—of modern corporations is yet another. The evolution of other-directed social character reinforces—and to a great degree stimulates—this same kind of awareness. Technoplanning is primarily concerned with spotting organization interrelationships. Electronic media stimulate in-depth involvement, which definitely results in an awareness of interrelationships. Computers and the whole field of cybernetics are based on the dynamics of interrelationships. As Allen Newell put it in *The Chess Machine,* so far as the use of computers is concerned, "the relevant information is inexhaustable"—which is to say, the interrelatedness of the factors in any given situation is limitless. Group therapy is, of course, based on the dynamics of interrelationships. All these amount to forms of large-scale integration. And the effects of drugs are basically similar in that they too stimulate this kind of awareness. Such use cannot be dismissed as a mere aberration or perversion. Drug use is in complete harmony with all these other developments—complementing them, stimulating them, and vibrating, like a metronome, in sympathy with them.

There is a strong tendency for any serious discussion of hallucinogenic drugs—particularly LSD—to lapse, as Duncan B. Blewett of the University of Saskatchewan put it, "into either the vague other-worldliness of mysticism or the sterile irrelevancy of scientism." Any such discussion must, in fact, tread a tightrope over these two chasms. The point about LSD which needs to be stressed is that its "humanizing influence" has scarcely been tapped. Among the people who have been either cured or considerably helped by LSD therapy are autistic children, alcoholics, neurotics, the sexually maladjusted, psychopaths, habitual criminals, and homosexuals. Dr. Blewett, one of the pioneers in the therapeutic use of LSD, summed up his feelings in the introduction to *LSD: The Problem-Solving Psychedelic,* by P. G. Stafford and B. H. Golightly:

> The discovery of LSD marked one of the three major scientific breakthroughs of the twentieth century. In physics, the splitting of the atom provided access to undreamed-of energy. The biologists are on the threshold of learning how to manipulate genetic structures and bringing the process of evolution under human control. In psychology, the psychedelics have provided the key to the unimaginable vastness of the unconscious mind. For, as Suzuki stated, "our consciousness is nothing but an insignificant floating piece of island in the ocean encircling the earth. But it is through this little fragment of land that we can look out to the immense expanse of the unconscious itself."
>
> In the last of these discoveries lies the key to survival. For if man is to cope with his newfound physical and biological power and responsibility, there must be an abrupt and decisive revision of human psychology. The motives that have made human history a chronicle of bloodshed and brutality will otherwise certainly and shortly lead to the annihilation of the species.
>
> The psychedelics offer the hope that we are on the threshold of a new renaissance in which man's view of himself will undergo dramatic change. Alienated and encapsulated, he has become trapped by his history in outmoded institutions which disfigure him with the creed of original sin; corrupt him with fear of economic insecurity; dement him with the delusion that mass murder is an inevitable outcome of his nature; debase him to believe that butchery in the name of the state is a sacred duty, and leave him so crippled that he is afraid to seek self-understanding or to love and trust himself, his neighbor, or his God.
>
> The models of man and the frames of reference involved in our technologically centered society are proving increasingly inadequate in the face of the profound revolutionary transformation of the times in which the dividing walls of social, political, and economic structures are rapidly being eroded. Only the psychedelics offer the hope that man *can* grow rapidly and fully enough to meet the challenge mounted by his technical accomplishments.

Dr. Blewett is discussing large-scale integration. But here again, we can see the fatal mental process of speciocentrism at work. Psychedelics do *not* offer the only hope. If they did, the hope would be a thin one indeed. As I have been stressing throughout this book, many other forces are at work—ranging from economic to characterological and technical—which similarly offer the hope that we are in the process—a self-regulated process—of overcoming the basically anarchic patterns of behavior that threaten us with annihilation. Considering the institutionalized resistance to it, the drug revolution could not on its own lead to an over-all social readjustment in time to avert disaster. Coupled with all the other examples of large-scale integration, however, the possibility that such a readjustment will be made in time is real—although by no means certain.

The point to be kept in mind is this: *the type of awareness made possible through the use of drugs renders most previous terms of reference irrelevant.* I will return to this factor later. Also, before leaving the topic, it is worth noting that most experts agree that a hundredfold increase in the types of drugs available is expected in the relatively near future. We are about to be engulfed, not only in a purely technological torrent, but in a torrent of drugs—which are, of course, aspects of the larger technological matrix. The resistance to drugs cannot help but collapse. The dam *will* break. The question, as ever, is whether it will crack apart more or less naturally —like an egg hatching a chick—or come apart in the midst of a social storm which causes untold grief, chaos, and disruption.

20

Encounter Groups and Sensitivity Training

Within a relatively short space of time, group psychotherapy was "discovered" by at least twenty different people acting independently of each other. According to Raymond J. Corsini, author of *Methods of Group Psychotherapy,* this was the case simply because there was a "cultural demand" for such a method of treatment. Corsini makes at least a tentative connection between Riesman's concept of the lonely crowd and the development of group-therapy techniques. "There seems to be no question that society in its development has isolated people from one another. Paradoxically, increases of communication and of transportation appear to decrease intimacy of relationships. It may be that group therapy represents a correction against social isolation engendered by technological improvements. In short, a strong need has developed for people to get closer together; it is met to some extent by group psychotherapy."

The above points are accurate, but they fail to make the crucial connections. Specifically, group psychotherapy is *perfectly adapted* to other-directed social character. It fits such social character like a tailored suit—which, in a sense, it is. Further, it encourages autonomy. The interrelationships between drugs and other modern phenomena are, if anything, even more applicable to the rapid growth of group therapy. Twenty-five years ago the concept did not exist. Today more than two hundred different techniques have been developed. At least 1700 articles, theses, and books have appeared on the subject. Group psychotherapy is now used in roughly one half of all mental hospitals in North America and in one quarter of all correctional institutions. Moreover, the group method is being used more and more frequently in schools, outpatient departments of somatic and mental hospitals, in the military, in social agencies, in industry, guidance clinics, prisons, and reformatories, and in institutions for the defective and the handicapped. "Group psychotherapy," as Corsini puts it, "is a significant factor in our cultural pattern. It is here to stay." Furthermore, as he takes care to note, it is a *part* of a yet larger "sociocultural matrix."

"Group psychotherapy," writes Corsini, "represents a procedure for the attainment of the ideal state wherein every individual maintains perfect harmony with others. The various goals sought by people who are involved in group psychotherapy may be summarized by the golden rule, and the particular means may be summarized by the admonitions, 'Love thy neighbor,' 'Know thyself,' and 'Do good works.' Group psychotherapy may be said to be the application of ideal relationships between people. . . ." It is worth noting that the term "group psychotherapy" was itself introduced by J. L. Moreno in 1932. "By it, Moreno meant the method of relocating people in a community by means of individual evaluations and placements into new groups, so that, as a result of the interactions of personalities, social and personal amelioration would occur. Moreover, it is *milieu therapy,* in which the entire community is established as a beneficial organism." Finally, the definition used by Corsini is as follows: "Group psychotherapy consists of processes occurring in formally organized, protected groups and calculated to attain rapid ameliorations in personality and behavior of individual members through specified and controlled group interactions."

Here, quite clearly, we can see the processes of large-scale integration being deliberately and *therapeutically* applied. A further characteristic of group therapy which perfectly matches the larger process is the nature of its development. It "evolves from religion, education, and the social sciences. It is therefore old and at the same time new. It is like a river, fed by old streams and penetrating into new territories." The same, of course, can be said of other-direction, the rise of technostructures, technique itself, electronic media, and so on. "Group psychotherapy"—like all the other parallel developments—"is the product of many minds." Corsini notes that "while people worked and played in groups throughout history, there was not, until recently, an explicit understanding of the importance of group association for the psychological health of the individual. It is not fanciful to say that people who entered various social groups in which they found pleasure were participating in informal group psychotherapy. . . . Natural groups that serve the same purposes as artificial groups are certainly the more desirable; formal groups merely provided a substitute for whatever can be obtained from natural groups. It is when the latter do not exist for an individual that formal, artificial, or contrived groups have a place." He is able to trace group psychotherapy, in its most primitive forms, to the healing temple at Epidaurus, from 600 B.C. to A.D. 200.

Traditionally, psychotherapy has been directed at curing mental illness. Nowadays, particularly since the setting up of the Esalen Institute at Big Sur in 1962, the emphasis is shifting from those who are obviously "sick" to those who are ostensibly "healthy." Today there are some fifty-odd "growth centers"—based, to varying degrees on the Esalen model—in North America. Loosely banded together under the American Association for Humanistic Psychology, these centers represent the most forward thrust of the whole group-therapy movement. And that thrust is aimed not *inward*—at patients already in mental hospitals or jails—but *outward,* directing itself in a snowballing attack against the "culturally patterned defects" that are the supporting props of contemporary industrial society. Like advertising, these growth centers are a frank declaration of war on society as it is presently constituted. The target is nothing less than the pathology of civilized communities which was referred to by Freud in *Civilization and Its Discontents.* As much as electronic media and drugs, the group-therapy movement is concerned with creating a new alignment between the individual and society.

The institutionalized social "virtues" which Erich Fromm has identified as being, in fact, pathological behavior patterns are in the line of fire. The linear patterns which are imposed on individuals by literacy and which have been shown to be root cause of alienation and anarchy are the first things to be assaulted in most

21

Further
Examples

Jacques Ellul makes the point that disintegration is a stage
must be passed through before integration can take place. The examples of disintegration, decay, social decomposition, and the
breakdown of law and order offered in the section dealing with environmental collapse all underline this point. The overwhelming impression of chaos and disorder which seems so characteristic of our
times is real—but it is mainly an overture to the new order. Our
institutions, ideals, values, and concepts of order *are* disintegrating.
But the seeds of a massively integrated social order have already
been planted. Obviously, these seeds cannot take root until the
moldering plants which are now choking the social landscape have
decayed or crumbled into compost. It would be possible to draw
any number of rough historic parallels—the fall of the Roman Empire and the rise of the Holy Roman Empire comprise only one of
the more obvious examples. However, these parallels have already
been noted, particularly by Arnold Toynbee, who makes it clear
that each civilization follows a certain pattern into the grave, and
that this pattern is being followed almost precisely by modern
Western civilization—a term, incidentally, which embraces Russia
as much as it does the United States.

183 *Encounter Groups and Sensitivity Training*

group-therapy situations. The individual is forced to redefine himself in view of his own neuroses or pathologies, which are quickly
dredged up by the group. The experience is frequently shattering.
Social virtues—such as thrift, loyalty, ambition, dedication—all
come under attack. In the language of psychology, these are not virtues so much as symptoms of deep emotional malaise. As such,
they are bombarded. The power of the group—to which the other-
directed person is already incredibly sensitive and before which he
is, by earlier inner-directed standards, pathetically vulnerable. As a result,
be fully unleashed. Few can withstand such a barrage. As a result,
the individual emerges more group-oriented, more "sensitive," and
more aware of subtle interactions, and certainly far more aware of
the dynamics of interrelationships. Among other things—if the
chic both in outlook and, to a lesser degree, in behavior. Group
treatment has had any success at all—he is, as a rule, far less anar-
therapy works cataclysmically when involved a long, painful accre-
niques of individual therapy which involved a long, painful accretion of results, rather than an emotional blitzkreig.

The second great advantage of group therapy follows from this.
It is a simple matter of logistics. Formerly, the supply of qualified
psychotherapists could never begin to match the supply of qualified
neurotics. Individual therapy was such a long process—and so
costly—that it could never have become a method of mass treatment. Its basic techniques could, of course, be exploited by advertisers, but this was never for therapeutic reasons. However, apart
from the ways in which psychology could be exploited for manipulative ends, as a therapeutic tool it was doomed to remain forever
beyond the economic reach of the masses. Group therapy reverses
this proposition. It came into existence, to a considerable extent,
simply *because* the older methods were so limited in scope. "Individual therapists were faced with case loads that were impossibly
large," writes Corsini: "Therefore, having heard about the group
method, they tried it out, sometimes in desperation, with little belief
in it and little understanding of it. Thus, out of necessity, the
method was developed."

Today it is possible to reach a whole classroom, a whole department, a whole ward, within a matter of hours. In short, group therapy offers the opportunity of making a quantum leap in treatment
of whole populations. An entire industry could be given therapy in

I am more concerned with showing the shape of the new order that is emerging. But before turning to that, it is necessary to extend the dimensions of large-scale integration just as the dimensions of environmental collapse were extended in the first half of this book. We have dealt at some length with characterological large-scale integration, which is characterized, in large urban areas, by the emergence of other-directed and autonomous social types, economic large-scale integration (taking the form primarily of technostructures), and technological large-scale integration (which involves, among other things, the rise of autonomous technostructures within governments and their agencies, within the military, educational, and police systems). We have seen how planning—whether economic, social, or military—leads invariably to large-scale integration, how electronic media stimulate further psychic large-scale integration (thus complementing all these other developments and generally speeding up the process), how environmental collapse is now forcing a massive acceleration of the process of applied techniques, and, finally, how psychedelic drugs and group-sensitivity training deepen the dimensions of all these other processes—thus adding a layer of psychic, characterological, psychological, and social large-scale integration to the technological, economic, military, and organizational layers.

The causes of large-scale integration range from the philosophic and religious to the economically expedient. And from the speciocentric viewpoint, certain particular causes appear to be the *only* ones. A good architect, for instance, will view the concept of city-planning as being a development in itself and as having no connection whatever with the ecumenical movement in the church. Similarly, a priest, rabbi, or minister will not see any connection between town-planning and a profoundly religious issue such as ecumenism. Each of the two developments will be viewed, from within, as being a logical reaction to trends that are peculiar to either the needs of the church or the needs of growing urban centers. However, it is precisely *because* each of these situations is dealt with on its own, with little or no over-all awareness of the parallels and interactions with other situations, that I refer to these changes as being self-regulated and spontaneous. Their net effect, built on millions of individual spontaneous reactions and thousands of spontaneous corporate or institutional reactions, betrays a recognizable pattern—the pattern that I have been referring to as large-scale integration.

Oddly enough, it is in the field of geography that this pattern has come closest to being recognized. In the March 1969 issue of *Harper's Magazine,* Peter R. Gould writes that "geographers today are intrigued by the order and regularity they find in the patterns, structures, arrangements, and relationships of man's work on the face of the earth. They want to find out how things hang together in geographic space. . . . Geography today has 'caught the vision of the study of the earth as a total system.' " What has emerged in the last few years is the "central place theory," which holds—and this point has been reinforced by computer studies—that "regularities exist even where patterns have been shaped by a host of individual decisions acting over long reaches of time." Large-scale integration is just such a pattern, and the individual decisions of architects, engineers, churchmen, industrialists, philosophers, generals, and politicians are the disparate parts that make up a cohesive whole. The "geography revolution," in fact, may be offered as a minor example of large-scale integration. Making use of computers and working with others in the fields of remote-sensing and pattern-recognition, geographers are now able to program harvest periods, to understand "perceptual surfaces"—i.e., the mental maps which we carry around in our heads—and, most important, to predict the impact of certain ideas in various areas. They are also able to figure out in advance where surplus and deficit food crops will be in relationship to human population. Thus, human needs and the carrying capacity of the land can now be integrated by computer programming. "Communication fields" can be studied in advance to predict the outcome of the introduction not only of techniques but of ideas as well.

It is possible to submit a long list of technological innovations, all of which amount to forms of large-scale integration. In *The Year 2000* Herman Kahn and Anthony J. Wiener listed one hundred technological breakthroughs which are likely to take place in the remaining years of this century. Of these, at least forty-nine are specific examples of large-scale integration, and all but a few contribute in a secondary manner to other forms of large-scale integration. The innovations range through more reliable and long-range weather forecasting, extensive use of cyborg techniques (mechanical aids or substitutes for human organs, senses, limbs, or other components), automated housekeeping, general use of automation and cybernation in management and production, "new and possibly pervasive techniques for surveillance, monitoring, and control of individuals and organizations," direct electronic stimulation of the brain, increased ability to "change" one's sex, broad-spectrum antibiotics and artificial blood plasma, extensive use of organ-transplant methods, automated universal (real time) credit, audit, and banking systems, inexpensive worldwide home and business communication, use of satellites, lasers, and light pipes, home education via video and programmed learning, new methods of rapid language-teaching, and flexible penology without the use of prisons. Kahn and Wiener also submitted a list of twenty-five less likely possibilities. Of the twenty-five, all but four were examples of large-scale integration. They included "true" artificial intelligence, the artificial growth of new limbs, direct input into human memory banks and electrical connection of the brain with a computer, verification of some extrasensory phenomena, telepathy, some direct control of individual thought processes, and, significantly, "production of a drug equivalent to Huxley's soma."

The integration of various scientific fields could also be expounded at great length. The interdisciplinary trend in the sciences is strong. Buckminster Fuller notes, in *Operating Manual for Spaceship Earth,* that early in the Second World War scientists began to realize that the use of powerful new instruments was breaking down the boundaries between their fields. "Each specialist suddenly realized that he was concerned alike with atoms, molecules, and cells. They found there was no real dividing line between their professional interests. They hadn't meant to do this, but their professional fields were being integrated—inadvertently, on their part, but apparently purposefully—by inexorable evolution."

In the case of geography, we have already seen how this converging of fields is taking place, bringing computer programmers, systems analysts, agriculturalists, behavioral scientists, and geographers into a team relationship. In *The Modeling of Mind* Kenneth M. Sayre and Frederick J. Crosson point out that "there is an increasing overlap between the fields of philosophy of mind and of computer simulation. Lines of communication already have been opened between technologists and social scientists involved in a study of mental behavior and brain functioning." These lines of communication have widened spectacularly in the past few years. In the April 1969 issue of *Psychology Today,* Robert L. Schwitzgebel was able to report:

> Psychologists have now begun to design electromechanical devices that one hopes will produce more predictable changes in human behavior. Although the efforts of these psychologists are not organized, there is little doubt that "behavioral electronics," "behavioral engineering," or "social instrumentation" will increasingly dominate the fields of psychotherapy, education, and social administration. We can define "behavioral engineering" as the application of electromechanical technology to the understanding, maintenance, and modification of human behavior. Such engineering will be, almost by definition, *interdisciplinary* and will utilize specialties as diverse as politics and biochemistry.

A long list of interdisciplinary trends, which are themselves further aspects of large-scale integration, should not be necessary, since they are everywhere obvious. And when seen in context, their meaning becomes clear. The use of computers, for instance, to act as legal counsel, diagnose illness, "match" couples, fight crime, organize election campaigns, plot the best route for a mailman, control traffic, detect the influence of one poet on the works of another, decipher ancient languages, analyze English syntax, and so on, is, in each case, an interdisciplinary affair. Electronic communications devices and computers amount, quite literally, to an electronic semiconducting material, making large-scale integration possible on an ever-expanding basis. Specifically, here are some of the large "blocs" of activity and endeavor in which large-scale integration is taking place:

Cities

Some of the general problems of the cities, stemming almost entirely from their unprecedented rate of growth, have already been pointed out. To the extent that they are virtually rudderless, that the bridge has little control over what goes on in the engine room, that the surrounding waters are filled with deficit-shaped icebergs, and that a storm of social forces is gathering, cities have become urban *Titanic*s. What, then, are the solutions?

John Kenneth Galbraith points out that planning is needed on an unprecedented scale. In effect, only a civic technostructure can cope with the problems of the city. That it will be forced into existence —and to a very considerable degree it is already taking shape in the large cities—is evident, given the whole complex of problems. This means technoplanning. Galbraith points to urban and interurban transportation as one area in which nothing less than "one corporation, that is to say, one planning instrument," is absolutely essential if we are to avoid complete paralysis of the cities. The "planning instrument" would have to cover the cities of an entire region, including the lines between cities. "The local system would then have [to be] developed in relation to the intercity and interregional systems with joint use of right-of-way, terminals, and other facilities. . . . The prospective growth of the entire system would have [to be] projected in a systematic and orderly way together with the investment requirements in the various parts and at various stages. A planning unit of such scope and power would have [to be] largely independent of the local influences and pressures." In other words, the system would have to have an autonomous technostructure.

The same applies, Galbraith notes, in the areas of housing and property development. "The proper instrument for urban and related land acquisition and administration is a strong planning, housing, and development authority. And no less than for the manufacturing of automobiles or the colonization of the moon, prices and opportunity to develop a technostructure are the requisites of effective planning. The remedy also carries a price. Only liberal Republicans on first coming to office imagine that there can be social gain with no cost. Although money is important, as elsewhere in the industrial system, power and organization are even more important. And, as elsewhere, individuals will have to surrender to the goals of organization."

The conservation of natural resources, the development of outdoor recreation, forestry, and agriculture are other areas in which the same imperatives exist. Paul and Percival Goodman make precisely this point. In *Communitas* they write: "Whatever the causes, from the earliest plans of the modern kind, seeking to remedy the evils of nuisance factories and urban congestion, and up to the most recent plans for regional development and physical science fiction, we find always the insistence that reintegration of the physical plant is an essential part of political, cultural, and moral reintegration." To describe this process, Greek architect Constantinos A. Doxiadis has, as stated before, coined the word "ekistics," which he defines as "the total science of human communities."

"Architecture in space," he writes, "plays a great role in minor units and a diminishing one as the units grow large. The development of architecture in the future will regulate the degree of its interrelation and interdependence with other disciplines." Clearly, "ekistics" is Doxiadis's word for large-scale integration. He even refers to the large developing urban centers as "ecumenopolises," and talks about "ecumenic architecture," which is the kind of integrated architecture "where we are able to have the same type of industry everywhere, the same economic conditions, as well as the same type of prefabrication, the same organization of production, and the same type of society." (That such circumstances are rapidly becoming reality will be argued in the following section.)

In *The Hidden Dimension* Edward T. Hall points out the need for controls in the cities. Design features need to be introduced in the cities "that will counteract the ill effects of the sink but not destroy the [ethnic] enclave in the process." Much of the conflict in the cities arises from the aggravated cultural mixing, with results similar to those obtained when members of different rat colonies are mixed together. "To increase density in a rat population," writes Hall, "and maintain healthy specimens, put them in boxes so they can't see each other, clean their cages, and give them enough to eat. You can pile the boxes up as many stories as you wish. Unfortunately, caged animals become stupid, which is a very heavy price to pay for a super filing system! The question we must ask ourselves is, How far can we afford to travel down the road of sensory deprivation in order to file people away? One of man's most critical needs, therefore, is for principles for designing spaces that will maintain a healthy density, a healthy interaction rate, a proper amount of involvement, and a continuing sense of ethnic identification. The creation of such principles will require the combined efforts of many diverse specialists all working closely together on a massive scale. . . . Psychologists, anthropologists, and ethologists are seldom, if ever, prominently featured as permanent members of city planning departments, but they should be. . . . Also, planning and renewal must not be separated; instead renewal must be an integral part of planning."

Hall is arguing strongly for large-scale integration. And in noting that "when good workable plans are developed, planners must not be forced to witness a breakdown of implementation which is often excused on the grounds of politics or expediency," he is also arguing for the establishment of an autonomous technostructure to guarantee the efficiency of the planning instrument. Also, in accurately pinpointing the need for a "continuing sense of ethnic identification," he is telling us, academically, what groups such as the Black Panthers are saying far more emphatically. Quite simply, in order for large-scale integration to be effective, the existing system must be broken down into its component parts. Only then can reintegration take place. Integration does *not* involve the homogenization of all components. Rather, it involves a precise definition of their function in relationship to other parts and *the organization of these relationships,* as opposed to any attempt to mold the separate parts into a single unit. Today militant Negroes are beginning, quite literally, to define themselves as component parts of American society as a whole.

In *The City as a System* John P. Eberhard argues that cities should be "conceived as *total* systems; they should be constructed as organic wholes. . . . Each subsystem [in a city] will need to be integrated with the others, rather than generated at random as in the past." He offers these general guidelines to integration of the city as a whole:

● A well-functioning, publicly owned transportation system, designed as an integral part of such a complex, to encourage a greater degree of participation in common events.

● A community money-credit-exchange system, to be modified if all stores were linked to a computer-based system which recorded purchases against banking accounts.

● The information system of a community could be enhanced by a linkage between the telephone and an information bank containing data on weather, transportation schedules, and schedules of current events.

● Advanced education programs could be designed based on programmed instruction and home consoles.

• Live music—open-air concerts and marching bands—could be woven into the fabric of the movement paths, as could displays of arts and crafts of various kinds.

Eberhard's vision may sound utopian, but it is an accurate assessment of some of the steps that need to be taken if cities are to remain—or once again become—habitable. Each of the suggestions can easily be seen to be a form of large-scale integration. And to a considerable extent, tentative moves in this direction have already taken place.

From this point onward, it would be redundant to cite other writers, thinkers, and planners with regard to the problems of the cities. All agree—using the peculiar images, metaphors, and jargon of their respective fields—on the basic need for large-scale integration. Spontaneously, although fitfully and spastically, steps are being taken in this direction. And they are being taken precisely because there is no other course. It is unrealistic, however, to imagine that the fundamental changes involved—the great shifts in the locus of power and the development of hundreds or thousands of powerful autonomous planning agencies—can be made simply on the basis of reasoned argument. They will come about, but only after the failure of the existing order has become glaringly apparent to everyone, including those whose own power bases are threatened by change. This failure, of course, will not become apparent to those in power and those with vested interests until the cycle of disintegration is more or less complete. The system will have to be shaken down, broken up, dismantled, wrecked. The fire, as suggested earlier, cannot be avoided, except in a liberal flight of fancy. The hard-edged reality is that a painful and costly period of transition must be experienced. What we are witnessing today are merely the first contractions of this great labor.

War

The dropping of the atomic bomb on Hiroshima unleashed far more than it contained. It can be compared to the dropping of a rock into a pail causing a tidal wave. Just one of the ramifications has been the breakdown of the world system of national defense. Of course, it may be argued that this was not so much a direct result of the bombing of Hiroshima. One might choose to regard 1949 as being the key date, since it was in 1949 that the United States lost its monopoly on nuclear weapons. At this point the nuclear stale-mate begins. The dropping of the bomb itself was a match flaring in the dark. Sooner or later, given universal access to the same infor-mation, it was inevitable that other countries would develop their own nuclear weapons. Back in 1939, Germany, Norway, the U.S.S.R., the United States, and France were all on the verge of de-veloping nuclear weapons. "But," as Ellul points out, "circum-stances upset European technical evolution and gave superiority to the United States."

As for the results of the development of the atomic bomb, Ken-neth Boulding states: "A system of national defense is only feasible if each nation is stronger at home than its enemies, so that it can preserve a relatively large area of peace within its critical bound-aries. Such a system is only possible, however, if the range of the deadly missile is short and if the armed forces of each nation lose power rapidly as they move away from home. The technological de-velopments of the twentieth century have destroyed these founda-tions of national defense and have replaced it with another social system altogether, which is 'deterrence.' " This is a profound, quali-tative switch. It may be viewed as a break boundary. "Deterrence," in the words of Maxwell D. Taylor, is designed "to assure that no [nuclear] war will ever be fought. In all probability, this purpose can be achieved provided there is an appropriate balance of de-structive capability between the two power blocs which will make the deliberate choice of general atomic war unthinkable to either."

In *The Atom and the West* George F. Kennan has referred to what he calls "the negative dynamics of the arms race." The nuclear weapon, he says:

> is a sterile and hopeless weapon which may for a time serve as an an-swer of sorts to itself and as an uncertain sort of shield against utter cataclysm, but which cannot in any way serve the purposes of a con-structive and hopeful foreign policy. The true end of political action, after all, is to affect the deeper convictions of men; this the atomic bomb cannot do. The suicidal nature of this weapon renders it un-suitable both as a sanction of diplomacy and as the basis for an alli-ance. Such a weapon is simply not one with which one readily springs to the defense of one's friends. There can be no coherent rela-tions between such weapons and the normal objects of national pol-icy. A defense posture built around a weapon suicidal in its implica-

tions can serve in the long run only to paralyze national policy, to undermine alliances, and to drive everyone deeper and deeper into the hopeless exertions of the weapons race.

This, indeed, has been its effect. Herman Kahn once remarked that the effect of the arms race was only to buy time, "and we are doing nothing with the time that we buy." On the contrary—as the reader should have grasped by now—we are doing quite a bit with the time we are buying, but little of it is deliberate or controlled. Apart from the internal processes already described, the existing international system, based on the deterrent principle, is being broken down into its component parts in precisely the same way that the large cities are being broken down. The balance of terror need only endure for another fifteen years or so for the way to be cleared for large-scale integration. The spontaneous drift in this direction, as will be shown in the next chapter, is well advanced.

In an article in *Harper's Magazine* historian Arthur Schlesinger, Jr., writes that the brief Age of the Superpowers is coming to an end. The concept of deterrence, it must be remembered, was basically a seesaw concept in which two great nuclear opponents were so armed that their more or less equal weight would keep them balanced. A threeway, fourway, or fiveway seesaw would be a very difficult machine to balance, since the additional factors would not only *add* to the probabilities of a breakdown, but would actually *compound* those probabilities.

Schlesinger notes "the contagion of nationalism" which is to be found everywhere, from Quebec to Indonesia, including Scotland and Wales. Accurately, he sees Black Power in the United States as being forced into existence by the same pressures, which are cultural and national only to the extent that they frequently approximate national boundaries. Wherever there is a cultural division within national boundaries, however, the tide of "nationalism" quickly sheds its political skin and emerges as a cultural phenomenon. I will argue later that this is a part of the larger critical phenomenon of our time—the process of self-definition—which is a prerequisite to large-scale integration and convergence. Schlesinger notes that this process is taking place in Czechoslovakia, Yugoslavia, Poland, Germany, France, Canada, Cuba, Africa, Asia, and South America. He does not appear to understand the roots of the phenomenon and is content to attribute it to new "spirit and audacity" and the urge for national autonomy.

This drive for autonomy can, in part, be seen as an inevitable response to the complex conditions of modern national existence— the same conditions which flushed the technostructure into existence in industry and is forcing it into existence elsewhere. On an altered scale—necessarily more flexible and necessarily less specific—the same process is going on within nations. No individual or even a group of individuals can cope with all of the exigencies of modern international relations, and to that degree an autonomous national technostructure is required. This factor can be examined at length on its own, but cannot be understood in isolation from the related phenomenon of "definition," which is also a response to complexity. Schlesinger misses all this, but nevertheless manages to identify "nationalism" as a crucial factor in the breakdown of the deterrent system and the end of the period of global dominance by the two superpowers, Russia and the United States. "Nationalism means, first of all, the determination to assert national identity, national dignity, and national freedom of action. It can also mean, as the memory of prewar Germany, Italy, and Japan remind us, the determination to assert these things at the expense of other nations; and in this sense, nationalism has been and will be a source of tremendous danger to the world. But the nationalism which arose after the Second World War was, in the main, not the aggressive and hysterical nationalism which led nations before the war to try to dominate other nations. It was rather the nationalism generated by the desire to create or restore a sense of nationhood."

Schlesinger is the first writer I have found who has taken the important step of recognizing the qualitative difference between modern versions of nationalism and the nationalism of earlier periods —even though the two play on the same basic emotions. Today, since it is based primarily on a drive for necessary autonomy, nationalism has a strong antianarchic undercurrent, even though in its extreme convulsive manifestations it can frequently slip into its older, more decidedly anarchic patterns. The drive, after all, is for internal unity, as Schlesinger points out, and for reintegration. The identities of the component parts are being defined, as they need to be, before integration on a larger scale can proceed.

Religion

The ecumenical movement need not be gone into at great length here. What needs to be stressed is that the movement cannot be isolated from the other developments which we have discussed so far.

Further, the ecumenical movement and the crumbling of church authority—particularly in the Catholic Church—offers us an opportunity to look at the role of authoritarianism in the process of large-scale integration.

Pope Paul VI was right when he said early in 1969 that "the Church suffers above all from the restless, critical, unruly, and demolishing rebellion of so many of its children—priests, the teachers, laymen, those devoted to the service and the testimony of Christ in the living Church—against its intimate and indispensable communion, against its institutional existence, against its canon rule, its tradition, its interior cohesion, against its authority, the unchangeable principle of truth, unity, and charity, against its very requirements of sanctity and sacrifice." The Catholic Church, he acknowledged, is being crucified.

Earlier on, I referred to the survey published by the *Journal of Marriage and Family* which showed that, despite the Church's unrelenting stand against birth control devices, by 1965, 53 per cent of Catholic women in the United States were using such devices. This was a *measurement*—not a "guesstimate"—of the degree to which the Church's authority had decayed.

McLuhan has observed that the "pattern" which applies to drug use and the use of computers applies equally well to the Church. In fact, "much greater efforts have been made, both in ecumenicism and liturgical reform, to accommodate the new impulse to involvement on the part of both priesthood and laity; but as in any of the other operations of the Western world, the patterns of parish and ecclesiastical organization are riddled with the old mechanical forms of specialism and delegation of responsibility and authority." McLuhan, it may be noted, recognizes here the existence of a pattern, but does not seem able to pin it down. The "pattern" is the process of large-scale integration in which individual components become highly defined and more unique than ever. The old authoritarian pattern—which has all but crumbled in the industrial and political spheres—has proved to be too fossilized to allow for adjustments within the Catholic Church. Not surprisingly, the defection rate is mounting, the Church is having more and more difficulty recruiting new priests, members ignore edicts from Rome, and nuns shed their habits and go out into the world to "get involved" in social issues, education, even politics. The Pope, for his part, grows ever more strident in his pleas for devotion and loyalty. One mass-circulation magazine recently posed the question: Will Pope Paul VI be the last pope? The pressures of environmental collapse, swirling in the vortex created by population growth, moves irresistibly against one of the central doctrines of the Church. These pressures cannot be resisted indefinitely, and any institution which decides that it would "rather fight than switch" is doomed to be swept into the ash can.

Authoritarian structures are pyramidal. They impose patterns and they are built on a base of homogeneity. In the case of the Catholic Church, for instance, it is imperative that all members share the same attitudes, beliefs, feelings, and reactions. The Church is totalitarian. Authority cannot be challenged and believers must respond like well-drilled soldiers. "The essence of totalitarianism," as Norman Mailer has remarked, "is that it beheads." Soldiers have their orders to follow, and believers have canons, traditions, and unchangeable principles. The image of the herd or flock is deeply bedded in such a structure. And this, as we have seen, is the very opposite of the whole drift of large-scale integration. The Church encourages sexual anarchy and is itself (as clearly indicated by its missionary zeal and the doctrine that *its* members alone will find salvation) an example of organized or institutional anarchy. Its "me first" compulsion is very strong, at least as strong as its self-survival instinct—which, we have seen, is the primary characteristic of anarchic organizations.

There may seem to be a contradiction here. On the one hand, I have been arguing that we are heading into a highly organized "control" situation where traditional freedoms will be severely diminished. On the other hand, I am also saying that authoritarian structures such as the Catholic Church are crumbling. This reflects, not a contradiction, but a *difference* in types of organization. L. J. Evenden has put it succinctly in an article in the charter issue of *Focos*. According to Evenden, a distinction must be sharply drawn between *order* and *organization*. "Medieval political philosophy was dominated by the ideal of unity. The implications of such an 'ideal of unity' are many. Believing that all Christian men comprised one great society dedicated to external purpose in life, medieval men were parts of a social organism in which each part in principle had internal autonomy. Such a system is conceivable where there is over-all allegiance and agreement as to eternal purpose. The difficulty . . . with complete agreement on ultimate purpose is that it becomes, on the one hand, allegiance to absolutism and, on the other, a blindness to alternative possibilities. Either way, choice is eliminated; but the merits are obvious: community and order are enhanced."

Harvey Cox notes, in *The Secular City,* that pluralism asserts itself "where once a closed system stood." Within society, Evenden adds, "the mere fact of town development carries the seeds of destruction for the order of life in unity: massive city development continues to carry and disperse such seeds. In the city, total community necessarily breaks down and there is a reduced acceptance of a teleological order of things." Cox describes urbanization and secularization as being twin processes. He sees them as being potentially enriching, rather than as leading everyone into the abyss.

Evenden also states:

> In the secular epoch man's groupings may be traced from the tribal to the town to the "technopolitan." The "ideals of town life" are that the town should be "fully open or fully universal," or a place of *freedom.* But how does this square with the idea of over-all order and community which necessarily constrain individual avarice, activity, and thought? The distinction is between *order* and *organization.* *Order* is total; it encompasses virtually all social life and is rooted in traditional commitment. *Organization* is partial; it affects individual life in segmented fashion and is characteristically secular, future-oriented, and flexible. Only limited and strictly defined claims are made upon its members' lives. . . . Now that life may be *organized* in various ways (instead of being *ordered* in prescribed ways), the scope for the individual is greater than ever before. *Organization,* though far from perfect, demands far less commitment than does *order;* but it offers far greater individual freedom.

Large-scale integration involves the *organization* of unique components and interconnections. It does not involve *order,* which demands an authoritarian superstructure. Order, based on the concept of unity and absolutism, requires uniformity and unswerving allegiance. Organization, on the other hand, based as it is on diversity and relativism, requires differences and flexibility. Order implies, at best, voluntary slavery.

At a time when order is everywhere being superseded by organization, the Catholic Church continues its attempt to impose order. Ecumenism, on the other hand, at least recognizes the relativity of different viewpoints. It acknowledges the possibility that other viewpoints are also valid. Furthermore, it underlines the basic similarities of the various religions, rather than stressing the superficial differences of interpretation, rite, and so forth. When the members of one church sit down in another church in order to participate in an exchange program, they are learning about relativism.

The impact of science and technology has also affected the traditional Western churches in much the same way. The impact of increasingly pervasive media forces older, less pervasive media to define themselves more precisely. Literature, art, theater, and radio have all reacted in this way to the impact of television. Similarly, churches are forced into a more precise self-definition. This definition forces them to stress their *essence*—rather than their rituals and window dressing. And as each religion is backed further into a corner by technology and science, it finds itself becoming "truer," in the sense that it has to deal more and more with the reasons for its existence. At this point, the superficial differences between religions become less and less important. As each religion defines itself, it necessarily arrives at the same definition—since all religions, after all, *are* similar at bottom.

The question that the churches attempt to answer is, therefore, the same question in every case. Their answers do not vary widely, except in details. And it is the details that are losing their meaning —which is exactly what the process of self-definition is all about. In their search for a true identity, the churches reflect the problem of modern man: If I seriously ask, "Who am I?" it is not enough to say merely that I am Canadian or American or Bantu; that I am white, orange, black, or green; that I am happy or sad. These are nothing more than descriptions of my exterior. The churches, like the rest of us, are being forced to go to the heart of the matter. And at the heart—like persons taking part in group therapy—they discover basic similarities, not differences.

The New Morality

Those who talk about the "collapse of morality" are referring, in fact, to the collapse of *authoritarian* morality. They are not aware that "collapse" is simply another word for change, and they are evidently blind to the basically anarchic nature of any authoritarian morality. Within its confines—which is to say, applied to its own members—authoritarian morality is antianarchic. Beyond those boundaries, however, it seeks to impose or rule or, failing this, to dismiss others. It is, by nature, exclusive and exploitative. The devout today tend to dismiss the horrors of the Inquisition, the Crusades, the slave trade, and the exploitation of Asians, Africans, Chinese, and North and South Americans by Christianity as, at worst, an aberration. They do not see that Western churches—with their authoritarian morality—are *perfect examples of organized anarchy.* It is possible to compile a long list of the atrocities that have been committed in the name of the church. The church, moreover, has seldom failed to endorse a war which was being conducted by its national "host."

Authoritarian morality today is collapsing, and this is a hopeful development. The so-called New Morality is, in fact, a humanistic—as opposed to authoritarian—morality. Dr. Renatus Hartogs writes: "Outwardly imposed, restrictive mores are waning. One may hope that an essentially self-imposed morality will take their place. . . . Formerly, patients came to me because they failed in adjusting to prevailing codes. Now they come because they fail in creating new codes. Theirs, I feel, is the nobler failure. And, surely, theirs is the more hopeful attempt."

It is not only a "more hopeful attempt," it is an integral part of the over-all process of large-scale integration. A humanistic morality is basically existential and, as such, it places responsibility squarely in the lap of the individual. In an earlier period this would have meant nothing but individual anarchy. Today, within the context of all the other pressures which are acting to force an awareness of interrelations, involvement, mutual interdependence, the need for approval, the necessity—economic as well as technological—for cooperative effort, teamwork, and a sharing in the complex decision-making process, the *opportunities* for anarchic individual behavior are already restrained by social and other pressures in ways that they have never been restrained before. Moreover, the awareness which is made possible—and necessary—by these other developments accentuates the need, as McLuhan points out, for a *role,* as opposed to marching orders or memos from the head office. This awareness is an awareness of one's role in relation to the roles of others. And this is precisely what a sense of responsibility is all about.

The "new" humanistic morality contains nothing that is truly new. A hippie poster accurately portrays Christ, if he lived today, as being an outlaw and rebel. Hippies, flower children, "love children" have accurately been called the "new Christians." Without doubt, many of the negative characteristics of other-direction— imitation of fashion setters, subservience to the peer group, and so on—are at work in the creation of the hippie subculture. But the movement is still strongly in the direction of autonomy. The New Morality, moreover, has not become the exclusive possession of the hippie subculture. Rebellious priests, nuns, clergy, and so on, all follow the same pattern of behavior. They are taking their beliefs —the *essence* of their beliefs—seriously. Each individual is motivated by his own sense of awareness, his own sense of responsibility, and his own sense of morality.

The assumption that without authoritarianism morality is not possible is based on the same ignorance of human nature as the political definition of anarchy. It is assumed—falsely—that human beings are vicious animals, each bent on his own self-gratification. Without some morality imposed from above, man automatically reverts to barbarism. This, however, is not the case. The need for order—not only in the human, but in the animal world as a whole —is now clearly recognized. Authoritarian morality merely approximates natural morality. Church rules merely imitate quite obvious and easily understood rules of human behavior. If these "natural rules" did not exist, the church could not exist—it would have no basis in reality. As it is, the main function of religion is to articulate the laws that control human relationships. Religions endure simply because they are on the right track. When we are told not to covet our neighbor's wife, we are being told an obvious social truth. It will make future relations between yourself and your neighbor awkward, to say the least. Most religious edicts are, in fact, rules of *social* behavior. They apply specifically to the organization of communal life, setting down guidelines of behavior. Once secularized, most of these canons and commandments hold up on their own, since they are simply social truisms. In short, stripped of their metaphysical rationalizations, most authoritarian moralities merely reflect sensible human behavior.

As indicated earlier, most anarchic, aggressive, and destructive behavior stems not from inherent aggression, but from the adverse effects of civilization. Unfortunately, it is a widespread belief that the psychotic and the criminal psychopath—not to mention the neurotic and the emotionally disturbed—are in some way responsible for their own illness. What we must bear in mind, however, is that acts of hostility, crimes of aggression, and so forth are plainly symptomatic of the deleterious effects of an unnatural and therefore unhealthy environment. In tribal villages thievery is almost unheard of. The locked door is a product of civilization, along with the burglar alarm, the squad car, and the prison cell. Under genuine tribal conditions there is no need for these artificial restrictions.

The New Morality reflects the emerging phase of retribalization, autonomy, and integration. It is based on the *natural* social character of human beings, as opposed to their *unnatural,* collective, anarchic impulses. Authoritarian morality, which began as an attempt to *reinforce* natural-behavior patterns, ended up *replacing* them with a bastard form. It is a crude model of the real thing. The "real thing," of course, was not possible in a fragmented, alienated, mechanical, and linear culture. Today police are more and more frequently called in to quell riots and disturbances involving people who profess to have adopted the New Morality. This is held up as proof that the New Morality is a sham. In fact, it proves nothing— except the degree to which such a natural morality is in conflict with the existing authoritarian forms.

On the basis of what the New Morality represents, it is now possible to redefine "obscenity." The increased use of obscenity in art, literature, and theater is not only a process of self-definition forced by the emergence of mass media. It is also an indication of the relatively abrupt shift away from authoritarian modes of morality to more humanistic ones. In terms of the New Morality, obscenity has been moving steadily upward from the area below the belt to the area above the collar. Those people who are most representative of the emerging social type of the future—students, for instance—

object to having their minds abused in the same way that their sexually repressed parents objected to having their bodies abused. It is not obscene to *fuck;* it is obscene to *mind*-fuck. What this represents is the coming into focus of a humanistic value system that is psychologically oriented. It is also a barometric reminder of the degree to which the economy has come to be dependent on psychological manipulation—as opposed to *physical* manipulation.

In *Four-Letter Word Games, The Psychology of Obscenity,* Dr. Hartogs writes:

> Rather than deplore the proliferation of four-letter words in casual usage, I regard it as a rising index of spiritual freedom. . . . The emergence of a new morality is, of course, a long and complex process which does not affect every social stratum to the same degree. Yet among my patients—especially those from the more enlightened segments of the middle class—I have noted encouraging signs of a change in our psychocultural climate. Where many of my patients in earlier years suffered essentially from guilt syndromes arising from their inability to come to terms with the proscriptions and taboos of the surrounding society, a significant percentage of my present patients is relatively free from such a sense of social oppression. Nowadays, their difficulties stem at least in part from an inability to formulate independent individual codes of conduct and values to establish a suitable self-concept.

He attributes the widespread usage of obscenity to "the growing pains of a culture that after some five thousand years of institutionalized sexual repression has finally reached a stage of awareness. With luck and a modicum of intelligence, we may outgrow this ambivalence of our sexual values in about one more generation."

Authoritarian morality is not integral. It is imposed, and demands obedience—not involvement. It is absolute, exclusive, and totalitarian. Conversely, the new existential, humanistic morality assists the process of large-scale integration by being relativistic, other-directed, inclusive, involving, and anti-totalitarian.

Existentialism

Fundamental to existentialist philosophy is the concept of responsibility. Existentialism's leading advocate, Jean-Paul Sartre, argues that the limitations of our lives are no excuse for failing to behave like men. Life is action, not apologetics. Man is a creature with no excuses. Existentialism, in Norman Mailer's view, "begins with the . . . notion that we live out our lives wandering among mysteries, and can guide ourselves only by what our inner voice tells us is true about the relations between the mysteries. The separate mysteries we may never seize, but to appropriate a meaning from their relationships is possible." Or, as another writer puts it, fundamental to the existential view of man is the idea "that the world as it appears to me is my creation, and for it I must assume responsibility."

Existentialism is an abyss. Most discussion about it tends to end in sterile abstraction. However, its essence is emerging as the line which separates the global village from the universal concentration camp. In an article which first appeared in the periodical *Explorations,* Peter Kosentenbaum made the following observation:

> The frontiers of knowledge in philosophy, psychiatry, and theology converge on one and the same image of man. Existential philosophy, associated with Kierkegaard, Nietzsche, Sartre, Heidegger, and Jaspers, agrees with the insights of depth psychology, such as those of Freud and C. G. Jung, and further leads to the kind of demythologized theology that has found acceptance with Buber, and is at the heart of the contemporary intellectual revival and revitalization of religion. . . . Existential philosophy has reconciled the insights of mankind's religious consciousness with the most advanced views in the philosophy of science and with the entire tradition of philosophic skepticism characteristic of the last three hundred years. It has become possible to teach the meaning of religion without violating the commitments of conscience of any man—theist, deist, atheist, or agnostic; Catholic, Protestant, Jew, or Buddhist. The religious meanings of God, soul, immortality, sin, guilt, salvation, etc., have been given an existential reinterpretation.

How is this miracle achieved? According to the existential view, "the nature of man, the meaning of human existence, the provenance and destiny of man, the essence and definition of man, all these are not found or discovered. They are *invented.*" We create meaning for ourselves. We organize the world around us by means of the choices we make. We *choose* to accept or not to accept a religion, tradition, or a culture. We *choose* whether to rebel or to accept what our environment has to offer. We *choose* whether to be depressed or to be spontaneously angry. And whether we like it or not, in each case we are responsible—completely responsible—for what we do, and therefore for what we are.

We see the existential philosophy emerging today on numerous fronts. Techniques of group therapy are based squarely on the existential position. A large number of modern counselors and therapists are, consciously or unconsciously, adopting similar positions. A patient or delinquent or criminal or whatever says: "I come from a broken home." To which the therapist replies: "Interesting. But what are you going to do *now?*" Many group-therapy encounters begin with a strict admonition from the therapist: "No archaeology." In other words: "Don't bore us with the squalid details of your background and childhood. We are only interested in what you intend to do with yourself right now, at this moment." Excuses are neither tolerated nor listened to. Existentialism is filtering into educational circles as well, as teachers come increasingly to feel involved with their students. McLuhan has noted that existentialism is perfectly in tune with the new electronic environment. "Existentialism," he writes, "offers a philosophy of structures, rather than categories, and of total social involvement instead of the bourgeois spirit of individual separateness or points of view."

Existentialism, in short, articulates the realities of a world in which large-scale integration is coming to be the dominant reality. The processes of self-definition mentioned earlier require a philosophic framework, and existentialism offers just that framework. Each individual unit is unique and highly discriminatory. The New Morality, of course, embodies the existential philosophy. Passivism —today rapidly emerging as a mass movement—is existential. Draft dodging, when it is done as a matter of conscience, is an existential act. The expression, "Do your own thing," is an existential statement, pure recognition of the fact that each individual creates his own meaning. The current popularity of "dialogue" is also based on this existential insight. The rise of a humanistic morality, even a humanistic psychology, is not an isolated phenomenon. Erich Fromm notes, in *The Revolution of Hope,* that "developments during the last ten, and especially the last five, years all over Europe and in America have shown a very strong trend toward the deeper values of the humanistic tradition. This new quest for a meaningful life did not arise only among small and isolated groups, but became a whole movement in countries of entirely different social and political structures, as well as within the Catholic and Protestant churches. What is common to the believers and the nonbelievers in this new movement is the conviction that concepts are only secondary to deeds and human attitudes."

Existentialism, seen as a dimension of the same development which leads to humanistic morality and humanistic psychology, is clearly a powerful force working against regimentation and homogenization. The other-directed social type described by David Riesman would not seem to be very existential—but Riesman foresaw, back in the early 1950s, the distinct possibility of an autonomous social type evolving organically out of other-direction. This evolution has proceeded more rapidly than Riesman had any reason to expect in 1950. Other-directed attitudes work like acid to break down attitudes and types of awareness which are far removed from the existential position. In this respect other-direction helps to create a social climate in which existentialism can take root. The first stage of involvement is *awareness* of others and awareness of one's self in relation to others. This is the takeoff point for the development of autonomy and the beginning of an existential attitude. The other-directed are quicker to pick up on existentialism than the inner-directed, who are "preprogrammed" and consequently less flexible.

The collapse of authoritarianism, the rise of technostructures, the multiplication of peer groups and veto groups, the crumbling of the corporate and political power pyramids—together these create an atmosphere in which the individual is forced to come out from behind the shield of institutionalized irresponsibility. He is forced to react, to participate, to be involved. These moves lead progressively in the direction of *responsibility*. Having been driven, step by step, in this direction, the individual is then in a position—consciously or unconsciously—to adopt spontaneously very existential attitudes.

Existentialism is therefore not a *cause* of social change. Rather, it is a very accurate reflection of the fact that all of the other processes which we have been discussing are acting in combination. The rapidly spreading influence of the philosophy indicates the degree to which large-scale integration has already taken place. Existentialism clearly works against organized anarchy.

Student Revolt

In dealing with the phenomenon of student unrest, we immediately see that the kind of interrelatedness which characterized the entire discussion of environmental collapse is also at work here. Each aspect of environmental collapse, we saw, was a part of the others. Working together, they had a synergistic effect which we referred to as "environmental collapse." Student revolt, to be understood, must be approached in the same light. It reflects the other pressures and disequilibriums that we have been discussing. It is *not* an independent phenomenon. Rather, it is a part of a larger phenomenon, one which we have been referring to as "large-scale integration."

Clearly, student rebels are at least other-directed, and frequently autonomous—as opposed to inner-directed, like those who, for the most part, run the universities. At this one level we see characterological conflict—which, as David Riesman points out, is one of "the great levers of change in society." Moreover, we see that the creation of an autonomous technostructure is being resisted by those in power, in the same way that the great entrepreneurs of a generation ago resisted the creation of technostructures in industry. Student demands for participation in the group decision-making apparatus constitute, in essence, demands for a large, more pervasive, and therefore more effective academic technostructure. A technostructure, in order to function effectively, must dissolve the old pyramidal organization chart and replace it with an integrated network of groups, each of which has its say in the decision-making process, and each of which contributes a unique and highly defined function. Students, as much as administrators and teachers, need to be brought into the technostructure in order to make it work. The ancient power structure which has collapsed—in terms of real functions—in industry has not yet collapsed on the campus.

A break-boundary has been passed in higher education. Universities have become multiversities. As Howard Adelman and Dennis Lee put it in *The University Game:* "There are so many faculties, divisions, schools, institutes, centers, departments, and councils which conflict in their claims for money and space, their notions of what education is all about, and the directions in which they want to propel the institution, that it is all but impossible to identify with the multiversity as a whole." It is "a juggernaut which may be out of control, but which at least is out of control in a spectacular and irresistible way." It is, in the words of Howard Adelman, "a fragmented agglomeration of elements held together by the homogenizing fist of technology."

These descriptions of the modern multiversity—and any number of other descriptions—could be applied as easily to cities as to multiversities. Universities, in fact, are tiny, brightly lit stages on which the larger conflicts and tensions in society are being acted out in miniature. And since the problems are basically the same, the solutions inevitably will follow the same pattern. The case made earlier for organization of the cities applies as well to universities. Also, as suggested, an autonomous technostructure will be flushed into existence. The crucial difference in higher education is that, unlike managers and industrial executives, the inhabitants of the academic corridors of power do not have sales charts to prod them, like electric rods, in the direction of maximum proficiency. The loss of talent and energy sustained by the community as the dropout rate increases is not as easily measured as is an abrupt drop in sales. University managers, unlike managers in industry or in the military, are not held accountable for such losses—even though their own failure to adjust their system to meet the new requirements is largely to blame for high dropout rates and continued overspecialization.

In short, universities refuse as yet to make the adjustment which has been made so successfully in industry. Medieval power structures are maintained. New members are not welcomed into the structure, and so no technostructure—which would embrace the whole of the academic organization, students included—is allowed to take shape. The process of fragmentation continues with little or no corresponding movement in the direction of integration. As a result, students are forced to lead the drive themselves. Few, of course, perceive that they are seeking the same kind of organizational structure as industry—their motivations could not be more different. Yet their objectives remain basically the same. They want integration, coordination, cooperation, and so on. They want to be involved in the decision-making apparatus, so that their views and needs will be taken into consideration in the over-all operational calculations. Further, the most radical among them want to integrate the university with the community at large.

It is worth noting that drugs are an important factor in student revolt. Without doubt, most student activists have had drug experiences and their *awareness* has been correspondingly altered. They are sensitive to interrelationships, oriented to seeing things in context, accustomed to perceiving patterns, to seeing the forest rather than the trees, and so on. It should be added that a far larger proportion of students other than those identified as activists have had drug experiences, and so, evidently, have a great number of teachers. Few administrators, on the other hand, give any indication of having had such experiences, and so they are quite out of tune with the type of interrelationship-responsive awareness engendered by the use of psychedelic drugs. Moreover, they are afraid of drugs and certainly afraid of the kind of awareness that drugs produce, all of which serves only to deepen the chasm between themselves and the students. The type of awareness germinated by psychedelic drugs makes earlier frames of reference meaningless. And it is precisely those frames of reference which administrators, almost universally, hold to be sacred.

The techniques of group therapy can also be seen to be working themselves out in university conflict. Based, as they are, on the idea of confrontation, they find a solid parallel on the campuses. Rebellious students are frequently criticized for not having specific goals and programs. As a rule, it turns out that they do. But much unrest stems simply from a belief—supported by the latest developments in psychotherapy—that confrontation is, in itself, a good thing. The kind of confrontation that takes place in group therapy forces the individual to define himself, to sort out his position in relationship to others, to sift the platitudes and rationalizations from the genuine beliefs. It involves feedback, which is a picture of himself as seen by others. In short, it is an educational process that operates on an emotional as well as an intellectual level. Students, of course, have picked up this technique. And the goals of many in their confrontations with administrations are simply to experience this kind of shaking-down and self-defining. The objective is an acquired knowledge of their own real positions as well as those of the administrators—as opposed to their *assumed* positions. Few administrators are willing, however, to take part in this process of mutual education. In many cases, this reluctance stems from their own uncertainty about their positions and goals. They have a vested interest in their own accomplishments, and few are willing to risk learning that their values and conceptions have become irrelevant in the new social context.

Finally, most rebellious students can be characterized as being responsive to the New Morality and all that this entails. Everything said earlier about the New Morality applies specifically to student rebels. There are exceptions, of course. But as a general characteristic, the description stands. And as should now be evident, they are, for the most part, existentialists. They take responsibility for themselves. To argue that they are "irresponsible," as the mass media usually does, is to ignore their *motivation,* which often stems from a profound sense of responsibility. They are not able to retreat behind an ideological shield in order to protect themselves from the consequences of their "collaboration" with the various forms of organized anarchy. Student demonstrations against the war in Vietnam, against firms that provide weapons for the war, and against politicians and parties that are associated with the war, support of peace candidates, and so on, stem not from a sense of irresponsibility, but from a deep existential sense of responsibility. The point need not be elaborated upon, since only those who are completely committed to various anarchic institutions can fail to see this.

It is worth noting that student groups have also been active in protesting pollution, sponsoring birth control programs, and objecting to the use of pesticides. They are also concerned with breaking down the economic, racial, and class barriers which bar others from entry to universities, with forcing universities to involve themselves in politics, social issues, and so on. In almost all student activism we see a clear antianarchic thrust—which is not surprising in view of the fact that such activism is a synergistic effect, the result of a large number of factors working in combination.

However, all of this is not to say that some students do not manage to act irrationally and destructively. Their response is extreme because the situation in which they find themselves—and in which we all find ourselves—is extreme. As a result, they often spend time and energy tilting at windmills or attacking the wrong enemy. A perfect example was the destruction, in early 1969, of the computer center at Sir George Williams University in Montreal by rebellious students. A more misdirected attack could not be imagined. Although few seem yet to have realized it, the computer is a rebellious student's best friend.

Computers

The role of computers has been referred to several times, but the degree to which they are assisting and stimulating the process of large-scale integration needs to be underlined. Before proceeding, however, we must add a few words concerning the metaphor around which this book is wrapped.

Large-scale integration, as stated, offers us a metaphorical frame of reference. More than that, as the reader will have gathered by now, the term also refers to a pattern. The choice of this particular development in computer technology to illustrate a larger pattern may be compared to the breaking-off of a piece of ice from an iceberg. The single piece will tell us much about the properties of the iceberg itself. It will also tell us much about its basic structure. It will tell us nothing, however, about its dimensions. To gain some sort of perspective on those dimensions, we will need to view the iceberg from different vantage points. This is precisely what this book has attempted to do.

By now, the dimensions of the iceberg will be apparent. The metaphorical value of large-scale integration will be clear. The meaning of self-regulation should also be clear. The process is obviously not controlled or guided. It is spontaneous, a kind of slow-motion spontaneous combustion involving the accretion of millions of detailed developments. Also, the pattern revealed by the rapid evolution of large-scale integration as a technique of computerization will have been seen to have broad, universal application. This should not be surprising, since, like the chunk of ice removed from the iceberg, it is an integral part of the larger picture.

Computers, so far viewed mainly as complex tools, will shortly become weapons. Environmental collapse is taking shape as the main enemy of mankind. As its dimensions deepen, the intertribal rivalries and ideological squabbles which occupy us at the moment are bound to diminish. Never before in history has the phrase, "United we stand, divided we fall," had so much meaning. Computers are unifiers. They pull us together in ways which have only begun to be tapped. In the section on environmental collapse, I stressed the interrelated nature of the problems confronting us. Hopefully, the point was made clear that no aspect of environmental collapse could be successfully tackled in isolation. The controls required to cope with environmental collapse will have to be pervasive and complex beyond anything yet attempted. Ultimately, these controls will have to approximate the near-infinite complexity of the natural ecological system—a system so intricate and sensitive that we have not yet come close to mapping its contours, let alone beginning to imitate it. In short, a "systems approach"—which is to say, a simultaneous, coordinated assault on all fronts—is the only effective strategy. And until the advent of computers, such a strategy would have been impossible. Today it is not only likely, it is inevitable.

Computers have not yet been brought to bear on the problems of environmental collapse, except for a few reconnaissance operations. To date, computers have been used largely to further the power of anarchic institutions. At the same time, however, they are distributing the seeds of interdisciplinary integration, decompartmentalizing sciences, expanding the awareness of industries, opening up government agencies to a steady flow of feedback, integrating subsystems (formerly thought of as systems in themselves), and pulling the whole world together in a communications network. When McLuhan refers to computers as the LSD of the business world, he is saying that they are, literally, mind-expanding. Computers increase the corporate consciousness of interrelationships as surely as psychedelic drugs increase individual consciousness. They bring more and more data into the ambit of any firm that makes use of them. Larger and larger patterns are detected. As knowledge accumulates, it tends to reveal trends, patterns, and larger and more complex realities. There is no ceiling on the accumulation of data, and each new fact makes the pile that much higher, thus giving the individual or corporation in command of such information a better vantage point from which to operate. In an informative little book called *Computers,* Stanley L. Englebardt refers to "the ability of the computer to cross departmental lines and interrelate results so that decisions are made for the benefit of the entire company—not just one department." The same may be said not only of companies but also of states and countries—and, finally, of the world. As the use of computers expands and the systems embraced by computers come increasingly to overlap, the point will quickly be reached where the globe itself is seen electronically as a system—which is precisely what it is.

Space flight would be impossible without computers. Existing defense systems would be impossible. Many avenues of research that were blocked because of the physical impossibility of making the necessary calculations are now wide open. Even back in 1950 the Los Alamos atomic energy laboratory was able to program a computer to do a massive mathematical calculation which called for nine million arithmetic solutions. The job was done in 150 hours. It would have taken a mathematician 1500 years to do it. And by present standards, the Selective Sequence Electronic Calculator used in that instance was a primitive device.

Clearly, a tremendous power is housed in computers. Already, every man, woman, and child in the United States is represented in the memory of one or more electronic computers as either a name, number, or statistic. Almost every transaction in the United States winds up, sooner or later, within the circuitry of electronic equipment. An estimated one billion "Your account is overdue" notices are written by data-processing machines every few months. All states use data-processing machines every few months. All states use data-processing systems. Major cities have two or three computers on hand, plus hundreds of punched-card machines. The Central Intelligence Agency has a computerized information retrieval system containing some one hundred million pages of material and three million index items.

It is possible to compile a long list of statistical evidence that would show the extent to which, in less than twenty years, computers have become essential to the organization of modern society. In all cases, the clear trend is to expand all systems into larger and larger overlapping units. Not only does data accumulate, but it transforms earlier fragmented pictures into *larger* integrated pictures. And through simulation, thousands of possibilities may be checked out in advance before any step—industrial, governmental, or whatever—is taken. Wars are fought on computer to forecast the outcome, drugs are tested, and so on. The margin of error is reduced by a fantastic percentage.

As observed earlier, computers are used mainly by industry and government. Increasingly, they are being used in research, medicine,

education, and so on. Shortly, they will be used to control environments, to tame them. They will be able to tell us, for instance, exactly when we can expect to run out of air. This discovery will be
one of the headlines of the future. But as McLuhan points out,
"computers are being asked to do things that belong to the old technology. The real job of the computer is *not* retrieval but discovery."
As every writer on computer agrees, computers are not yet being
properly applied. They are being used, for the most part, to extend
the power of exploiters and militarists, and only incidentally to *discover* anything.

In Russia the use of computers has leaped ahead in the last few
years, to the point where the Russians are very close to "government by computers." In Moscow, Leningrad, Kiev, Yerevan, and
Riga, state-operated computer training centers are turning out programmers by the thousands. Russia has already divided her land
into economic sectors, each of which has several computer centers
overseeing production, manpower requirements, and so on. A central installation in Moscow coordinates the flow of data from these
various sectors. The Russians, in short, have gone a long way toward programming and orchestrating their environment. Which
possibly accounts for the fact that in recent years they have moved
decisively against some aspects of pollution. They have already
begun the battle against environmental collapse.

According to Richard Kostelanetz in *Beyond Left & Right,*
"even by now, institutional policy-makers could have access to
computers whose simulation capacities, allied with software techniques of systems analysis, would enable them to regard the behavior in time of any organization or activity, even the most multifar-
iously complex, as an integrated unit; and this makes computers an
indispensable aid in planning for complex systems. They can
fantastically extend and expand the human intellect's capacities for
retrieving relevant precedents, remembering a multitude of specifi-
cations, processing numerous variables, considering more plentiful
combinations, and even envisioning approximate models. . . .
Moreover, in any system of cybernetic control, the relevant information is integrated into a feedback loop, which likewise reduces
[information] lag by insuring that the machine gets to consider its
output and perhaps to adjust itself accordingly, just as the human
brain constantly considers the results of its own directives. 'Im-

provements in control,' as John von Neumann said, 'are really improvements in communicating information within an organization or mechanism.' "

Computers, in short, do everything that group therapy, technostructures, psychedelic drugs, technique, town-planning, other-direction, television, the New Morality, existentialism, the ecumenical movement, and student revolt have always attempted to do. And computers do it on a larger scale, more specifically, more effectively, and more thoroughly. The great strength of computers is that *they work from within*. They alter consciousness in a corporate sense, thus transforming organized anarchy into pure organization. They bring to light the effects of organized anarchy and force readjustments at the heart of those very organizations and institutions that are the most dangerous. Initially, when computer systems are small and are programmed to answer only those questions which increase the possibilities of manipulation and exploitation, that is all they succeed in doing. But as systems grow larger, they embrace larger and larger environments. Industry is quite suddenly confronted, thanks to its computers, with "neighborhood effects." Trends can be projected ahead. Cutoff points can be established in advance. Destructive effects or suicidal behavior can be anticipated. Slowly, the whole of industry is being diverted from its suicidal course by the DEW-line computers which are built into its structure.

Computers act, among other things, as fail-safe systems. They are the greatest source of change in society today, interacting with all the other forces that I have been describing. They unify, they integrate, and they coordinate. Student rebels may be dismissed by corporation heads and politicians. Groups and group therapy may be similarly dismissed. Warnings from the academic left may be brushed aside. The protests of ecologists and biologists may be ignored. But the electronic voice of the computer that is working *for* —not *against*—a corporation or government is not so easily written off. Computers will prove to be not only the great weapon in the war against environmental collapse, but also the greatest built-in brake on organized anarchy ever devised.

It is only fitting to add, at this point, that the dimensions of large-scale integration have not been exhausted by the above survey. The cutoff point is arbitrary. Lengthy discussions could follow along several lines from here, but they would tend to be redundant. I have attempted to pick out the examples which are most widely based. But this does not mean that other, similar movements are not afoot.

The dropout community, for instance, is becoming ever more popular. Some estimates place the number of people in North America who have moved into such communities at roughly one million. Some of the better-known communities include the Boston School for Human Resources, the School of Living at Heathcote Center, Freeland, Maryland; Walnut Acres, Tolstoy Farm, the Bruderhof, Tanguy Homestead, Sons of Levi, May Valley Co-op, Argenta, Drop City, The Lama Foundation, Libre, and so on. They are scattered from Colorado and New Mexico to Vermont, New Jersey, New York State, and back across the continent to British Columbia. The literature, including periodicals such as *The Green Revolution* and the *Northern California Almanac of the Changes,* embraces books ranging from Ralph Borsodi's *Flight from the City* to *How to Get Out of the Rat Race and Live on $10 a Month,* published by Herter's, Inc., Waseca, Minnesota.

At first glance, dropout communities would seem to represent anything *but* large-scale integration. Yet their objectives are, in fact, the same. They are attempts to create an integrated community, to involve people with each other at many levels, and, primarily, to allow people to define themselves in relationship to their environment. They are, for the most part, existential. Some are composed of drug-users (although many dropouts look upon drugs with the same revulsion as university administrators), and finally, they are based on cooperation. They are all antianarchic, in that they deeply resent organized anarchy. The search, in every case, is for an alternative existence. The fact that such an alternative existence is emerging in society as a whole either fails to register on them or else they don't believe that it has a chance of developing fast enough. Most members of dropout communities regard the cities as being doomed and existing society as being suicidal, and most members are acutely aware of the problems of environmental collapse.

In art, it is also possible to detect many signs of large-scale integration. Kingsley Widmer, author of *The Literary Rebel,* has pointed out that "the underground arts mostly demand group rather than private responsiveness. . . . Not the 'artistic career' but the group art-action becomes the essential focus. . . . Masterpieces, or the attempt at drastically individualized art, are largely irrelevant to working on a communal style." Widmer refers to this as a "new neolithic culture," thus making the connection with tribal as opposed to detribalized, "civilized" forms of art. He refers, as well, to "the deep longing for a culture of communal involvement," which he believes is reflected in underground art. "Generally," he writes, "in our society, 'sophisticated' and 'cultivated'—and even 'educated'— are terms used to praise the ability to lead a schizophrenic life, to separate culture and politics, consciousness and social function. Much of the rebellion is about that forced and painful disparity between awareness and daily activity. Social necessity once seemed to mandate that fragmentation, the opposing styles of dress and morality and ideas in public and private. No more schizophrenia, say the cultural rebels, who thus simultaneously become social radicals."

The rapid growth of antipollution groups is, of course, yet another critical dimension of large-scale integration, one which contains all of the characteristics listed above. Nowhere is the homeostatic or self-regulated nature of the reaction more evident. Most of antipollution groups evolved out of other groups whose attention was focused on other matters. For example, the militant Ecology Action groups based in Berkeley, California, started out as the ecology branch of the Peace and Freedom Party. After the 1968 Presidential election it grew into an organization in its own right. In California alone there are some ninety-odd organizations devoted to fighting environmental collapse. To varying degrees, all of them adopt an existential position; they are acutely sensitive to the organic nature of the interrelationships around them; their attitudes toward the environment can best be described as "gestaltian"; and *all* are moving with increasing vigor and determination against organized anarchy. The sudden emergence of an "ecological consciousness" reflected in the rapid proliferation of such organizations is one of the most striking indications of the extent to which large-scale integration has progressed.

Underground art, antipollution groups, legislation to stimulate racial integration, the development of "think tanks," integrated educational programs, organ transplants, the rise of small-crafts shops, the emergence of the underground press, and so on—all betray, at bottom, the same basic pattern, the same basic goals, the same imperatives. And each is a variation—and the variations are limitless —on the theme of large-scale integration.

Convergence

*The world of human thought today
presents a very remarkable spectacle,
if we choose to take note of it. Joined in
an inexplicable unifying movement,
men who are utterly opposed in
education and in faith find themselves
brought together, intermingled, in their
common passion for a double truth;
namely, that there exists a physical
unity of beings, and that they themselves
are living and active parts of it. It is
as though a new and formidable
mountain chain had arisen in the
landscape of the soul, causing ancient
categories to be reshuffled and uniting
higgledy-piggledy, on every slope,
the friends and enemies of yesterday.*

—Pierre Teilhard de Chardin
  The Future of Man

NORMAN MAILER once remarked that a profound idea is sometimes found in a particularly ugly notion. To many, large-scale integration will seem an ugly notion. Its effect, after all, is to render meaningless individualism as we have come to know it since the Middle Ages. Another effect of large-scale integration is to stimulate Balkanization, to break down monolithic structures into a rubble heap of impotent veto groups. Leon Trotsky once prophesied that the final revolution would consist of a series of small and violent upheavals going on everywhere at once. It would appear that Trotsky was right. Human beings lose the power to shape their destinies; when large-scale integration has taken hold, revolution becomes impossible—and it is already impossible in the highly industrialized nations. The system, so loathed by Herbert Marcuse, becomes impregnable, due to the force of technique, so loathed by Jacques Ellul. The romantic hero, like the great entrepreneur, goes the way of the dinosaur. Leadership is transformed into Management, risk is replaced by programming, and adventure by security. The administrative concentration camp takes shape. Something that looks very much like Huxley's Brave New World arrives. And because the historic means of revolution have been absorbed and abolished, there is nothing we can do about it.

This would appear to be the state into which we are being driven by large-scale integration, the state which I would describe as "convergence," the point at which all lines of large-scale integration finally meet. The argument has been advanced, in the preceding pages, that organized anarchy (which is the best that we have been able to achieve through the medium called "civilization") has succeeded in triggering an environmental collapse. This collapse, already well advanced, will lead inevitably to our extinction unless we are able to reverse our basic approach to the organization of human life. Since we really have no choice in the matter, we are forced collectively to adopt attitudes and techniques which are antianarchic—which move, that is, *against* organized anarchy. Those forces, movements, developments, and trends which I have characterized as being facets of large-scale integration move precisely in this direction. But they move not only *against* organized anarchy; they move, simultaneously, toward convergence.

Convergence is the ultimate result of precise definition. Like environmental collapse and large-scale integration, it is a synergistic effect. Convergence is the state arrived at when the collective anarchic impulses of organizations and institutions have been eroded, and they are eroded through a process of definition. Large-scale integration, in this context, can be seen as the process of self-definition, and convergence is the state reached when that process is complete. Our model remains that of an organism in which the functions of its individual parts are precisely defined in relation to the functions of other parts. The heart makes no attempt to make the liver or lungs behave like a heart, nor do the liver and lungs seek to impose their method of functioning on the heart. Organs, in short, do not behave anarchically. Within an organism their functions are highly defined and these *functions* converge—that is, they are processes going on in relation to each other. Insofar as the behavior of the cells within these various organs is concerned, it can easily be seen that they possess the biological equivalent of a technostructure, that all decisions are made by groups of cells, and that these groups are autonomous within the superstructure of the entire organism.

The organism is here used as a model—an example or blueprint —for convergence. The thrust of the integrative processes that have been described in the second part of this book is in this direction

—that is, in the direction of organic and highly defined organization. Heart cells work *for* the heart, but not in opposition to the cells that work for other organs. Only cancer cells work for themselves *at the expense of other cells.* With the organization of anarchic impulses in human society—the formation, that is, of institutions, nations, and organizations—we see the exploitative logic of cancer becoming the model on which our progress and development are based. "Progress," when it is cheered by organizational anarchists, means cancer. It is not the healthy, balanced growth of the social organism. It is, rather, the healthy growth of one part of the organism at the expense of other parts.

We see today that the struggles that are now boiling to the surface—between the haves and the have-nots, blacks and whites, young and old, humanists and authoritarians, freedom-loving and freedom-fearing—are more organic than the struggles with which we were concerned in earlier periods. This is a developmental stage in the appreciation of differences. It signals the beginning of real contact between people, with people supporting basically different ideas about the organization of human society. Thus, much of the conflict which appears to be threatening us threatens nothing more than our outmoded concepts. It is an early and prerequisite stage of making contact. And contact must be made before any sort of organic relationships can develop. *Making contact is the beginning of self-definition,* which is the process of finding one's own identity in relation to one's group and, further, in relation to other groups and individuals within those groups. Self-definition can be an individual experience—a "journey to the center of the self," such as is liable to occur in an encounter group—or it can be a collective experience, a journey to the center of the corporate self. The search for identity that is going on in so many different areas today is an essential step in the process of self-definition. Large-scale integration—whether it takes the form of group encounters and sensitivity training, technostructures, other-directed or autonomous social character, use of psychotropic drugs, or whatever—assists (and in some cases forces) higher definition, not only of functions but of needs and aims.

The proposition can be put simply. In a neolithic village a man's function was clearly defined. He was a hunter, a builder, and a beast of burden. Introduce the mule, the camel, or whatever, and the man's function must be redefined. He is no longer effective as a beast of burden, at least not in relation to the mule or the camel. So the man is forced to define himself more precisely. If he is no longer a beast of burden, what is he? Freed of one chore by technology—the domestication of animals was one of the earliest technological breakthroughs—he turns his attention to new endeavors: painting, developing a language, inventing better weapons and tools, and so on. *Each refinement on existing life styles forces a similar redefinition of the functions of man. And at each stage we see the definition becoming stricter, more precise, and always in relation to the "change agent"—be it a mule, a hammer, an assembly line, or a communications satellite. Thus, one of the most significant effects of technology is to force man into ever-higher levels of self-definition. Our machines, in other words, force us forward.*

A man who has been replaced as a beast of burden must become something else. He therefore reaches for a new role, a new function. He becomes a scribe. Then the printing press comes along, and he is forced to seek another function, one that cannot be performed by the printing press. Having discovered that farming is a better way of ensuring a supply of food, he abandons hunting. But then the Industrial Revolution comes along and he is forced to redefine himself in relation to a more advanced technology. He concentrates on educating himself. Then comes the computer, and he finds that there are machines whose capacity for linear thinking is greater than his. So he must redefine his role once again, and he becomes a creator, an innovator, a programmer, an analyst, a discoverer. We say that men are replaced by machines, but what actually happens is that men are *displaced,* forced to seek new roles and functions, forced to discover new resources, forced to explore their potential. And when these new functions are, in turn, displaced, men are forced to dig even deeper into their potential, to mine their resources still further. The collective journey to the center of the self is therefore something of a forced march, during which we are herded along by our own creations—which keep snapping at our heels like sheep dogs.

Let me give some specific examples. What is the effect of television, say, on the older communications media of literature, theater, and radio? Clearly, all have been forced to redefine themselves. Previously radio settled for low definition—that is, there were variety programs, programs that appealed to children, drama for adults, comedy—in short, something for everyone. The impact of television has been to force radio stations to move from a position of low definition to one of higher definition. Now, for the most part, radio stations adopt a single, intense position. There are rock stations, candelight-and-wine stations, hard-news stations, "quality" stations (which emphasize background analysis of the news and classical music), and stations that feature country music and Bible talks. There are even psychedelic-sound stations, as opposed to pop-music stations. Radio stations, particularly in North America, have found that the only way to survive in relation to television is to define themselves as precisely—which is to say, as intensely—as possible. It is no longer possible for radio to appeal to all of the people all of the time. Television, with its extra powers, can do that much more effectively.

Similarly, theater and literature are affected not only by television but by television *and* radio. Books become more information-packed—i.e., they fill in the background spaces which neither television nor radio can handle. They give details and analysis which neither of the other media can manage. At the same time, literature goes looking for areas that cannot be explored successfully on television, radio, or through the medium of movies. Thus, there is more obscenity, novels become more surrealistic, the novelist abandons the exterior world (which can be depicted in living color and Cinerama much more effectively by a camera) and advances into the "night life," dreams, fantasies, the subconscious. Books on psychology become a regular fixture on the best-seller lists. As for theater, it tries to push itself outward from the stage, to engage the audience, to touch its viewers and thus to move them in ways in which none of the more-pervasive and mobile media are able to do.

One may see too that *power* is also forced to redefine itself. The reason the British Empire collapsed so much more quickly than the Roman Empire was due not simply to the flabbiness of the Briton as compared to the Roman. It was due mainly to a much-accelerated rate of change and technological innovation. The British Empire felt the impact of new technologies much more quickly than did Rome, and was forced to redefine itself that much sooner. The atomic bomb and technoplanning were just two of these new technologies. The same rapid pace of change has already wiped out the

American Empire (which has been even more short-lived than the British Empire) and has similarly broken up the Communist monolith. French intellectual Jean-Jacques Servan-Schreiber has pointed out that the turmoil in the United States today is a sign not of decay but of growth, painfully rapid growth, which is forcing "a new *definition* of the relationship between man and society with this second industrial revolution."

This is the point apparently overlooked by pessimists like Ellul —namely, that technique is a tide which forces us further and further up the beach. We are driven along the path to self-discovery, at each turn finding a new self, a new definition of ourselves in relation to the world which we have created. If the trip into our own inner space—through the medium of psychotherapy, drugs, art, or whatever—suddenly assumes infinitely more relevance than the trip into outer space, it is only because space travel is an extension of already developed techniques. Inner space is the unexplored area into which we are really being driven in the search for potentials and talents which have not yet been matched or overtaken by our machines. The most creative among the young in North America today have instinctively grasped the need to move into new territories. And the moon is already an old territory. What is new and mysterious lies within. This, in part, accounts for the sudden interest in psychotropic drugs. These drugs are inner-space vehicles, just like the "hot seats" used in group therapy. And further, they are vehicles that are being taken to like Noah's ark at a time when technology has literally flooded the land.

A critical aspect of the process of being forced into higher and higher definition is the fact that—as Pierre Teilhard de Chardin has noted—"men who are utterly opposed in education and in faith find themselves brought together, intermingled." Ancient categories are reshuffled, and the friends and enemies of yesterday are united higgledy-piggledy on every slope. Exactly. As the level of definition rises—particularly in the collective or corporate sense—those institutions and nations which previously held themselves to be diametrically opposed find themselves moving into phase with each other. Other institutions and nations, whose roles, needs, and internal organization are different, surface in a new relationship to these first groups. What is happening in Europe is a clear-cut example. There the bitterly divided nations whose history has been one of endless territorial conflict are suddenly forced into one economic entity, with the pressure mounting steadily for a final political union. The Common Market was flushed into existence because the squabbling nations of Europe were forced to redefine themselves in relation to the emergence of the two great powers. Since the social structures of the countries of western Europe were basically the same, they quickly began to converge. Similarly, many of the emerging nations of Africa and Asia have begun to converge, forming a Third World bloc.

In short, nonorganic (which is to say, ideological) differences are no longer the differences that truly divide. Higher levels of definition and the antianarchic thrust of large-scale integration are both aspects of the on-going process that tends to produce convergence. *Real* differences come to be recognized. Thus, Cuba—a nation which is struggling to industrialize itself—identifies with China, another nation which is struggling to industrialize itself. Russia, a highly industrialized nation, loses influence among the nonindustrialized nations, except in those cases in which Russian aid can be used advantageously. Even then, the recipient nations cling fiercely to their independence. The Kremlin, as much as the Pentagon, ceases to be the head office from which memos are dispatched to subsidiaries around the globe.

The most spectacular instance of convergence, however, remains that of the United States and Russia. In many respects large-scale integration is proceeding at a much more rapid rate in the United States than in Russia. But in terms of social organization, economics, the use of computers, and most kinds of technology, the pace is about even. If—in terms of social character, drug use, psychotherapy, and the resistance of identity-conscious minorities to assimilation—Russia does not appear to be as far along the path of large-scale integration, it must be remembered that Russia is still well behind the United States on the trajectory that is shaped by technique. It can be seen, however, that Russia is moving in the same direction. David Riesman's study of social character in large urban centers was limited to the United States, where urbanization has proceeded more rapidly than anywhere else. In Russia today, only 54 per cent of the population lives in cities, but that figure will have grown to 70 per cent by 1980—bringing the urban population close to the percentage which existed in the United States at the time that Riesman began work on *The Lonely Crowd*. Passenger-car production in Russia (now at about 344,000 a year) is expected to increase fourfold in the near future—still well behind the more than 90 million cars on the roads of America in 1972, but moving up. That Russia will, before long, have to face the enormous social consequences of increased mobility and urbanization cannot be denied. Increasingly, it will come to mirror the United States. It is, in fact, already doing so.

Few writers have made this as clear as has Erich Fromm. In *May Man Prevail?* he points out that the methods of production in all industrialized nations are the same, regardless of whether the nation is a communist state or a democracy. The main features of industrialized production are "centralization, bureaucratization, and manipulation," and these characteristics apply equally on both sides of the Iron Curtain. Fromm argues that the Soviet position is no longer revolutionary—an argument that has been echoed from London to Havana to Peking. He notes that the Russians did not take advantage of the postwar situation in France and Italy and that they did not, later on, attempt to take over Finland, Austria, Greece, Turkey, Iraq, Iran, Lebanon, Egypt, Cambodia, or Laos—all of which are places where she could have, at various stages, made such an attempt "without any great risk." The Soviet Union's policy "is strategically a defensive one." Fromm's main point is that Russia has become "a state managerial bureaucracy" and that in this respect it is virtually identical to the United States.

John Kenneth Galbraith has shown how the industrial systems in the two nations—indeed, in *all* industrialized nations—operate in basically the same way. Functions that are controlled by the state in socialist or communist nations are controlled, circumspectly, by large corporations in democratic nations. "The reality," Galbraith writes, "in the case of the United States and the Soviet Union is of two large industrial nations. Both, it has been amply shown, can achieve success by their very similar economic tests of success at the same time. . . . There is a large and unquestioned difference in the two systems in the role of politicians, writers, artists, and scientists. None may minimize the difference made by the First Amendment. But it is less clear that the contrast in the systems of economic management is so great. Both systems are subject to the imperatives of industrialization. This, for both, means planning.

And while each uses different techniques for dealing with the individual who contracts out of the planning, planning in all cases means setting aside the market mechanism in favor of the control of prices and individual economic behavior. Both countries, quite clearly, solicit belief for what serves the goals of the industrial mechanism. *Instead of contrast leading to implacable conflict, a more evident economic tendency is convergence* [my italics]."

Jacques Ellul also recognizes the convergent aspects of technique. "From the geographic point of view, it is easy to see that technique is constantly gaining ground, country by country, and that its area of action is the whole world. In all countries, whatever their degree of 'civilization,' there is a tendency to apply the same technical procedures. . . . In the past, different civilizations took different 'paths'; today, all peoples follow the same road and the same impulse. This does not mean that they have reached the same point, but that they are situated at different points along the same trajectory. The United States represents the type that France will represent in thirty years, and China in possibly eighty."

We have seen now that there is a strong tendency for societies—industrialized societies, at any rate—to converge both economically and technologically. As Kenneth Boulding phrased it: "Civilization is haunted by the specter of decline and fall, though it is noteworthy that in spite of the rise and fall of particular civilizations, civilization itself expanded steadily in geographical coverage, from its very beginnings. We must face the fact, however, that post-civilized society will be worldwide, if only because of its ease of communication and transportation. I flew last year from Kennedy to Brussels, and on glimpsing the new Brussels Airport out of the corner of my eye, I thought for a moment that we had come back and landed at Kennedy again." This is a remark echoed by Alan Watts: "Faster intercommunication between points makes all points the same. Waikiki Beach is just a mongrelized version of Atlantic City, Brighton, and Miami." Both men are simply observing the physical evidence of the ecumenical impact of technologies and industrialization.

This impact has a "leveling" or "homogenizing" effect, which has generally been taken to be its *only* effect. And from this observation stem all the protests about "mass society." Since technology is at the root of social change, it is technology that is usually accused of being totalitarian. As Norman Mailer has put it, technology "obliterates distinctions. It makes factories look like college campuses. It makes the new buildings on college campuses look like factories. It depresses the average American with the unconscious recognition that he is installed in a gelatin of totalitarian environment which is bound to deaden his most individual efforts. This new architecture, this totalitarian architecture, destroys the past. There is no trace of the forms which lived in the centuries before us, none of their arrogance, their privileges, their aspirations, their canniness, their creations, their vulgarities. We are left with less and less sense of the lives of men and women who came before us. So we are less able to judge the sheer psychotic values of the present."

Here, Mailer has summed up the feeling of revulsion that is directed, from both the left and the right, against the world that is now taking shape. The past is mythologized. Its brutalities and its sheer waste of human life, the numbing, pointless rituals in which most people were forced to live out their lives—all these are conveniently overlooked. Galbraith has noted that "the wretched freedoms of the slums are the counterpart of the individualism of the buggy-maker." Everyone bemoans the decay of sharply distinctive cultures under the impact of technology, although most admit that the death rate is cut, physical suffering is eased, hunger is reduced, and fewer infants grow sick and die.

Watts puts the matter clearly: "Advances in one field are interlocked with advances in all others. I could not have penicillin or modern anesthesia without aviation, electronics, mass communication, superhighways, and industrial agriculture—not to mention the atomic bomb and biological warfare." Technology is indeed totalitarian. It does level and homogenize. However, the evidence is that electronic technology is qualitatively different from mechanical technology and that it *reverses* the process. This reversal has only begun—and it is most evident in those countries, such as the United States, where electronic technology is most advanced. Elsewhere, where the impact of the *first* industrial revolution is only beginning to be felt, it is too much to expect that the effects of the *second* industrial revolution will be having any noticeable impact as yet—although McLuhan argues that "backward" nations stand a good chance of being able to make the transition from tribal to electronic civilization without having to follow the step-by-step process of mechanization and industrialization which the West has had to endure.

Thus, the picture that emerges is one in which (thanks to the process of large-scale integration) the end result will be a technological civilization in which techniques are standardized and universally applied. The economic systems of each country will emerge as variations of the same post-industrial theme. Electronic communications, computers, and so on will knit each complex national unit into an integrated whole. Further, international alliances and arrangements—the European Common Market is only one example of the many that are rapidly coming into being—will be worked out so as to assure markets and to make small economic systems into larger, more predictable, and more controllable ones. Health standards, environmental controls, population controls, and so on will be, of necessity, worldwide. *In all the technical details each corporate body will come to mirror the others.* Autonomous technostructures will emerge in every sphere of large-scale endeavor, from the administrative to the economic. Planning will become absolutely essential in all areas. Organization—and the organizations will all be basically the same—will replace social order. Ecological controls—taking the form of land and resource management—will eventually be global in scope, since pollution, as we have seen, ignores political boundaries. Integration will be carried out on all fronts, and global management will become a reality. A global concentration camp will have come into existence—in the administrative sense—and individuals everywhere will be organized into integral units and the relationships between these units will be programmed—orchestrated, if you like—by large planning agencies using electronic data-processing systems.

At the same time, however, border lines, languages, customs, and so on will not disappear. They will, in fact, acquire new importance as dimensions of cultural self-definition. Negroes will be "blacker" and whites will be "whiter." As this happens, each group will be more capable of accepting the other's positions, needs, and beliefs without fear of having its own ground under. The process of large-scale integration, particularly in the way in which it forces a more and more precise definition of roles and function, creates a climate in which self-awareness comes to have increasing application.

Moreover, from the rise of technostructures to the use of psychedelic drugs—through the whole gamut of technoplanning, group therapy, New Morality, student revolt, and, particularly, the increased use of computers—we see that it is *the irrationality in social life* that is being attacked. Anarchic behavior is irrational, and organized anarchy is organized irrationality, working itself out in the form of culturally patterned defects. The global group therapy session which is now under way has the effect of breaking down, or at least bringing to light, those premises, ideologies, and positions that are irrational and anarchic. Convergence, based as it must be on precise definition and organization, will leave very little room for the irrational—although the word "irrational" must be used cautiously, since what is "rational" at one level of awareness frequently appears "irrational" at the level just below it.

It is possible to continue at considerable length on the subject of convergence, citing Herman Kahn's and Anthony J. Wiener's concept of a "standard world," or Arnold Toynbee's tentative forecast of a "world order," or, for that matter, the predictions of a large number of thinkers, writers, scientists, and philosophers. The main points, however, have already been made, and there remains but to add one other dimension—the dimension of *religious* convergence.

Erich Fromm, for one, says that he believes a revitalization of religion is just around the corner. He is not the only one saying this. In early 1969 Alan Watts "humorously" predicted that Asia would soon be covered with hotdog stands and superhighways, while North Americans would be wandering around in yellow robes droning "Om." He was exaggerating in the finest McLuhan tradition of hyperbole. Yet the theme of religious convergence recurs. In the early part of the century Carl Jung was saying that the East, with its psychic proficiency, was even then throwing our psychic world into disorder at the very time that the West, with its mechanical proficiency, was disrupting the East.

"The viewpont of Zen," wrote Watts, back in 1957, "lies close to the growing edge of Western thought. . . . The more alarming and destructive aspects of Western civilization should not blind us to the fact that at this very time it is also in one of its most creative periods. Ideas and insights of the greatest fascination are appearing in some of the newer fields of Western science—in psychology and psychotherapy, in logic and the philosophy of science, in semantics and communications theory. Some of these developments may be due to suggestive influences from Asian philosophy, but on the whole I am inclined to feel that there is more a parallelism than a direct influence. We are, however, becoming aware of the parallelism, and it promises an exchange of views which should be extremely stimulating." Watts also points out that the second largest Zen monastery in the world today is in California. Moreover, many leading technologists—Buckminster Fuller is a notable example—hold pantheistic viewpoints which are similar to Asian conceptions.

To go further than to note the convergent aspects of Western science and Eastern mysticism is to venture into uncharted territory —a bottomless realm of mysticism, spiritualism, and so on. It cannot be approached unless the writer is willing to plunge headfirst into the abyss. This is not the place for such an exploration. However, it is worth quoting, on this score, the remarks of Pierre Teilhard de Chardin in *The Future of Man:*

> [It] is possible for us to envisage a future state of the Earth in which human consciousness, reaching the climax of its evolution, will have attained a maximum of complexity, and, as a result, of concentration by total "reflexion" (or *planetization*) of itself upon itself. Although our individualistic instincts may rebel against this drive toward the collective, they do so in vain and wrongly. In vain, because no power in the world can enable us to escape from what is in itself the power in the world. And wrongly because the real nature of this impulse that is sweeping us toward a state of super-organization is such as to make us more completely personalized and human. The very fact of our becoming aware of this profound ordering of things will enable human collectivization to pass beyond the *enforced* phase, where it now is, into the *free* phase: that in which (men having at last understood that they are inseparably joined elements of a converging Whole, and having learned in consequence to *love* the preordained forces that unite them) a natural union of affinity and sympathy will supersede the forces of compulsion.

This vision is shared by Buckminster Fuller, Alan Watts, Carl Jung, Marshall McLuhan, and Arnold Toynbee—men who, on the surface, are as individual and as different as men can possibly be. And the theme which it embodies is to be found in the prophetic writings of many religions, including Christianity. In short, the theme of religious convergence is not at odds with the other developments that have been described in this book. Economic and technological forces need not be viewed as being in opposition to religion. They show every sign, in fact, of being in harmony. Further, we have seen in this "overview" that the new social type that is emerging at the heart of the revolution in our times is, in many respects, far more meek than the "rugged individual" whom we have come to revere in the West. And after all, the idea that the meek shall inherit the earth is not really at odds with Christian concepts.

Since the Second World War our attention has been held by spectacles of violence which most of us regarded as representing violent *change*. Since 1945 there have been 60 wars, 48 *coups d'état*, 74 rebellions of independence, 162 social revolutions, and an uncounted number of racial, religious, and language riots. However, almost none of these has had the effect of real change. Rather, they have been conflicts stemming from the organization of anarchic impulses. The hauling down of one flag and the hoisting of another represents no fundamental change at all, although we have always assumed that a switch in symbols means something more. It does not. One form of organized anarchy supplants another—and rather than representing change, this represents only a vicious circle. The processes that I have been describing in the latter part of this book as processes of large-scale integration have been less visible—in fact, invisible to most. But more than all the wars, *coups d'état*, rebellions, revolutions, and riots taken together, they signify the beginnings of real, as opposed to illusory, change. They are changes that strike at the very heart of our civilization.

Bibliography

Adelman, Howard, and Lee, Dennis. *The University Game.* Toronto: House of Anansi, 1968.

Ardrey, Robert. *African Genesis.* New York: Atheneum, 1961.

Berry, Brewton. *Race and Ethnic Relations.* Boston: Houghton Mifflin Co., 1951.

Bocking, Richard C. *Canada's Water: For Sale?* Toronto: James Lewis & Samuel, 1972.

Boulding, Kenneth E. "After Civilization What?" *Bulletin of the Atomic Scientists,* October 1962.

————. *The Meaning of the Twentieth Century.* New York: Harper & Row, 1964.

Calder, Ritchie. *How Long Have We Got?* Montreal: McGill–Queens University Press, 1972.

Carrington, Richard. *A Million Years of Man.* New York: World Publishing Co., 1963.

Carson, Rachel. *Silent Spring.* Boston: Houghton Mifflin Co., 1962.

Clark, John R. "Thermal Pollution and Aquatic Life." *Scientific American,* Vol. 220, No. 3, 1968.

Cox, Harvey. *The Secular City.* New York: The Macmillan Co., 1965.

Darlington, C. D. *Genetics and Man.* London: Allen and Unwin, 1964.

de Chardin, Pierre Teilhard. *The Future of Man.* New York: Harper & Row, 1959.

Douglas, William O. *The Three Hundred Year War: A Chronicle of Ecological Disease.* New York: Random House, 1972.

Doxiadis, Constantinos A. *Architecture in Transition.* New York: Oxford University Press, 1963.

Dreskin, Nathan. "And Now, in Living Color, Television Brings You Radioactivity in the Living Room." *The Star Weekly,* March 2, 1968.

Eberhard, John P. "The City as a System." *International Science and Technology,* 1966.

The Editors of *The Ecologist. A Blueprint for Survival.* London: Penguin Books, 1972.

Ehrlich, Paul R. *The Population Bomb.* New York: Ballantine Books, 1968.

Ellul, Jacques. *The Technological Society.* New York: Alfred A. Knopf, 1954.

Englebardt, Stanley L. *Computers.* New York: Pyramid Publications, 1962.

Evenden, L. J. "And What About Our Cities?" *Focos Magazine.* Media Research Society, Simon Fraser University, Burnaby, B. C., Canada.

Foss, Daniel. *Freak Culture: Life Style and Politics.* New York: E. P. Dutton & Co., Inc., 1972.

Foucault, Michel. *Madness and Civilization.* New York: Pantheon Books, 1965.

Fromm, Erich. *The Sane Society.* New York: Fawcett World Library, 1955.

———. *May Man Prevail?* New York: Doubleday & Co., 1961.

———. *The Revolution of Hope,* New York: Harper & Row, 1968.

Fuller, R. Buckminster. *Operating Manual for Spaceship Earth.* Carbondale: Southern Illinois University Press, 1969.

Galbraith, John Kenneth. *The New Industrial State.* Boston: Houghton Mifflin Co., 1967.

Gavin, James M. *Crisis Now*. New York: Alfred A. Knopf, 1968.

Guillain, Robert. *When China Wakes*. New York: Walker & Company, 1966.

Gustavson, Carl G. *A Preface to History*. New York: McGraw–Hill, 1955.

Hall, Edward T. *The Hidden Dimension*. New York: Doubleday & Co., 1966.

Hampden–Turner, Charles. *Radical Man*. New York: Doubleday & Co., 1971.

Hartogs, Renatus. *Four-Letter Word Games*. New York: Dell Publishing Co., 1967.

Josephson, Eric, and Josephson, Mary. *Man Alone: Alienation in Modern Society*. New York: Dell Publishing Co., 1962.

Jung, C. G. *Modern Man in Search of a Soul*. New York: Harcourt Brace and World, 1933.

Kahn, Herman, and Wiener, Anthony J. *The Year 2000*. New York: The Macmillan Co., 1967.

Kostelanetz, Richard. *Beyond Left & Right*. New York: William Morrow and Co., 1968.

Landau, Norman J., and Rheingold, Paul D. *The Environmental Law Handbook*. New York: Ballantine Books, 1971.

Lawton, A. T., and Abrook, G. E. "Large-scale Integration." *Science Journal*, August 1968.

Mailer, Norman. *The Idol and the Octopus*. New York: Dell Publishing Co., 1968.

Malthus, Thomas; Huxley, Julian; and Osborn, Frederick. *On Population: Three Essays*. New York: New American Library, 1960.

McLuhan, Marshall. *Understanding Media*. New York: McGraw–Hill, 1964.

———. *The Medium Is the Message*. New York: Bantam Books, 1967.

———, and Fiore, Quentin. *War and Peace in the Global Village*. New York: Bantam Books, 1968.

Mills, C. Wright. *The Power Elite*. New York: Oxford University Press, 1956.

Montagu, M. F. Ashley. *Man and Aggression.* New York: Oxford University Press, 1968.

Mumford, Lewis. *The City in History.* New York: Harcourt Brace and World, 1961.

Nicholson, Max. *The Environmental Revolution—A Guide for the New Masters of the World.* London: Penguin Books, 1972.

Osborn, Fairfield. *Our Plundered Planet.* New York: Pyramid Books, 1948.

Overstreet, Bonaro W. *Understanding Fear in Ourselves and Others.* New York: Harper and Bros., 1951.

Packard, Vance. *The Waste Makers.* New York: Simon and Schuster, 1960.

Price, Daniel O. *The 99th Hour: The Population Crisis in the United States.* Chapel Hill: University of North Carolina Press, 1967.

A Report of the Commission of Inquiry into the Non-Medical Use of Drugs, Cannabis. Ottawa: Information Canada, 1972.

(SCEP) Report of the Study of Critical Environmental Problems, *Man's Impact on the Global Environment.* Cambridge, Massachusetts: The MIT Press, 1970.

Riesman, David. *The Lonely Crowd.* New Haven: Yale University Press, 1950.

Sayre, Kenneth M., and Crosson, Frederick J., eds. *The Modeling of Mind.* Notre Dame: University of Notre Dame Press, 1963.

Schlesinger, Arthur J., Jr. *Violence: America in the Sixties.* New York: New American Library, 1968.

Simpson, David. "The Dimensions of World Poverty." *Scientific American,* Vol. 219, No, 5, 1968.

Skinner, B. F. *Beyond Freedom and Dignity.* New York: Alfred A. Knopf, 1971.

Stafford, P. G., and Golightly, B. H. *LSD: The Problem-Solving Psychedelic.* New York: Universal Publishing & Distributing Corp., 1967.

Stearn, Gerald Emanuel, ed. *McLuhan: Hot and Cool.* New York: New American Library, 1967.

Storer, John H. *Man in the Web of Life.* New York: New American Library, 1968.

Toynbee, Arnold. *A Study of History*. New York: Oxford University Press.

Watts, Alan W. *The Wisdom of Insecurity*. New York: Pantheon, 1949.

————. *The Way of Zen*. New York: New American Library, 1959.

————. *The Book*. New York: Collier Books, 1966.

Weisberg, Barry. *Beyond Repair—The Ecology of Capitalism*. Boston: Beacon Press, 1971.

Wickenden, Leonard. *Our Daily Poison*. New York: Bartholomew House, 1955.

Index